Praise for Robert Wainwright's books

... ents the

... emained ... *Weekly*

... what ... a

... *rier* on

... deniably ... *Sheila* ... nd.'

...'

... highly

... never

Wainwright has done a fine job of rescuing his protagonist from the footnotes of climbing history. He has restored the reputation of a man whose achievements were frequently overshadowed by the romantic fate of Mallory and the later triumph of Edmund Hillary.' *The Telegraph* on *The Maverick Mountaineer*

Robert Wainwright has been a journalist for more than 30 years, rising from the grassroots of country journalism in Western Australia to a senior writer with the *Sydney Morning Herald*, where he was a three-time finalist in the prestigious Walkley Awards. His career has ranged from politics to crime, always focusing on the people behind the major news of the day. He is the author, amongst others, of *Rose: The unauthorised biography of Rose Hancock Porteous*, *The Lost Boy*, *The Killing of Caroline Byrne*, *Born or Bred* (the story of killer Martin Bryant), the best-selling *Sheila*, the award-winning *Maverick Mountaineer* and *Miss Muriel Matters*. *Rocky Road* is his twelfth book.

Rocky Road

The incredible true story of the
fractured family behind the
Darrell Lea chocolate empire

ROBERT WAINWRIGHT

ALLEN&UNWIN
SYDNEY·MELBOURNE·AUCKLAND·LONDON

Allen & Unwin
83 Alexander Street
Crows Nest NSW 2065
Australia
Phone: (61 2) 8425 0100
Email: info@allenandunwin.com
Web: www.allenandunwin.com

A catalogue record for this book is available from the National Library of Australia

ISBN 978 1 76029 155 6

Set in 12.5/18 pt Minion Pro by Post Pre-press Group, Australia
Printed and bound in Australia by Griffin Press

10 9 8 7 6 5 4 3 2 1

The paper in this book is FSC® certified. FSC® promotes environmentally responsible, socially beneficial and economically viable management of the world's forests.

To Andy and Dave. Special friends who made a difference
in my life. Sadly missed.

CONTENTS

Foreword

It is often said that nothing in life is ever black and white, an idiom particularly apt when applied to families. Two children who share the same parents and upbringing can look back, as adults, and describe entirely different experiences.

A mother who insists on adherence to rules and routine can be perceived as a maternal rock to one child and a cruel autocrat to another. A gentle, distracted father can be seen as kind and loving to his eldest son or distant and uninvolved to the youngest.

There is no absolute truth, just life—and events—experienced differently.

Add divorce, stepchildren or the complexities of adoption and it is inevitable that the intimate, often fragile dynamics of the family are affected—and an objective analysis of events becomes almost impossible to discern. Every life experience is valid, acceptance of difference necessary.

Rocky Road is the story of Monty and Valerie Lea and their blended family of four biological and three adopted children. On the surface, at least, it seemed a success, with dozens of photo albums and cannisters of film showing smiling children and happy times. But the reality was much more complex.

The four biological children would recall mostly happy childhoods under an engaging if slightly eccentric mother who taught them right from wrong and filled their lives with opportunity, although even their accounts would differ.

By contrast, the recollections of their adopted brothers and sister were rather darker, growing up in a household in which they were told they were 'not real Leas'. Their inevitable difficulties as adolescents were misunderstood and mismanaged by a woman who diarised her own frustrations.

This is primarily the story of Valerie Lea and her three adopted children, their lives and search for identity and answers, set against the backdrop of the rise and fall of the Darrell Lea empire.

1

GAYLE

September 1953

The girl in the cotton dress stood alone in the white-walled room, clutching a paper bag and the tattered remains of her security blanket.

Instinct had told her, even at the age of four, that something was desperately wrong. Why was she here, in a city doctor's surgery? Why had a man taken her photograph when they arrived and why did her mother, whom she rarely saw, hold her so tightly as they sat in the waiting room?

A woman in a nurse's uniform appeared and knelt in front of the chair. 'Do you like sweets?'

She nodded, unsure how to react.

The nurse offered her hand. 'Then come with me. There are chocolates in the next room.'

The girl felt the grip around her waist ease, the warmth of her mother's arms gone. Taking it as a sign to go, she slipped off her lap and followed the woman into the other room.

The nurse pointed to the chocolates in a bowl on a table and quickly retreated. The door closed and the girl was alone. She eyed the sweets but did not touch them, something inside telling her they were rotten. In hindsight, many years later, the offering of those chocolates wrapped in shiny paper would take on a significant meaning.

The windows on the far side beckoned—a possible escape route. She crossed the room, passed a giant desk, and stared through a towering pane of glass at the street beyond, the noise and bustle of the city of Melbourne in sharp contrast to the silence within. It offered no comfort.

The girl could hear voices in another room, the deeper tones of a man and a woman whose voices signified authority. The woman was not her mother, and they were coming for her. She sensed it. In that moment of utter despair, she decided that they, whoever *they* were, would never get her. She might be trapped physically, and in their control, but they couldn't touch her inside. She would never forget the feeling.

Gayle turned and faced the door.

A tall lady with a shining smile and steely eyes walked into the room. The lady was with the doctor, but he didn't bother to examine her. Instead, he told her that she was going home with the lady. She was her new mummy.

The lady called herself Valerie. She held Gayle's hand as they walked down Collins Street and talked about all the wonderful things that would now happen and how it would be better for her.

A car like a small bus was waiting nearby, filled with children who stared at her through the windows. They were her new brothers and sisters, the lady named Valerie told her, and they were all going to her new home.

It was the colours Gayle would remember when they arrived at the house—the red brick walls sharply outlined with their clean white grouting and spring-green leaves tinged orange at their edges by the late afternoon sunshine filtering through the trees on either side of the road. She was in Toorak, one of Melbourne's wealthiest suburbs, five kilometres south-east of the city centre.

The children gathered behind Valerie: 'What do you think we should call her?' she asked her brood as they followed her to the front gate.

Gayle almost froze. What did Valerie mean? She already had a name. She was Gayle Lesley Johns.

A boy's voice behind her piped up: 'I know, let's call her Honey because her hair is golden, like honey.' The others excitedly agreed.

2

THE CANDY MAN

It is said that to be a London Cockney you must be born within earshot of the famed Bow Bells of St Mary-le-Bow Church, whose chimes welcomed the real-life Dick Whittington and his famous cat to London in the seventeenth century.

There could be no doubt then that despite his birth name, Manesseh Jablinovich was every inch an East Londoner, not just for his accent and colourful vocabulary but also for his jaunty demeanour and propensity for wearing dapper hats.

Manesseh was born in 1876, the fifth of eight children of a Polish bootmaker and tailor who had anglicised his own name to Harris Levy. The family lived in Spitalfields, near the impoverished streets of London's Whitechapel district where Jack the Ripper would carve his barbaric reputation.

In 1886 Harris set off for Australia alone, presumably to make a better life, leaving his heavily pregnant wife, Hannah, and their children in London. He settled in Sydney where he resumed his trade and raised the money needed to bring out his family. Two years later Hannah arrived with the children, including Manesseh who, now aged twelve, was already working in the shoe trade.

But Manesseh wanted to be more than a bootmaker. Following his father's example, he changed his name to Harry Levy, a name that better matched his East London accent and gregarious nature, then set off to find fame and fortune.

After working for a time in a cigar factory he began to wander across the vast Australian continent, ending up in the West Australian capital of Perth where he tried his hand at gold prospecting, shooting kangaroos and breeding rabbits. An entrepreneur in spirit, he enjoyed some measure of success.

By the turn of the century, after the gold rush of the 1890s, Harry had settled in the West Australian mining town of Kalgoorlie, where he went into business with a man named Albert 'Jack' Abadee. The two men ran a 'marine store dealership', a colourful name for what was essentially a scrap metal yard, although they appear to have been involved in a broad range of businesses, including horse and dray rental.

Theirs was a murky partnership. The partners were accused of public brawling, keeping shoddy accounts and even charged (and later cleared after a court case) with knowingly buying stolen brass fittings from a mine site. Abadee's adventurous spirit was still apparent years later, when he made headlines by driving his wife and son across Australia, from Sydney to Perth and back.

Harry and Jack were so close that they co-ordinated their marriages. Harry was married first, to nineteen-year-old Esther

Goldman, daughter of a prominent Adelaide pawnbroker, in March 1905. The wedding photographs show a short but handsome man who wooed his much taller wife with his piercing gaze and impressive handlebar moustache; Harry won over his future mother-in-law by parading as a man of substance up and down Adelaide's streets in his horse and sulky.

Esther seemed to aim higher, socially and financially, than a Kalgoorlie 'dealer', as Harry Levy described his profession at the time. She had been keen on a 'Mr Alexander of the Imperial Hotel, Adelaide', and had also been engaged for a time to a man named Cohen, but both relationships had fallen through. As one of three sisters in a widowed household, Esther—encouraged by a mother who was eager to see her daughter settled into marital security—regarded Harry as an opportunity worth taking.

The Lea family records describe Esther as a beautiful but tough individual: 'Tall, straight backed with piercing eyes and clipped speech, not given to dollops of tact or gentleness—a woman who left her mark on her children and grandchildren, referred to as "aahh, one of the beautiful Goldman girls".' Esther maintained this was the result of religiously washing her face daily in buttermilk as well as bathing in it every Friday.

Harry was the opposite in many ways, and not just physically. He was a man with a wanderlust, 'a basic survival instinct which didn't appear to translate into physically settling down roots', as the family history, *How Sweet It Is: The Darrell Lea story*, would later note. Despite their differences and the pragmatic nature of their relationship, Harry and Esther were well suited, and for the next 50 years would be devoted to one another and their dreams.

The *Jewish Herald* reported a wedding celebration at the Goldman house in Hindley Street, Adelaide, that matched the sober nature of the union: 'The ceremony was of a pleasing and impressive character in the presence of relatives and a few friends. A happy time was spent during the evening, and although the occasion was not largely festive, it lacked nothing in joyfulness.'

ଓଌ

The following month the newlyweds returned to Kalgoorlie for Abadee's nuptials. This was another practical alliance, with Jack hitching himself to the Sydney niece of a business associate. The two men then resumed their business partnership.

Harry and Esther's first two children, Maurice and Nona, were born in Kalgoorlie beneath a tin roof that their father had covered with wet sacks to ward off the searing desert heat. But after two years Esther had had enough; she insisted on returning to South Australia. So in June 1907 Harry sold his share of the business to Abadee, packed up his family and headed back to Adelaide where their third child, Montague, would be born in 1909. But Harry remained unfulfilled and the family headed for Kadina, a bustling town founded on copper mining, located on the Yorke Peninsula north-west of Adelaide. Here Harry set up a catering business, Levy's Café, in Graves Street.

The family lived upstairs. In later years, the boys would remember the summer months and the 150-kilometre journey by horse and dray to Glenelg, a beachside suburb of Adelaide where they would camp. Childhood accidents would always be remembered with mirth. Like the day Monty fell out of a window and was saved by landing on a grapevine, and the time a naked Maurice leaned too close to the cocky cage and was bitten. 'The cocky bit the cocky,' he would later write.

But, once again, their time in Kadina would be brief—barely three years—although successful judging by the house full of expensive furniture sold as they left town, including a walnut bedroom suite, rosewood chairs and even a bath heater. The family moved to Melbourne in August 1914, just as the Great War was about to break out; a third son, named Harris after his grandfather, was born soon afterwards. Harry started various business ventures in Melbourne but success continued to elude him, and by 1916 the family was back in Sydney, where his journey had begun.

Ever willing to try his hand at something new, Harry bought into a fruit and vegetable business on Manly's The Corso, the iconic thoroughfare that links Sydney Harbour to the Pacific Ocean. The construction of the Harbour Bridge was still two decades away, so commuter and tourist traffic to and from the ferry port made The Corso, named after Rome's iconic Via del Corso, the centre of commercial life on the northern beaches.

The shop was situated close to the beach end of The Corso, and Harry stocked it high with colourful displays to lure the summer crowds who flocked to the area in their tens of thousands for weekend carnivals. He even won competitions for his displays, showcasing skills that would soon come to the fore in promoting another product.

But in the winter months Manly was whipped by rain and wild winds that came off the ocean. Those who braved the streets kept their heads down beneath umbrellas. Many shops closed and trade was slow for those shopkeepers, like Harry Levy, who remained open.

Harry had to find something different to keep his business alive. In Kalgoorlie, where he and Jack Abadee had traded in almost everything that came their way, Harry had learned to diversify. He decided to try making confectionery, using old European recipes.

Family stories, like memories, can become twisted in the telling and retelling. There are various versions of Harry Levy's start in candy-making, including his parents having him indentured as a young boy to a London relative who made 'European-style' chocolates and caramels.

His son Harris told a slightly different version—that his father had watched his aunt and uncle making toffees, taking notes as he did so.

Either way, Harry began making a variety of hard candies, caramels, toffees and chocolates, even peanut brittle. Instead of piling apples high on tables at the front of his shop, Harry made candy pyramids and adopted a new business cry that would endure for the next 90 years: 'Stack 'em high and watch 'em buy!'

Harry Levy had finally found a winner. If business was slow on The Corso, he would load up a handbarrow with confectionery and brave the storm-tossed harbour on the ferry to the city, where he would trundle the streets, spruiking and selling as he went in his ready-made Cockney accent.

Such was his success that within a year Harry was able to quit his fruit and vegetable shop and make a permanent home in the city, where he leased a tiny milk bar, barely two metres wide, jammed between a hotel and a theatre in Haymarket at the southern end of George Street. He called it The King of Sweets and relied on theatre and restaurant patrons for sales.

The family worked in rotation, making the sweets in the back of the shop. Much like a bakery business, they would start in the early hours of the morning, making fresh produce, then sell well into the night to catch the crowds during interval in the cinema next door. Their top seller was a Bulgarian Rock called Almond Rocca, a hard nougat embedded with almonds that was boiled in copper vats, cooled and tempered on steel benches, then packed into paper bags. Business became so brisk that the tables and chairs in the milk bar were shifted onto the footpath to make room for queuing customers.

It was during this time that Harry's business model changed. Until now he had been a man searching for success with various business partners but, now that he had stumbled onto a winner, he wanted to harness the biggest asset on his doorstep—his family. Maurice, Nona and Monty were now teenagers and their father, who'd had little or no formal education and had been working since the age of ten, could not see any value in keeping them at school: 'Business kept you alive, not books', the family history would note of Harry's attitude.

The Levy family provided not only a ready-made workforce but also one that didn't require formal wages. Any living expenses were taken from the till, and everything else was poured back into the business. Esther, who shared her husband's outlook despite her very different and formal upbringing, kept tight control of the purse strings. Family loyalty, diligence and thrift became the hallmarks of their operation.

☙

A fourth son was born in 1927. Blond and blue-eyed, with a mop of curly hair, Darrell had taken after his mother's side of the family—unlike his siblings, including his sister Nona, who all had their father's dark-eyed looks. There was the equivalent of a generation between Maurice, now aged twenty-one, and his baby brother yet, despite the age gap, in later years the family bond would bridge the difference when the brothers shared management of their burgeoning confectionery empire.

The business was growing rapidly, thanks largely to a marketing philosophy of selling chocolates, which they had now started to produce alongside candies, at one shilling for a half pound rather than charging two, or even three, shillings as their competitors did for the same weight; it demonstrated the benefit of keeping down costs by using family members to make and sell their wares, and even to make deliveries. Display was also critical. In comparison to their competition, their store was lit up, attracting customers like moths to a flame: 'We knew the value of lighting,' Monty would reflect many years later. 'Alongside us, the other stores were very drab.'

They expanded beyond the Haymarket store in 1928, when Maurice noticed that a shirt shop in Pitt Street, opposite the GPO in the heart of the city's business district, had gone bust. The family was happy to rent it cheaply and even reuse the shop's display units. The canniness of their move was rewarded almost immediately when the takings for a one-day sale at Christmas totalled £211, a significant amount at a time when the world was teetering on the brink of the Great Depression.

To cope with the increasing demand—for more volume as well as for new varieties—Harry found a factory site in Surry Hills, at the southern edge of the city centre. To their range they added toasted marshmallows, marzipan, coconut ice, honey malt, peanut brittle, old-time rock and barley sugar. And they found that customers wanted boxes of chocolates, rather than candies spooned into paper bags.

At the time there were many small family-based confectionery companies along the east coast experimenting with new flavours and textures. Some introduced unique products that would become known across the world: Sweetacres made Minties and Fantales, MacRobertson's invented Freddo Frogs and Cherry Ripe, and Hoadley's introduced the Violet Crumble. Americans called them 'candies' and Brits called them 'sweets', but Australians had their own word—lollies. There was serious international competition from overseas giants such as Cadbury, Nestlé and Rowntree; most local companies tended to be wholesale operations rather than retail ones.

What set the Levy brothers apart from the others was their involvement in every aspect of the business—from production to retail, and everything in between. Their range was bigger, their prices cheaper and they had more shopfronts than anyone else. By 1934 there were a dozen stores in and around the city, including several on Pitt Street and others at Wynyard station and on King, Market and George streets.

Their window displays were bold. 'Freshness and Affordability' was their slogan at a time when production meant a limited shelf life; their competitive pricing became even more important as the Great Depression took hold.

Years later, Harris would look back on the early days: 'The answer to our success was family. They were tough times but we had a family that was prepared to work hard. We worked fourteen hours a day, seven days a week so our product could be fresh and families could afford it, even in the Depression.'

By 1936 the business had outgrown the Surry Hills factory. So Harry and his sons, who had now assumed the day-to-day management, took space beneath the arches on the southern approaches of the Sydney Harbour Bridge, which had opened four years before, revolutionising the city. This move was followed eagerly by the media, which seemed entranced by the technology, as the *Sydney Morning Herald* reported enthusiastically on 5 May 1936:

In keeping with modern factory practice, the layout has been designed to permit of an orderly sequence of operations which is conducive to maximum efficiency. Raw materials will be brought into the building through a vehicle entrance, stored in a raw materials room, whence they will proceed to the various boilers etc. and onto the dipping room. Conveyers will take the dipped chocolates etc. to the cool room where the temperature is adjusted to permit of hardening the chocolate coatings in the space of about fifteen minutes. The trays will be withdrawn from the cool room and goods packed ready for dispatch, the whole process of manufacture being thus arranged on a progressive nature. Highly-glazed enamel wall surfaces are provided in all parts of the building, where goods are in process of manufacture, and all floors are of concrete, steel-troweled. A considerable amount of plant will be installed. Mechanical ventilation is being provided to deal with the fumes and steam from boilers and the refrigeration plant. This floor is designed to take an eight-ton lorry over the whole area.

But there was one thing missing from the business—a catchy name.

The window displays played on word associations such as Super Luscious, Nutty Nice, Wholesome Goodness and Melting Moments, but there was nothing to identify who had made them. This had to change. 'The Boys', as they were known, decided they needed to shed their Jewish association and 'sound' more akin to what they were selling.

Harry agreed. It would require another identity change, but this time it would be something that would recall his childhood in London. He wanted the sense of a rural paradise, of pasture and cows and milk, and settled on a term for an English meadow.

The word he chose was 'lea'.

There are several versions among family members of what happened next.

The most oft-repeated is that in late June 1935 Maurice and Monty (as Montague would always be known) went to the austere government registry office to register a new name for the company. Their brother Darrell, now aged eight, was in tow as they entered. The duty clerk seemed less than impressed with their proposed new name—Lea Brothers.

Noticing the curly head of a young boy just visible above the counter, he leaned over and enquired: 'Who's this?'

'That's our brother Darrell,' Maurice replied.

'Why don't you name the company after him? It's much more interesting.'

But Valerie would tell a different story, claiming that it was she who came up with the new company name and that the registry office tale was simply that—a tale: 'It was something that she remained very proud of,' her youngest daughter, Charryce, would insist.

Either way, the *Daily Commercial News* carried the registration details a few days later: 'Darrell Lea Chocolates Ltd. Nominal capital £10,000 in £1 shares. Objects: To carry on the business of chocolate manufacturers.'

The family name change was also announced, not publicly but in the minutes of the second meeting of the company directors in July 1935. It read, in part: 'Mr Montague Lea reported that the surname "Levy" had been abandoned by himself and his family, and in lieu therefore the surname "Lea" adopted.'

The boy named Manesseh Jablinovich who began life as a Bow-Bell Cockney was now Harry Lea, a successful Sydney businessman. Harry would not become mayor of the city he had conquered, as Dick Whittington did, but he had created an iconic symbol of migrant success and a bloodline that would carry on his legacy for the next three generations.

3

THE TICKET WRITER

Even before the Wall Street Crash of 1929 plunged the world into the Great Depression, Australia's economy was fragile. Falling commodity prices and a splurge of borrowing to fund post-war infrastructure were a toxic mix. Frustration fuelled industrial anger and a series of crippling strikes heralded a federal election that tossed out Stanley Bruce's conservative government and cost the prime minister his own seat.

Swimming against the economic tide, the then Levy family was seeking to expand its business. The Pitt Street store had just opened to great success and the brothers couldn't handle the operation by themselves. In April 1930 a series of newspaper ads were taken out calling for staff, both front of house and behind the scenes:

Girls 18 wanted of good appearance for high class candy shop. Must have sales ability.

Another read:

TICKET WRITER—Young girl required. Apply after 10.30.

Hopefuls queued for hours. Among them was Valerie Everitt, a sixteen-year-old from the inner western suburb of Petersham. She'd been attending East Sydney Technical College on a scholar-ship, studying art and dressmaking, when her mother noticed the advert and pushed her to apply.

Earlier that morning Valerie had knocked on the door in the hope that her eagerness would secure her the job, but she was turned away by a handsome young man with wavy black hair holding a toffee hammer. By the time she returned an hour later, the queue had stretched around the block into King Street. Annoyed, she spied a back door and, by slipping inside, reached the front of the queue. Those waiting outside were none-the-wiser as she faced the same young man she had met earlier, but he was now sitting with another man.

'This is the girl I was telling you about,' Monty Levy said to his older brother Maurice, who eyed the young woman flashing her best smile.

Maurice looked her up and down. A pretty foreigner, he guessed incorrectly. He gave her a task: 'Write the words "Candy Kitchen" on that card for me.'

Valerie gulped. This was a test of her calligraphy skills and, if there was one letter she hated writing, it was a capital 'K'. In a moment of inspiration, she ignored the brief and, with a flourish, wrote 'Tokyo Mixture'.

The brothers conferred. She had a good hand and they liked her feistiness, not to mention her curves. She could have the job, which paid £2 per week, but she might have to serve behind the counter as well. Valerie eagerly agreed.

Monty would recall in an interview with *The Age* newspaper in 1997 that Valerie fitted perfectly the physical mould sought by the company: 'They had to be tall, they had to be smilers and they had to have personality. If they hadn't been tall they couldn't see over the top of the counter because we used to build the counters up with lollies to such a height. We had such a reputation for girls. It got so bad that outside the shop at knockoff time there were up to thirty boys waiting for them.'

The queue-jumping later became an oft-told story at family gatherings. Valerie's son Lael reckoned it summed up his mother's character perfectly:

I can imagine it happening. The queues for jobs were long. It was [the] Depression period. She wouldn't have cared what anyone else thought about jumping queues. She was just someone who got in there. The brothers would have been there interviewing for two reasons: one to pick up a sheila, and, secondly, to get the best person possible. My father took one look at her and said: 'She's the one.'

Lael knows this not because his father told him but because his mother related the story. Valerie was proud of her appearance; she was keenly aware of the power of her presence and of the competition between Maurice and Monty for her attention. 'Maurice had eyes for Mum too,' Lael said. 'She was the one who told me.'

Among dozens of photographs of a young Valerie pasted into family albums is a series of photo booth shots, taken on the morning of the interview. Valerie is dressed demurely, a tie hung loosely and fashionably around her neck, her hair smoothed to one side in a ponytail. But it is her smile that shines, at once shy and alluring—she is a young woman who commands attention.

'The morning I met Monty in 1930,' one of the captions reads. 'He tells me now after 54 married years that he decided he'd marry me then and there. I always thought I'd caught him at a weak moment.'

CƐ

Valerie Everitt was more than a desirable and precocious teenager. She also had creative skills and was not afraid to voice her opinion in an environment that fostered fresh ideas. According to Lael, 'pushing her own barrow' came naturally to Valerie, and she was soon offering her own suggestions about the business.

The ticket writers, considered critical to the marketing success of the store, were stationed on the second floor of the Pitt Street building. There was a rough science behind the art, one that the company cleverly exploited. The brothers had unashamedly identified their market share as lower to middle class—in fact, more lower than middle—and they wanted their storefront advertising to reflect this careful positioning.

The process would start with a blank card, usually with yellow as the background colour, and then some hand-painted words in a bright red. This was a colour combination that the hamburger chain McDonald's would recognise many years later; it evoked feelings of appetite (red) and friendliness (yellow).

It was then a question of proportion—the ratio between words and price. The Darrell Lea philosophy was that the price should take up two-thirds of the card, with the remaining one-third devoted to words about its taste and quality. They believed that men mainly bought on price while women took into account the quality of the product itself. Given that the biggest share of sales in the city was to men on their way home, it was logical that the tickets highlighted the price.

Placement was also an art. There was the size of the ticket to consider, in proportion to the 'stack' of confectionery, and how it might be positioned in order to catch the light. And there were seasonal choices to make for goods that had a shelf life of a few days at best. For example, chocolates didn't sell well during Sydney's sticky summer heat, so in that season the family concentrated on toffees. Conversely, chocolates were favoured in the colder months.

Whatever they were selling, the displays were a kaleidoscope of colour—a shopfront version of a flamboyant Busby Berkeley Hollywood movie, as one writer would describe it—as if rebelling against the sad drabness of the Depression. There was affordable joy in a Darrell Lea window that made customers forget about their troubles—a year-round Christmas at a time when chocolate was not only a delicious treat but also considered a 'health-giving food' that was 'wholesome, fresh and nutritious'.

Monty, the creative talent among the Levy brothers, was always looking for new opportunities and techniques. He shared the management of the company with Maurice as their father, now approaching sixty, retreated further and further from the operation. While Maurice provided business leadership, it was Monty who pushed the marketing boundaries. As Lael put it, his father was a born entrepreneur—just as his own father, Harry, had been—and that meant he would taste success and swallow failure in equal measure.

And Valerie was by his side, although she was far from a wilting violet. One day, when Monty accused her of giving another girl a hard time, she gave him a black eye. She recorded the incident in a diary she kept, on and off, for more than 40 years:

Did I ever tell you about the time I was about eighteen, when I knocked Monty out cold with an uppercut under the chin? He had accused me of being unfair to Miss Murtagh who was very keen about him and WHO HE TOOK OUT a couple of times, and he claimed that was why I'd reprimanded her and it made me SO mad because I hadn't, and we were both standing in the doorway of 128 Pitt Street, leaning on the jamb and I let fly with my fist. He told me years later that he actually was out cold and couldn't even mop or blink the eye and, of course, I kept on talking and didn't know. It was only the doorjamb that held him up.

Valerie was quickly promoted from shop assistant to the senior management team, even helping to pen the *Salesgirls Guide to Better Salesmanship and Serving Your Customer*, the company rulebook on employee behaviour, which specified how a salesgirl should look and behave. The serving technique was precise.

'Sweets must be handled daintily and cleanly, and with the left hand so as to leave the right hand free and clean to handle money and bag,' it read in part. There were instructions on how to hold a bag of toffees 'with the left hand . . . close to your side so the customer won't reach out for it until the sale is ended' and how to focus on the customer. Eye contact was vital, as was the need to ensure the company logo on the bag's label was always facing the customer.

The tone of the voice and the message were also critical:

Don't quote the prices. She might ask 'How much?' and then you may say 'Six pence' and do try to get that correct inflection in your voice when quoting prices try not to sound scared, try not to sound as though you were frightened. When you give prices, give them as a FACT, drop the voice on the end syllable, don't raise it.

The notion of order and proper behaviour suited Valerie's personality. She was a woman who demanded attention as well as an immediate response to her orders, as she later demonstrated over and over in the way she ran her household, her marriage and her family.

 beta

It is not hard to see why Monty Lea fell hard for Valerie Everitt. She blew into the Lea family's life and business on a wave of bosomed confidence, turning heads from the moment she stepped into the Pitt Street store, lapping up the attention as men ogled her through the window while she served customers. Likewise, Valerie shone in a family home movie made during the 1930s, spinning and swirling in a white dress as she played to the camera with a toothpaste smile while the other women faded into the background.

Monty looked on in adulation. Despite his adventurous style in business, he was generally quiet and gentle, and happy to allow his girlfriend to take the spotlight. Short in stature, he had a 'kind Jewish face', one observer noted.

For her part, Valerie enjoyed the competition between Maurice and Monty for her attention, but she would quickly decide that Monty was the man for her, even though he could be 'picky and naggy'. This behaviour, she later wrote, once drove her to fantasise about 'sinking an iron toffee hammer into his head'. It would not be the only time she wrote about her dark thoughts and violent impulses.

The relationship would not be easy. Valerie was no pushover and resisted Monty's invitations for at least a year before agreeing to accompany him to a nearby theatre one night. And neither mother was keen on the union. Esther wanted her son to marry a Jewish girl while Harriet didn't want Valerie involved with a 'Jew boy'.

Monty was sent overseas and Valerie, now nineteen and managing one of the company's city stores, was dismissed. She opened a dressmaking business, calling herself Valerie Dallas. The separation lasted only a few months as Monty, on his return, defied his mother and drew Valerie back into the business. A marriage proposal soon followed.

Given the opposition of their respective parents as well as Monty's concern that his brothers would also object, the couple decided to keep their union secret, marrying quietly at the registry office inside Marrickville Town Hall on 24 May 1935 in the afternoon, just before the doors were closed for the day. Their honeymoon was a café meal and an evening at the pictures in George Street before they went home separately.

Harriet, unaware of her oldest daughter's elopement, was busy organising the wedding of her younger daughter, Lola. Three months later, in contrast to Valerie's clandestine ceremony, Lola was married in a glamorous traditional church service that made the social pages of the *Sydney Morning Herald*, which noted inaccurately that *Miss* Valerie Everitt was a bridesmaid. Valerie had also designed and made her sister's wedding dress, complete with a four-metre-long train.

Likewise, the Darrell Lea board members seemed to be none the wiser. Minutes of an August 1935 board meeting record that the idea of women staff members dressing in multi-coloured smocks, to make them stand out, was raised. Responsibility for the design was handed to the secretary, a Miss Featherstone, and to *Miss Everitt*, both of whom were asked to report back to the next board meeting.

A month later Valerie presented a design based on the attire customarily worn by artists—a smock with a giant bow at the front, which gave the impression that the salesgirl was wrapped up like a box of chocolates. Not only did the smocks look smart and add a sense of showmanship to the store, but they were also practical—a virtual one-size-fits-all garment that could be worn by all the women, even pregnant staff members. They were also deliberately made without pockets, to discourage staff from stealing.

Valerie and Monty, meanwhile, continued to live separately, relying on carefully planned liaisons, somehow managing to keep their marriage hidden from Harriet until 1939, when they accompanied Harris to the United States to scout for business and seek new ideas. Valerie told her mother that she was going along as an assistant. This enraged Harriet who, already suspicious, had managed to obtain the marriage certificate from the registry office.

When Monty and Valerie arrived in Honolulu several weeks later, they were detained by officials and questioned separately about their relationship and why they were travelling as Mr Lea and Miss Everitt—company director and salesgirl. They had been 'potted' by Harriet, who told officials that Monty had kidnapped her daughter and was planning to sell her into 'white slavery':

> Monty was held 'incommunicado' in Honolulu for a whole day until they finally elicited the information that we had been married for four years by having me swear on a Bible and THEN asked me for my true lawful name, and I had to give in.

The US trip would be a turning point for both the marriage and the company. The trio drove across the States, visiting confectionery factories and filling their heads with ideas, but when they returned to Sydney in September, forced to return by the declaration of World War II, older brother Maurice, now ensconced as chairman, promptly poured cold water on their ideas, preferring to stick with the company's successful formula.

The following year Harris enlisted in the army. Meantime Valerie and Monty headed to Melbourne, where they would concentrate on taking the Darrell Lea name to the southern capital and enjoy the freedom to pursue their own business ideas.

It was also time to start a family of their own, one of Valerie's few joyful expectations of marriage, as she would later reveal:

I expected to have a positively terrible and frustrating and hard-working married life . . . but I was always of the opinion that I'd rather be miserable with him than happy with someone else! But I do wish I'd started having children sooner and had more.

4

A NEW IDENTITY

The house was enormous, or so it seemed to four-year-old Gayle. She wouldn't have noticed the sign on the door, but 'The Lodge' suited the building—room after room of beds and bookshelves and toys. Even a rocking horse! To a child who had arrived with only a paper bag, a security blanket and a notepad the house seemed endless—a wonderland of children and noise. Gayle's fears were suddenly replaced by wide-eyed excitement.

There were seven other children. The loudest of them were seven-year-old Lael, who jumped and swayed in front of her with monkey-like energy, and six-year-old Brett, the boy who had called her Honey as they walked down the front path. He had a wash of freckles across his face and a wide, broken-toothed grin.

The other children were quieter. Jason, eleven years old and almost as tall as his mother, looked at Gayle curiously with his dark eyes. His sister Gaela, aged nine, said nothing and went to her room. There was another girl named June, who, she was told, was Gaela's playmate and new to the house, just like her. But June would not stay long. She had already run away once and would do so again a few weeks later so Valerie returned her to child welfare authorities.

There was also another seven-year-old boy named Shelton, but he was sick in bed. Gayle peeped into his darkened room and saw his pale face and curly dark hair against the white pillowcase. She decided he looked like an angel.

Finally, there was Charryce who, like Gayle, was also four years old. They were to share a room and be playmates, just like Gaela and June. Valerie called Charryce 'Bubbie', but Gayle didn't know what to make of her.

The enormity of the change struck her at dinner that night when her new family sat around a huge table in a room off the kitchen. Valerie sat at one end of the table next to her husband, whose name was Monty. He had a nice smile, she decided.

Around them on both sides sat the eight children, from oldest to youngest. Gayle was told to sit next to Valerie and gazed around the room. There were women in uniforms serving the food. It felt like a fairytale.

At one point Gayle stood up and left the room. The others stopped, wondering where the little girl had gone and what she was doing. She was back a minute later with the paper bag she had been carrying when she arrived. Gayle reached into it and pulled out her notepad, then solemnly walked around the table, presenting each person with a blank, carefully torn-out page.

'I wanted to show them all that I was excited,' she would later recall. 'And blank pages from a notepad was all I had to give them.'

After dinner Valerie showed Gayle to the bedroom she would be sharing with Charryce on the second floor. When they were standing at the top of the staircase, her new mother made another announcement: 'From now on your name will be Kestin.'

The little girl was confused. 'But my name is Gayle.'

'Yes, but we already have a Gaela, so you can't be Gayle anymore.'

It was all too much. Why did she need a new name and why did she need a new mother? What was going to happen to her? In the early hours of the morning Gayle woke in fright. She must have been screaming in her sleep because the lights were on and it seemed as if every member of the family was crowded around her bed, peering at her.

Valerie was the closest, crouched next to the bed in her dressing-gown. There was no attempt to console her, no words of comfort or understanding that she was distressed. The expression on the face of her new protector was annoyance.

CB

Giving birth didn't come easily for Valerie Lea, at least not the first time, in 1942, the year World War II reached Australia's shores. Darwin was bombed in February and Sydney Harbour infiltrated by three Japanese midget submarines in June. As the year progressed, the fear of invasion spread as far south as Melbourne, where residents began digging air raid shelters in their backyards.

Valerie's baby was due on 18 September. But when the day came, although she was packed and ready for the trip to hospital, there was no sign that the baby was ready to enter the world. Instead, Valerie spent an anxious day waiting at home before ringing the office of her paediatrician, Dr Wilson, in a panic. The surgery receptionist seemed amused by her naïve discomfort, brusquely telling her to ring back in a week if nothing had happened. Valerie felt like a sook. Monty shrugged his shoulders.

As instructed, she called again seven days later when there was still no movement. It was a Monday and the receptionist was kinder this time. First pregnancies were often late, she reassured her. There was nothing to worry about. Dr Wilson wanted her to be at the hospital in three days' time. If her waters hadn't broken by then, he would induce her.

At 5 am on 28 September, now ten days overdue, Valerie reached for the castor oil in the hope it would act as a laxative and kick-start the contractions. Nothing. When she was admitted to hospital four hours later she was promptly given a large white tablet. God knows what was in it. She didn't bother to ask, so keen was she to get the baby out. Nothing. Another pill the size of a tuppenny piece an hour later. Again, nothing. Another at 11 am. Still nothing, and the nurses started to look slightly worried.

The first injection was given at 1 pm, then another at 2 pm, after which she finally felt the contraction pains begin. Sudden and fierce, they hurt like hell, but the pain was a welcome relief from the worry. But by 6 pm it had all become too much. She was aching but the contractions were still a long way apart and delivery seemed no closer. Then came the sedative—Twilight

Sleep it was called, a combination of morphine and scopolamine to obliterate memory. Valerie blacked out.

When she woke up three hours later the baby was still inside her but delivery had begun. Not that she knew anything about it; there was no pain, only the blurred vision of Dr Wilson and the nurses around her. Valerie thought she had died, she would later write, with 'end of the world' noises buzzing in her head. It turned out to be noises from the labour ward next door, where they had taken her baby.

Jason Durard Lea weighed almost ten pounds. Little wonder that, six days earlier, Monty had strained hard as he heaved his heavily pregnant wife over the threshold of 22 Lambert Road. Their first house together, it had been bought to celebrate the beginning of what they hoped would be a big family to match the thriving business. Monty had been planning to welcome mother and baby to a new home that would be bright and fresh and gleaming but, as is often the way, the renovations were not quite finished and they would have to begin their new life amid mess and chaos.

By contrast, when Gaela was born on 9 August 1944—Valerie's own birthday—it was an easy delivery. The labour pains started at about 4 am and Gaela slipped into the world four hours later. How wonderful to have a child as a birthday present, Valerie thought. A gift from God. There was no great pain or discomfort that she could recall; the day before she'd even worked in the garden planting tomato bushes. She was twenty-nine years old and eager for more children, despite the continued horror of war that seemed no closer to resolution.

It was the same with Lael, due in the first week of August 1946 but arriving three weeks later. The day before he was born, Valerie went shopping, pushing Gaela in a pram. On reflection, it was not a good idea, but it seemed to do the trick. At 4 o'clock the following morning she felt the first contraction and went straight into hospital. Lael was born at 10 am, such a big baby that she swore he damaged her back.

The arrival of Charryce two years later, also detailed in her diary, was a different matter. Due in early December 1948, she was late, like the others, and her doctor decided to put Valerie into hospital, where they gave her the works: castor oil, hot baths, tablets and six injections. All to no avail. She was sent home but returned a week later to undergo the same procedure.

At 9 am Valerie swallowed castor oil and took a hot bath. The first contraction came as she stepped out of the water at 9.20. Bang. The midwife gave her a needle at 9.30 and forty minutes later Charryce appeared. Just one push, one squawk of pain, and she was out.

Then the problems began. The nursing sister who, she wrote, 'had just arrived from delivering black babies in South Africa'— began pummelling her stomach to help remove the afterbirth. But it wouldn't come away and she began losing blood at a rapid rate. A transfusion specialist and the Red Cross were called while Valerie's doctor tried to measure the amount of blood she was losing by scooping it up in dishes.

The maternity ward had become a trauma unit. The situation was serious, Monty was told as he paced the corridors, wondering if his wife was going to make it. (When Valerie, with her trademark sense of dark humour, retold this story many times over the years, she reckoned Monty was also wondering where he was going to find another woman to take care of their six children if she didn't make it.) When Red Cross nurses walked in carrying bags of blood, Monty's worry turned to anger because they weren't running.

Inside the delivery room Valerie was in a daze; she was vaguely aware of the panic around her, but physically unable to respond, other than to hold her doctor's hand as his colleague struggled to find a vein. She felt her body fizz with pins and needles as the blood flowed into her veins, coupled with the strange sensation that she had become too heavy and the bed wouldn't hold her. Then, mercifully, the ether took hold and she passed out.

When Valerie woke three hours later, the emergency was over. Two pints of saline and four pints of blood had been pumped into her as nursing staff worked to remove the retained placenta. The doctor told her he had never seen anyone lose so much blood so quickly. Valerie was lucky to be alive but she would struggle with back pain for the next seven months.

But the baby was worth it, she would write in her diary, even if Charryce was 'the plainest one of the lot, with all of Monty's and my worst points and none of our good ones'. Not that her initial disappointment lessened her love for the child. Quite the opposite, in fact, as 'Bubbie' quickly became her favourite.

She would also be her last natural child.

ભ

October 1953

For the first few days after leaving the Collins Street surgery, Shirley Newman had done nothing, unsure of how she felt or what she wanted in life. The reality that she had given away her own daughter was now setting in, and so was the regret. She had decided to act.

On the day she handed Gayle over, a friend of Shirley's had followed the little girl and the woman to a house in Toorak. Now she was outside that home, watching quietly, hoping to see Gayle and maybe talk to her, to find out how she felt. If she wasn't happy, then maybe she would demand her back. If Gayle said she was happy, then maybe it was all right and she could walk away, content that her daughter would have a good life. Better than she could provide anyway.

Gayle wasn't her only child. There was a two-year-old boy and another child on the way. She touched her belly, the bulge hidden beneath her coat. The 24-year-old was several months pregnant.

There were also others to consider. Gayle was an unplanned pregnancy, the result of a fleeting romance with a man named Leslie Rough, who had offered to marry her 'to do the right thing'. But she'd said no, unwilling to 'make the same mistake my mother did', as she would later offer in defence of her decision.

Instead of giving birth in a hospital surrounded by her lover, family and friends, she had done so alone at The Haven, a Salvation Army home in North Fitzroy, an inner-city working-class suburb of Melbourne.

Inside she had found herself among forty or so other young

women—victims of bad timing rather than bad character, she would say—who slept in dormitories of ten and were kept by the quasi-military Salvationists to a rigid schedule that included daily chores, cleaning, cooking, laundry and minding babies in the crèche. The staff were kind, but everything came at a cost— even the second-hand light blue cardigan she was forced to buy for a few pence to ward off the winter cold.

On 10 April 1949, Shirley was on her hands and knees in a corridor scrubbing floors when she felt the first labour pains. Gayle was born a few hours later, the delivery less complicated than what was to follow. She had nowhere to go, so they stayed at the home until Shirley's mother agreed to take in her and the baby.

But that arrangement wouldn't last; by the time she had turned one, Gayle was living with Dot and Jack Quinlan, an aunt and uncle of Gayle's father. She would live with the Quinlans for three years until one evening in September 1953 when Shirley turned up with a police officer. She wanted Gayle back—not to keep, but to give away.

Now she was unsure. The first time she went to the Lea house, Shirley stayed outside a short while, then a bit longer the second time. But she did not see her daughter on either occasion.

Then, on the third occasion, Gayle was alone on the porch, sitting on a chair with a blanket covering her lap. Shirley was unaware that her daughter had been in bed with pneumonia the previous week.

Shirley ventured near the gate and called softly, in case someone inside the house heard her. Gayle looked up in surprise.

Recognising her mother, she dropped the blanket and walked to the front gate. Her hair was tied back in pigtails and she was dressed in a white top and tartan skirt that her mother didn't recognise. Shirley bent down so she'd be at the girl's eye line. 'Are you happy?' she asked her. 'Are they treating you well?'

Gayle was thinking about the playroom, the rocking horse and the other children. 'Yes,' she nodded.

Shirley didn't know what to say. 'Can I take a photo of you, please?' she said finally.

Gayle stood at the gate, arms behind her back as if embarrassed, and grinned at her mother. The smile turned to a look of confusion when, after taking the photo, Shirley waved and walked away. It was the second time that her mother had abandoned her.

Ω

When Shirley was out of sight, Gayle ran into the house and found Valerie. 'My mummy was just outside the house!' she squealed excitedly.

Valerie stopped what she was doing and looked down, an angry expression on her face. 'Don't be silly, Kestin, you're imagining it.'

Valerie's diary entry for that day says the opposite. She believed the little girl, or at least feared she might be right, and telephoned the adoption officer, a public servant named Basil Rush, to have him warn off Shirley Newman. As if to cement her situation, she also phoned her solicitor to formally register Gayle's new name— Kestin Ferne Melani Lea.

There was another diary entry written later the same day. It read: 'Honey tonight had to be restrained from throwing the table and chairs at the other children upstairs.'

Decades later, when she applied for her birth certificate, Gayle would find that the true details of her birth had been altered. Her certificate stated that she had been born not to Shirley Newman but to Valerie and Monty Lea, and had six siblings. The 'informant' was Valerie.

She could vividly recall Shirley coming to the house. 'She asked me if I was happy. I probably was; after all, I was four years old and there were other kids and a rocking horse and billy carts to play with. I had ribbons in my hair. Why didn't she ask me if I wanted to stay?'

ଓଃ

Valerie Lea started adopting children in 1947, when a young factory worker named Louise O'Brien confided in her boss that she was pregnant, unmarried and considering an abortion. Valerie was between babies at the time, having given birth to Lael the previous August, and she saw it as an opportunity to add a kitten to the litter without any effort, particularly as she still dreamed of having a dozen or more children. What difference would it make if one of them wasn't her own flesh and blood?

She had convinced the young woman to continue the pregnancy by promising to take the child when he or she was born. She had then watched over her like a hawk, supplying her with calcium and vitamins until the birth on 5 July. The adoption of the boy she would name Bretton Carrick Grantham Lea was made official a few weeks later through the Child Welfare Agency, where Valerie told the officer, the same Basil Rush who would organise Honey's adoption, that she was in the market for more 'orphans'.

Unlike Gayle, Brett of course had no memory of his real mother. As far as he was concerned, Valerie was his mother and Monty his father; he called them Mum and Dad. Yet they never hid the fact that he was adopted—in fact the point that he was 'not a real Lea' would be made constantly. But the only information he was ever given about his natural mother—that she was Spanish—was not true.

Four months after Brett's arrival at Lambert Road, another 'orphan' would join him in the family home.

℃ß

Gwyneth Roberts, like Shirley Newman, gave birth to a child at The Haven in North Fitzroy. But the birth certificate of Philip Anthony Roberts, born on 25 August 1946, made no mention of his father.

Gwyneth—'a refined type of girl', as staff would later recall—was twenty years old. When her dreams of marriage and a family had been shattered, she had fled her home city of Perth and made a three-day train journey across the Nullarbor to ensure she could have her illegitimate baby in secret.

The story she gave authorities sounded plausible: the father was a man named Anthony Edwin de Havilland, a Royal Engineer with the British Army, whom she had met at a party in the last months of 1945 as the world celebrated the end of World War II.

A relationship of sorts quickly developed and, when Gwyneth fell pregnant in early December, he responded by promising to marry her. The wedding date was set for January 1946 and the arrangements were well under way when he suddenly disappeared. De Havilland was found in Sydney soon afterwards and shipped back to England. Gwyneth was told that her errant fiancé, who had spent time in a Japanese prisoner of war camp, had suffered a nervous breakdown. She was left alone and in shame.

There was one problem with Gwyneth's account. Anthony Edwin de Havilland did not exist, or at least his name had never been registered in birth records or in British Armed Forces lists. Either he had given her a false name and hope, or she had made up the name and the account to cover the embarrassment of an out-of-wedlock pregnancy. Whether they was genuine or not, the aristocratic-sounding name and dramatic story also gave Gwyneth and her baby a social status that made an adoption to a good home more likely.

The boy arrived a few days prematurely and, as was the practice at the time, was moved on his own to Queen Victoria Hospital in William Street, Melbourne, for observation. In his absence, Gwyneth checked out of The Haven, but refused to sign adoption consent forms. She seemed undecided about the future. Instead of returning to Perth, she remained in Melbourne, got a job as a secretary, and within six months met and married the man with whom she would spend the rest of her life and raise a family.

But her secret son would not be part of the plan with her new husband, an engineer named Noel Lennard, deciding that a fresh start was her only option. Gwyneth never told Lennard of her illegitimate son, whose existence would remain a secret until long after she died.

In the meantime, she had fallen behind in her payments to The Haven, which charged twelve shillings and sixpence per week to take care of babies left by their mothers. The law at that time was cruel: if a mother fell more than four weeks behind in her payments, then the child automatically became a ward of the state and would be adopted out, like a stray dog from a kennel.

A suitable couple was found almost immediately but Gwyneth changed her mind and once again refused to sign the consent forms. The couple was turned away and Philip remained at The Haven, although his mother, now embarked on a new life, hardly visited him. She finally relented and signed the consent forms on 14 November 1947.

Again, the middleman was Basil Rush who, recalling Valerie Lea's enthusiasm for more children, telephoned to offer her 'a nice type of child, always contented, appears to be a normal child'.

Valerie was happy to accept. 'I have never believed in the idea of *choosing* one's own product and preferred to take just what was offered to us.' Monty was not about to refuse his wife: 'Okay, one more won't hurt,' he said.

In her diary, many years later, Valerie would recall the day that Basil Rush drove her and her sister-in-law Sheila to The Haven to pick up the child, whom she would name Shelton Giles Kimball Lea: 'I had on a hat piled high with flowers and when they brought Shelton in he gave it one look and yelled and didn't stop. It must have been the hat.'

What worried her more though were the scabs, each as big as a one-shilling piece, on the top and back of his head. She said the nurses told her they were the result of 'a little habit' of bumping his head and assured her that, with time, he would grow out of it. (Staff who nursed the boy at The Haven would describe the marks as sores, not bruises. His head thrashing would only occur after he had left The Haven and was placed in the care of the Leas.)

Although the marks on his head bothered her, Valerie was pleased that Shelton and Lael were virtually twins, born only a day apart, which meant that not only had she added another child to her brood but they could be playmates: 'Two dogs play better than one,' she would say.

But the head bumping was a worry. It was accompanied by a rhythmic moaning as he hit his head on the side of the cot for what seemed like hours each night. She bought him a rubber pillow to soften the blows but he didn't stop, instead increasing the force to compensate the muffled sound by crossing his arms in front of his face and throwing his head in a big arc so his head came down with a thump.

He seemed to be aware of what he was doing because, if anyone came into the room, he would suddenly stop, only starting up again when they left. Valerie took Shelton to see a GP who assessed the boy as normal and prescribed drugs he hoped would calm Shelton.

'Nothing seemed to help. Not even whacking,' Valerie recalled.

5

THE BULWARK AGAINST DISASTER

Walter Henry Everitt's childhood was not unlike Manesseh Jablinovich's. He grew up as one of ten children to Arthur Everitt, a Coventry watchmaker. His father emigrated to Australia in 1881 with a wife and four children, but he was widowed soon after. When Arthur married again, he and his second wife had another six children, whom they raised in Lithgow, a relatively new and isolated settlement beyond the Blue Mountains. Everitt opened a jeweller's shop and became a prominent businessman in the district, serving on the local council for many years.

One of the youngest of his brood, Walter was born in 1888. By his mid-teens he had made his way to Sydney, where he was apprenticed as a carpenter, a sturdy trade in a growing and newly federated colony. Later he expanded into general construction.

Walter had strange feet, according to his eldest daughter,

Valerie: 'Web toes on his right foot and lesser on his left,' she would comment in her diary many years later.

But that was largely it, at least in her diary. There were few other references to her father—no mention of his war service or celebration of his building skills that would help build a family fortune, let alone declarations of fatherly love, although she described herself as 'daddy's girl' and was always defending him to her mother.

Most notably, she did not appear to mourn his death in 1955, only mentioning that he cheated her out of her share of a jointly held property in Sydney and making a passing reference to her father when discussing hereditary hairlines, observing: 'My father still had hair in a "V" to the front till he died of cirrhosis of the liver at 66.'

And perhaps that was the clue. Walter Everitt was a problem drinker and frequently disappeared for weeks at a time. There was certainly evidence of that in 1916 when his wife Harriet reported her errant man to police for desertion. They had been married for five years; their daughter Valerie had just turned three and Harriet was four months pregnant. It was little wonder that she acted swiftly when Walter disappeared.

The *NSW Police Gazette* of 11 October 1916 noted:

Marrickville—A warrant has been issued by the Newtown bench for the arrest of Walter Henry Everitt, charged with wife desertion. He is 28 years of age, 5 feet 10 inches high, medium build, dark complexion and hair, thin features, clean shaved, has "Biddy" tattooed on one forearm; dressed in a navy-blue suit and grey soft-felt hat; a carpenter. Complainant: Harriet Everitt, Church Street, Marrickville.

There is no record of why Walter went AWOL, where he had gone and when he returned, but he wasn't gone for long. On 10 July 1917, less than four months after the birth of his second child, Lola, he signed up and went to war. Valerie was about to turn four.

His enlistment papers noted that the couple was now renting a house in Manly near Harriet's parents, a long ferry ride across Sydney Harbour. It says much about the transient nature of their early years together and the obvious lack of financial and physical security, which played on his wife's mind. The couple had already lived at four different addresses, mostly around the city's inner west, but war had sent Harriet scurrying back to the comfort of her mother, with whom she would remain until his return.

Walter's army medical report is strangely inadequate, given that it missed his webbed toes and makes no mention of the tattoo described in the police report. But it does note that he had a mole on his right cheek, a wart under his right arm and acne between his shoulder blades.

Whatever prompted his decision to sign up three years after the conflict began, Walter joined the Eighth Field Company Royal Australian Engineers and in November sailed from Melbourne aboard the troop ship *Nestor*. He disembarked at Suez before sailing to Southampton in January 1918; he finally reached the French front in May, just as the first American troops joined the war and Germany wilted.

Walter saw action around the town of Rouelles, but on Armistice Day he was in London on leave. However, although the war had ended, it would be eleven months before Walter headed back to Australia, taking a six-month position in an engineering firm in London rather than going straight home. His army file shows that during this time both his father and his wife made attempts to contact him; Harriet eventually wrote in annoyance to his superiors. The letter remains on file and says in part: 'Should you receive word of my husband's embarkation I would be much obliged if you would let me know when to expect him home.'

Valerie was aged six when her father finally returned from war. He declared to the army brass that he was free of any physical or psychological disabilities from war and ready to settle into the role of family man. The couple and their two daughters moved back to the inner west and Walter began re-establishing himself as a builder, building houses in a sweep of suburbs from Belmore to Kogarah and Glebe, as reunited families began the work of rebuilding a nation torn by conflict but now revitalised by an influx of European migrants eager for a new life. The young family would move into the finished property while Walter started on the next. It would then be sold for a small profit and the family would move again. As a result, Valerie would recall attending a dozen different schools.

ଓ

Harriet, Valerie's mother, was a year older than her husband and had broken off four engagements by the time she met Walter, who drove a horse and gig and had a pet fox. She had been born to a Welsh carpenter named Joshua Evans and his wife, Maria, who had been scooped up by Australia's migrant program and given assisted passage, arriving in the promised land in 1877 after a three-month voyage aboard the wool clipper *La Hogue*.

Maria was as feisty as she was striking, with blue, blue eyes and a mane of curly jet-black hair. She would give birth to fourteen children, including two sets of twins, although most of them would not survive childhood. In all likelihood it was Maria who inspired Valerie's desire to have a large family, given that she offered no other explanation for it and made reference to her grandmother's large brood.

The third youngest of Maria's children, Harriet was particularly close to her mother, embracing her very firm ideas about the demands of life and the bonds of marriage. In her world, everyone was expected to make their own way. As Valerie would later write:

Harriet's expressed demand—I cannot find the correct word for it—was that everybody should stand on their own two feet, that husbands should support the wives and the wives should do their utmost, as she had done all her life, to improve themselves and their children's futures, but that what SHE had worked hard for should be left to GROW and to ultimately be a 'BULWARK AGAINST DISASTER' for a large number of people—HER DESCENDANTS. She wanted each child, as it arrived, to have a little security for its future, which she did for her grandchildren and expected them to continue to do with theirs.

It was a simple enough ethos and one by which Harriet would live as she set up house with Walter Everitt. She clearly wasn't interested in following her own mother's desire for a large family and, even if she'd had maternal aspirations, the war got in the way. The potential for disaster was around every corner. She had spent the war years scrimping and saving but, by the mid-1920s, with the gradual success of her husband's one-man business and the help of her mother, she had managed to save £1000. Then she saw an opportunity to buy a family home rather than keep moving every six months.

Petersham is roughly six kilometres from Sydney's central business district, tucked between Parramatta Road and the Cooks River. Cleared and tilled by convict labourers in the last years of the eighteenth century, it provided the colony's prime agricultural land for wheat and corn and was named after the home village in Surrey of the then lieutenant-governor, Francis Grose.

Over the next century the area was initially carved into large private estates then slowly subdivided as the city's population spread. A rail line was opened in the mid-1800s. Horse-drawn and, later, motorised omnibus services followed as road surfaces were improved. As a consequence, the housing stock was a mixture of grand residences interspersed with more modest terraced housing for the middle class and a smattering of tiny workmen's cottages.

John Street, in the middle of the suburb, is a pleasant tree-lined avenue made up mostly of middle-class housing—two-storey terraces with filigree iron balconies, and large rooms and high ceilings, which could be configured in a variety of ways for different purposes, depending on the occupancy. Twenty-five John Street, a typical house of the late Victorian era, was built before the nation plunged into the Great Depression.

In June 1924 it was advertised by the *Sydney Morning Herald* as a 'gentleman's residence', with all the modern conveniences of the time, including a bath heater, but Harriet was more interested in its rental potential. The owner wanted to sell it for £1300, but it was estimated that it could be rented out for £150 per year. At one-third of the average wage for a working man, this would be a tidy return but one that could be doubled or better if the house was turned into a series of one-bedroom flats.

Rather than working on other people's houses, Harriet wanted her husband to work on *their* house. Besides, she could keep an eye on him. They bought number 25 and moved into the bottom half of the building while Walter converted the second storey and the rear into flats. Harriet Everitt had begun to build her legacy.

In 1929, now flush with the rental money earned, which had been carefully saved as capital, Harriet spied another terrace house in the same street. It was a bargain—cheaper than their first purchase for a house of similar size. The advertisement in the *Herald* of Monday, 23 December 1929, read:

Enmore Minute Terminus. Double-front tuck-pointed cottage. 6 rooms, garage. Good locality corner position. Needs slight repairs reduced from £1300 to £1025. Worth inspection. 17 John Street, Petersham.

The Everitts moved again and Walter began work on the new house, keeping the bottom half as the family home while creating flats above and behind. Advertisements for tenants began to appear in newspapers the following year and the rental income started to flow in. Harriet did not move again for more than two decades.

Harriet and Walter would buy at least twenty more properties, many using the same formula as the John Street houses—creating flats from large houses—but sometimes keeping them as they were, to be rented as family homes. There were two side by side in Lincoln Street, Stanmore; another in Neville Street, Marrickville; and one in Eltham Street, Lewisham. Harriet even ventured into the city's eastern suburbs to snap up a cottage in Jersey Road, Woollahra. There would be other houses, mostly bought in the names of her daughters, Valerie and Lola, who would ultimately inherit the properties and be expected to expand the empire.

Harriet rarely bought anything other than residential properties but there were a few exceptions, including a group of shops across the road from a nearby railway station. Her reasoning was simple and logical: in the Depression of the 1930s factories closed, and people lost their jobs and didn't have money to spend, but everyone still needed 'a pound of butter, a loaf of bread and a roof over their head'. And that became her maxim.

When Harriet divorced Walter in 1939, they divided the properties. Harriet kept on building the financial sandbag she called her Bulwark Against Disaster, a fund that would become the family treasure trove. She remarried, but it lasted only a few years and Harriet would spend the last 30 years of her extraordinary life frugally managing her property empire and drip-feeding her daughters money to educate and house their children—her bloodline.

Harriet and Harriet's mother, Maria Evans, were Valerie's heroes—women with a physical and moral backbone who left a mark through self-sacrifice. Harriet had worked hard all her life and kept nothing for herself, eschewing luxuries, wearing hand-me-down clothing from her daughters, managing tenants, sweeping yards and emptying rubbish bins, even choosing to walk around the streets of Marrickville and Petersham to collect rents each week rather than take a bus. To others it might have looked excessive, but for Harriet it was a way of life—to sustain not just her life but the lives of those who would follow. Valerie watched and followed her mother's example, squirrelling away ten shillings of her £2 Darrell Lea wages and even making her own clothes to save money.

Years later, when a grandchild was to be named Everitt in honour of the maternal line, Valerie exploded: 'I said "no"! I have done nought and neither did the Everitts. It was the EVANS who really did the scraping and working and saving . . . Harriet and her mother started the Bulwark Against Disaster.'

To her grandchildren, Harriet was known as Mungah, from Jason's garbled attempt to say 'Grandma'. To Lael and the others, the nickname seemed to fit a woman who dressed like a bag lady but was the modern equivalent of a millionaire.

As Lael later recalled:

She was tiny but she was a tough lady. Nobody dared cross her. I remember going around with her once to help collect the rents. It was all about cash. She would even empty the gas meters, a penny at a time, and take it back to 25 John Street to be counted and banked.

She had some strange ideas, including that poo had to be white to be healthy. That's why she drank a lot of milk.

6

SHATTERED DREAMS

18 May 1951

Valerie was in a hurry to get home after work. She had just hired a cook named 'Woody' and didn't want to disappoint her by letting dinner go cold. It was a rush to lock up the Swanston Street store and she was in no mood to argue with her brother-in-law. Darrell was in town from Sydney for a few days and had leapt into the front seat of the jeep alongside Monty.

Valerie had little doubt that Darrell was baiting her. After all, he was well aware of her often stated desire to sit in the middle of the bench seat next to her husband, where she felt safe. Valerie and Darrell had a testy relationship at the best of times, not helped by his extravagant lifestyle and what she regarded as his spendthrift ways. She had often made this abundantly clear.

But on this occasion Valerie thought better of rising to the bait and instead accepted the discomfort of climbing in beside

Darrell, next to the window. They were late as it was, she reminded Monty, who roared off down the city streets towards Toorak.

Darkness was descending as they drove with the late evening commuters out of the CBD, across the Yarra and past the Royal Botanic Gardens before swinging left into Domain Road, where the traffic began to thin as they followed the river towards Lambeth Road.

Valerie's thoughts had turned to her family and what she might find when she got home when the headlights of a car suddenly appeared behind them. It was clear the driver was speeding towards them, but Monty was unprepared for the dangerous manoeuvre that followed as the unseen driver closed in and then tried to overtake, clipping the rear wheel of the jeep and sending the lighter vehicle into a furious spin.

Like the two men, Valerie was not wearing a seatbelt, so she was catapulted from her seat and flung against the rail of the seat behind. Even years later she would remember the crunching force of the impact as she fell on the boards at the base of the seat and then literally bounced out the rear door of the car, which had been thrown open on impact, and onto the road.

Valerie's corsetry, underclothes and stockings had been ripped to pieces, and her dress and coat thrown over her head as she slumped in an ungainly pose, wondering if she had internal injuries. She had also lost control of her bladder.

All she could think about was that her face and teeth hadn't been smashed. She climbed slowly out of the gutter and screamed in the direction of the jeep, which was now at rest by the side of the road with steam issuing from its bonnet. The car that had struck them was gone; it was recovered later and found to have been stolen. The driver was never identified.

'Monty! Monty!' she screamed, fearing the worst. Then she was flooded with relief as her husband and his brother clambered from the wreckage, miraculously unharmed except for a few bruises, but afraid that their car might burst into flames.

Valerie collapsed onto the road again; the adrenalin that had been released into her system was no longer able to mask the sharp pain that now began to spread up her back. She had the bilious taste of fear in her mouth, a sensation that was foreign to a woman so in charge of her own life: 'I sat on the kerb and could feel the hysteria rising up in my chest, so I started talking about anything and everything,' she would later write.

The noise of the accident attracted crowds and an ambulance. The three of them were taken to the nearby Alfred Hospital, where they were treated before being sent home six hours later, dinner forgotten but their lives changed forever. Somehow the seriousness of Valerie's injury was missed, because of either an inaccurate X-ray or a careless examination. Her back would never be the same again, affecting her life physically and emotionally. Henceforth she experienced frequent bursts of pain, which forever and understandably affected her moods.

All her children would recall mornings where she would call them to help her lash herself into a heavy corset, clinging to the bedpost while they threaded and pulled, tightened and tied the long strings that pressed the canvas to her injured frame. It would be two decades before improved techniques and equipment, as well as attentive specialists, would not only discover a sea of floating bone chips and re-formed bones but conclude that, when she had been thrown from the jeep, Valerie must have landed in a doubled-over position that had stretched her spine and crushed its base. It explained why at times she described the discomfort as feeling as if she were a rag doll, shuffling on rubber heels and walking with a stick.

In the meantime, she would comfort herself with her belief that the unselfish decision not to challenge Darrell that night had probably saved him from far more serious injury, if not death: 'Had he been in my position he'd have definitely been badly or even fatally injured, but I was wearing a thick pad right on the spot where I was hit, so that my skirt would lie flat on my bum. My spine would have been smashed up completely if it had not been for the six-inch pad and heavy corsets.'

CB

Henceforth Valerie's movement around the house and the company's places of business was restricted, but it did not dull her greatest desire—to have children—and she was pregnant before the end of the year: 'I lost another baby at 3 months— pregnant Xmas 1951.'

It was her tenth pregnancy in as many years, four producing children in the even years—1942, '44, '46 and '48. The miscar- riages in the alternate years all happened late in the pregnancy, despite drugs being prescribed to try to help her 'hold' the baby as she entered the last trimester. It didn't occur to her that her body simply wasn't ready for another pregnancy.

When questioned by her daughter Gaela years later, Valerie

described the drugs she took in the successful pregnancies as 'injections', without supplying any detail, but admitted opting on occasions to take 'little mauve pills' widely prescribed at the time to help prevent miscarriages. Not only did they not help but they were actually dangerous, it was later discovered, hence Gaela's concern when she learned that some children born to women who had used the synthetic oestrogen called diethylstilbestrol, or DES, were found to have developed cervical cancer.

Valerie described in her diary how she took DES in 1950 and 1951, and in both cases had been bedridden for a fortnight, unable to move or utter more than a breathy whisper. The tablets had affected her mind in such a way that she could not stand the slightest noise, forcing Monty to tiptoe around the house. Both pregnancies ended in miscarriage.

The depth of Valerie's desire for a large brood was hard to fathom, complicated as it was by her devotion to the business and her constant worry about money. She would refer on occasion to her belief that wives should contribute in the home while having an external role that contributed financially; this was what her mother continued to do.

In later years Valerie would look back on the moment she realised her dream of motherhood was over. She felt she had failed somehow: 'When I look at the measly little family I produced, just the four of them, it breaks my heart that I didn't start earlier than I did. I might have had a dozen. I'm so thrilled and happy with the ones I have that I'd have loved to have had more. I remember I was quite morbid for a couple of years after Bubbie when I'd had my tubes tied. I felt like a blot on the landscape.

I felt like I was not of any use at all unless I was producing and bringing up progeny.'

There was no mention of Shelton, Brett or Honey. Somehow, they didn't figure in her notion of being productive. A mother in name only.

7

DISPLEASING GOD

Valerie Lea was a maternal enigma, a woman who wanted twelve or thirteen or fourteen or even fifteen children, depending on who asked and when. Just as strange, and unexplained, was her choice of names. Her eldest child's name, Jason Durard, was mundane by comparison to his younger siblings: Gaela Sherrin Carissa, Leighland Blythe Courtney, Shelton Giles Kimball, Bretton Carrick Grantham, Charryce Laleen Yolana and Kestin Ferne Melani.

Yet it was strange that someone so passionate about family did not appear to be interested in the hands-on role and day-to-day details of motherhood. As Australia entered the 1950s, an era in which most families operated on the notion of men going to work and women staying at home, the matriarch of Lambert Road had an obligation of far greater importance—the family business.

So the children were looked after by a cavalcade of staff, up to a dozen working three at a time on a rotation of two eight-hour shifts per day. Some were hired locally but many were recruited from the shiploads of post-war European migrants arriving in Melbourne each week. Valerie would go down to the docks herself and interview likely employees as they came down the gangplank, offering them room and board, a small wage and English classes at the local language school twice a week in exchange for caring for the children.

They were mostly 'Balts', as Valerie described the collective of Yugoslavs, Russians and Lithuanians she would employ over the years. They had names like Zofia, Bronislava and Bronica, and slept out the back in bungalows, with their own outside toilet and bathroom. Some lasted a few months and others several years: 'Nobody has such bad luck as I do with those Balts,' she would complain.

There was a strict domestic routine prescribed by Valerie; staff described her as 'very particular'. When they were young, the children would be walked to the local kindergarten and primary school while Valerie and Monty, who didn't rise until after 9 am, went to work.

Charryce would often go into her parents' bedroom to say goodbye on her way to school: 'They would be sitting up in bed eating toast and jam and talking about the day to come,' she recalled in an interview. 'They would even take the first phone calls of the day in bed, a bit like Winston Churchill.'

The younger children would be picked up again at noon and fed, then put to bed until 3.30 when they were allowed to play while the older children were escorted home from primary school. By the time Valerie arrived home, after 6 pm, they were all bathed and ready for dinner.

Jason would remember the routine with mixed emotions. He could understand his parents' investment in the business, but it had repercussions for their family life as well as enormous ramifications for his own parenting: 'If we didn't have a housekeeper, the house would have looked like a second-hand Chinese brothel. If we didn't have a cook we would have all starved to death,' he told the ABC's *Dynasties* program in 2005.

'My first image of the business was my old man coming home. Probably at the age of four or five. I'd throw my face into his hands because you could smell the chocolate on the back of his mitts. I used to just hold his hands and smell his hands. That was my first image of the business. When you grow up and you're close to something from a very, very early age, you become emotionally involved in it. I know I was.'

But Monty was never a 'proper' father in Jason's eyes: 'He never did anything to help me. I used to tag along and go to the factory with him but I just did it probably because I had nothing else to do.'

Meals were always eaten in silence and by 7 pm the children were in bed, where they were forced to listen to Bible lessons read by Valerie over an intercom known as 'The Pixies'; she had installed speakers in every bedroom. This system also enabled her to eavesdrop: 'Can hear footsteps to 40 feet away and voices too. It's really marvellous,' she would write.

Although the routine would ease as the children grew older, it never changed in terms of Valerie's involvement, or lack of it. Later on, the Bible stories were replaced by a safety lecture around the dinner table: Valerie would read aloud newspaper articles she had clipped that morning that focused on children who had suffered some sort of trauma—scalded with boiling water, or hit by a car when crossing a road. She would often go into harrowing details.

Brett remembered the lectures as life lessons, as he told author Diana Georgeff who would write a biography about Shelton: 'Valerie would sit us all down with the housekeeper and read out all these road accidents and other terrible news and stress: "The person is in critical condition in hospital. Critical." That was a big thing. It meant you were just about gone. "Don't ever cross the road without looking." Really harping on about it. And she used to say, in case you have had an accident, you have to be clean.'

Valerie was reliving the horrors of her 1951 car accident, in which she ended up soiling herself, sprawled on the road with her dress over her head. She would come back time and again in her diaries to the event and to her fears for the children. Although some of her beliefs and methods might be questioned, Valerie Lea was a woman who believed she was doing the right thing for her children.

Typical was an entry almost three decades later. Valerie sticky-taped into her diary a copy of comments made in an interview with *The Age* by the surgeon of a large Melbourne hospital. He warned that too few parents took accidents personally: 'We read that a youngster is hurt by a car, and we shake our heads, hope fleetingly that it will never happen to our own kids, and then turn the page,' he told the newspaper. 'We don't let ourselves understand that a once-carefree child has had a dark world of pain thrust upon him in one shattering instant, and that nothing will ever be quite the same for him again.'

This was all too real for Valerie and justified her confrontational approach:

> I cut out of the papers all of the accidents that happened and read them out to the children at dinnertime. I have always felt that all those examples must have sunk in and made them just that bit more cautious. Nobody could ever, of their own accord, think to tell their children of the quite extraordinary accidents that can happen.

While Brett and Honey hated Valerie's lectures and the intrusion of The Pixies, Charryce applauded her mother's common sense and luxuriated in her nightly bedtime stories: 'Her voice would come over the airwaves as I lay in bed. She couldn't walk up the stairs, because of her bad back, but she wanted to sing us and storybook us to sleep. I loved it and yet others saw it as odd.'

Gaela, like Charryce, took their mother's warnings of dangers to heart, wary not just of the potential for accidents but of the dangers of strange men in the street. What they missed out on with Valerie's long working hours was replaced by a mother who gave them attention, made costumes, sang songs and told stories.

Gaela recalls her mother's version of how she adopted Shelton and Brett. In it, Valerie enters a long room at the hospital with beds on either side, and has to walk the length of the room examining the tags before she finds one identifying *Baby Lea*: 'She made it suspenseful, building our excitement. We would get her to tell the story again and again.'

Despite Valerie's warnings, the Lea household was far from being orderly or a place of discipline. When their parents weren't home, the kids ran wild, and the staff, whose command of English was poor, often screamed in frustration at such behaviour and their own inability to cope.

Valerie Lea was a riddle. She was a frugal woman who constantly worried about money, who insisted on handing down clothes from one child to another and making handmade nightdresses from leftover cotton. And yet she was someone who took nutrition seriously, insisted on the children wearing good shoes and ensured they slept in cotton sheets.

She devoured the writings of American paediatrician Dr Benjamin Spock, whose 1946 revolutionary guide to childcare, *The Common Sense Book of Baby and Childcare*, encouraged mothers to trust their own instinct, writing: 'You know more than you think you know.'

'We were raised on Dr Spock,' says Gaela.

And yet Valerie appeared to ignore one of the book's central tenets, that there was not a one-size-fits-all approach to raising children and that they should be treated as individuals, a philosophy even more relevant in a household mixed with natural and adopted children. Instead, she was frustrated by their differences and parented by lecturing and berating them so they would fall into line.

She did not trust them enough to let them use chalk on a blackboard in case they drew on the doors. She insisted that it was useless to give them dolls or plastic toys because they would get broken, and she placed books on a high shelf out of their reach for fear the pages would be torn.

∞

In 1949 the world was changing and the Lea household with it. Although memories of the war were beginning to fade, its impact was still being felt in the rationing of food products, such as tea and butter. Robert Menzies would be swept to power on his promise to end rationing and protect the nation from communism.

The election was one issue on Valerie's mind as she began penning her diary in earnest, and it was hardly surprising that she cheered the end of Chifley's Labor Government. But there were also more personal issues at hand. Her doctor had put her on thyroid tablets and told her that Charryce would be her last child. Her dreams of having a large brood were over, as they were for Monty's brother Harris and his wife, Sheila, who had written from Canada to say that they could not have children. Adoption was their only recourse.

It's strange then that Valerie did not mention in her diary the issue that was troubling her most—Shelton. His head-banging and bad behaviour were continuing unabated, and Monty had even attempted to calm him by sleeping in his room. In desperation, Valerie sought professional help.

The Travancore clinic in Flemington, just north of the city centre, had been set up a decade before by the strangely named Department of Mental Hygiene specifically to help 'mentally defective' children.

Shelton Lea would be case number 3268, but it was to his parents that staff first turned their attention. Physically, Valerie appeared to be the perfect mother, according to a staff member's report of the visit: 'Very attractive appearance—dark hair, regular features, pink cheeks, dark eyes. Attractive smile and voice. The physical type that is often painted holding a child and entitled *Motherhood*.'

They also liked Monty, describing him as 'solidly built, good-looking, dark Jewish appearance, pleasant manner'. But Monty was sceptical about what the clinic could achieve.

The clinic staff were less impressed by the way the Leas ran the household, more like 'a small children's institution' than a family home. Valerie insisted that she left the care of the children to staff because she had a bad back, caused by Lael's birth and exacerbated by the accident. But the Travancore staff didn't believe this excuse: 'This is probably largely a rationalisation. She is a good businesswoman who probably prefers her work to the task of bringing up children which is eventually left to the nurses.'

It was clear that Valerie's daily absence from the family home was cause for concern. She tried to explain her rationale to the social worker, who reported: 'Mrs Lea stresses her desire for her children to grow up "good people", and tries very hard to instil moral principles for which the children are still too young.'

That wasn't to say that Valerie was a bad mother, the report stressed: 'She is obviously not a hard, puritanical or punitive mother. She has had a good deal of advice from doctors and others about the bringing up of her children and has been expecting to receive the same thing at Travencore, perhaps to better effect.'

And it was immediately obvious to the clinic staff that Valerie disliked Shelton; she was unable to recognise that the behaviour of her own children was just unruly as what she claimed about his. This was borne out on the occasion when she brought four of them, including Shelton, to the clinic; according to the staff's subsequent report, it was the other children who were 'hyperactive, aggressive and non-constructive'. Of Shelton they observed: 'A pleasant-looking child who behaved perfectly during examination and seemed unafraid. There was nothing to suggest that he was a likely behaviour problem.'

Over the next six months a team of social workers observed Shelton, visiting Lambert Road and the kindergarten: 'Shelton is not nearly as disturbed as his mother portrays him,' one social worker concluded. 'However there are factors in his history which would lead one to suspect some disturbance, eg: adoption and the twelve-plus unsatisfactory people looking after children at the Lea's and the present undivided control with shifts of adults looking after the children. Also, the degree of rejection.'

Neither was Shelton backward intellectually, let alone mentally defective. His reports from the kindergarten show he was above average and one social worker, identified only as SW, remarked how eloquent he was for a three-year-old: 'Are you going yabbying this afternoon, Jason?' Shelton asked his brother while they sat having lunch one day. Later, in a sad tone, he said to himself: 'I'm not a naughty boy.' To SW, this was a telling statement, because it showed that the boy already felt misunderstood and increasingly isolated.

The clinic staff pondered whether Valerie's absence from

the family home meant she was unconsciously rejecting her own children, who also showed signs of instability—particularly Gaela, who was quiet and withdrawn, and Lael, who was struggling verbally and well behind Bretton and Shelton developmentally.

Jason—dark and handsome but sullen and bored—was going to the local state primary school. A report noted: 'Mother said she wanted him to go to state school so he would have to mix with the type of child he'd work with later.' Valerie wanted her oldest son to get used to dealing with people she regarded as likely factory staff.

☙

By May 1950, the Travancore team had confirmed their opinions: Shelton wasn't the problem; Valerie was. She clearly had a deep underlying hostility towards the boy, feelings of which she was probably unaware: 'The conversation confirmed our opinion that Shelton really ought to be taken out of this family.'

But there was another option. Perhaps he could be sent to Sydney to stay with Monty's parents, Harry and Esther, who lived in 'comfortable circumstances', had little in the way of a social life and would welcome him: 'It seems entirely practical and may be the best solution of this difficulty as Shelton would remain in the family and share in its advantages. His adopted father [Monty] is particularly fond of him and does not want to part with him but would probably agree to do so if it was felt that the continued association of Shelton with his brothers and sisters was inevitably going to be damaging to all of them.'

Valerie initially poured cold water on the idea—'She felt it would be pointed out as a failure on her part', the Travancore staff noted—but her attitude softened once she was convinced that Shelton would be able to stay within the family and not be estranged. By the end of the day she was excited by the plan but the next morning staff were having second thoughts, worried that the move might merely serve to isolate Shelton even further and entrench his self-harming behaviour.

But it was too late. His air ticket had been bought and he was already on his way. Valerie, as was her wont, filmed him departing on the tarmac at the airport. Her camera followed the little boy in a yellow top and black beret as he posed with his brothers and showed them the address of his new 'home' written on an envelope.

At one point Valerie appears in front of the lens, her camera smile firmly fixed in place as she pecks the boy she cannot abide on the cheek and says goodbye before he climbs the steps to the plane with the help of an Australian National Airways hostess. Finally, Shelton appears at the window, his hand raised as his mother encourages him to wave, but his eyes and the tilt of his head betray his confusion.

Valerie telephoned the clinic the next day to tell them that Shelton had left for Harry and Esther's home. The report noted: 'Mrs Lea is very pleased about Shelton going to Sydney and says that she does not miss him.'

The experiment lasted just five weeks. Nothing had changed; Shelton's head-banging continued and Harry, now aged 65, was finding it impossible to cope. The fears expressed by the staff had been confirmed and inevitably Shelton returned to his family in Melbourne.

Travancore decided to send a member of their staff and her young daughter to live with the Leas for twelve days. Mrs Miller's observations were less than glowing. She noted that a Lithuanian worker named Barbara had 'almost non-existent' English and struggled to maintain control, mostly resorting to screaming at the children. A Russian woman in her late fifties was 'a lawyer, teacher and countess', but she didn't stay long and was replaced by an elderly Australian woman who 'believed in a sound smack and no nonsense'. None of them were suitable, Mrs Miller concluded.

Valerie thought she had been clever. But Mrs Miller thought otherwise. By hiring a disparate group of migrants who lacked English-speaking skills and a talent for child-minding, Valerie had created an environment of confusion and insecurity: 'Uniformity of treatment is impossible as no one has control,' wrote Mrs Miller.

Shelton had railed against Barbara when she tried to put him to bed, but he seemed to respond when she allowed him to be independent and take off his own shoes and wee in a potty. Likewise, her attempts to bathe Shelton and the other children often ended in her smacking them to regain control.

Mrs Miller's conclusion about Valerie was lengthy and damning:

She [Valerie] felt Shelton was already marked out as a criminal. When I agreed with Monty who thought Shelton would grow up like other children she accepted this for the time being and dwelt instead on my own daughter's shortcomings. She was sure I was spoiling her. I did not insist on her eating up her food or smack her if she did not come when she was called, nor even hit her when she hit Bretton.

She worried especially about Shelton when he was playing with others. She thought the others gave in to him and that he bullied them (this was not so). His nervous habit of pulling his upper lip irritates her and so does his bumping. She says she nearly bursts with pride over the children. She has a warm glow in her heart at the thought of all, except Shelton. But she believes God would be displeased with her if she gave him up. Should something happen to any of the others after giving up Shelton, she would know it was her punishment sent from God.

She says her children respect her because they know if they don't do as she says, they would get a good hard smack on their bums. Actually, she threatens and moralises and fails to carry out her threats. She is not obeyed in spite of a fair amount of smacking. She admitted once she is helpless if left with them. She has a vision of herself as a prolific and adequate mother, but she is in retreat all the way along the line.

Mrs Lea is high-minded towards all of the children. The thought forces itself upon one that the arthritis in her back is the price exacted by her conscience for her failure, and the secondary gains are very obvious. With the help of the paging system, and the arthritis in her back, the line of retreat is marked out. She withdraws bed-ward.

During this entire period Valerie only mentioned the Travancore investigation in her diary once and, even then, it was a passing remark about one of the experts accompanying the family to Sydney for a summer holiday. Nor did she mention Shelton's bad behaviour.

ಀ

When Valerie telephoned the Travancore staff in early 1952 to tell them about her miscarriage, she complained that Shelton was still problematic. He had stolen money from Woody the cook— something he would always vehemently deny—and had been punished with 'a good walloping' before being left at home alone while the others went on an excursion. Valerie was desperate and defensive.

It is not hard to imagine that the pain from the car accident, coupled with the disappointment of this latest miscarriage, played a part in her demeanour and antipathy towards Shelton, but Valerie refused to believe the Travancore psychiatrist when he suggested that her attitude towards the five-year-old was 'moralistic and ambivalent'. Although she conceded that she felt a lack of love for Shelton, she insisted it was 'only when he was wicked' which, she added, was 'always'.

'Mrs Lea is unable to look at Shelton without a feeling of distaste,' the psychiatrist concluded.

Valerie was also angry that at a previous meeting the staff had presented her with their initial observations, made at the Guidance Playgroup, about the behaviour of her other children. Upset that she hadn't been told about this earlier, she flatly rejected their conclusion that Jason, Galea and Lael had misbehaved.

She had brought with her a page-long list of her complaints

about Shelton, including bed-wetting, head-bumping and stealing toys. It would not be the last time she resorted to writing lists in situations where she believed she had been wronged by others.

In her mind, Shelton's behaviour justified the almost constant punishments she was now doling out: 'She cheerfully described how she took him and shook him by the hair for a misdemeanour,' they noted. 'A passer-by interfered.'

When the clinic suggested that Shelton be admitted for in-patient observation, Valerie agreed, and he was admitted in mid-March, just as the Darrell Lea factory was gearing up for its Easter rush. The team's observations were stark: six-year-old Shelton, constantly harangued at home, now accepted that he was the rebel of the family. He did not miss the other siblings and was in no rush to go home.

Valerie phoned the clinic and became angry when she was told that they were no closer to solving the problem. After a fortnight, he was sent back to Lambert Road. Monty came, alone, to collect him. Their last report came a week later, on 22 April: Shelton had wet the bed three nights in a row and they had put him on phenobarb, a drug normally used to treat epilepsy in children. The clinic advised her to stop giving him the drug.

For more than two years Travancore had studied a young boy they believed to be normal, even highly intelligent, at the request of a woman who professed to hate him and who had rejected their pleas to treat him with affection and kindness. There was no more they could do. Presumably the clinic was unsurprised by the extraordinary trajectory of Shelton's life in later years.

A week later Valerie was admitted to hospital to be treated for haemorrhoids and to have her tubes tied. Her hopes of more children had finally been dashed.

8

LINE UP, CAMERA, ACTION

Valerie Lea was a film-maker. Amateurish, but persistent and determined to document more than four decades of her version of family life. The footage has now been digitised from the 16-millimetre film she used and lasts roughly four hours, taking the viewer from her life as a young bride to a doting grandmother in her seventies. It is riveting viewing.

The focus throughout is family, from the births of her four children and the adoption of three more, to formal celebrations, joyful and carefree summer holidays, off-to-school pride and backyard skylarking. It is all there in a glowing tribute to maternal triumph.

Little of it is natural. It's mostly smiling faces hamming it up for the camera in eerie silence because the 1950s Bell and Howell camera she used had no microphone. The subjects chat happily to her, obeying instructions to turn this way or that, to smile, pose, swivel and walk. There are numerous retakes of the same scene, as if she intended at some point to edit the disparate footage into a single polished movie.

Each can of film has been carefully indexed and referenced—*Gaela eats peas . . . Shelton, Lael with sand castles . . . Bretton in bath aged three weeks . . . Jason home from Sunday school*—just in case she wanted to retrieve one of the twenty-one spools from its place in the library and remind herself, or visitors, of the wonderful life they led. Family movie nights were frequent, a reinforcement of the picture of domestic harmony, as Charryce would recall in an interview: 'We would sit there and laugh at our antics. This was us as a happy family and that's how I remember it. A family that was functioning well.'

Surprisingly, there is scant vision of the Darrell Lea business itself—just one sequence shot inside the factory of staff mixing, stirring, pouring and moulding the various candies. And there is no vision of either the Darrell Lea stores in central Melbourne or the spectacular window decorations that Valerie helped to design and install. It is as if Valerie did not recognise this achievement and her central role in the development of one of Australia's most iconic businesses, or simply didn't think it important enough to document.

Perhaps she felt guilty about the dichotomy of her life—her genuine desire for a large, happy family conflicted by an overwhelming devotion to the business and the realisation that some of her children probably suffered because of it. Charryce and sister Gaela remembered the vision with affection but their older son, Jason, regarded the films as a facade as he said in an interview with the ABC in 2005: 'It may have looked like a very happy bunch, there's terrific old footage in there, but Mum and Dad were workaholics. They'd go off to work, that was their life.'

The film collection stretches back to the late 1930s, before Valerie and Monty shifted to Melbourne and began their family. A ten-minute section captures what appears to be a gathering of family and friends at the grand Stanmore home of Harry and Esther. Valerie is the star, in front of the camera as well as behind it—a *femme fatale* in a summer frock, confident of her body and her beauty, beckoning and cajoling, languid while others appear stiff, always with Monty as her admiring sidekick.

But the films mostly follow the story of the Leas of Melbourne, from the days in late 1947 when two young boys, unwanted by their birth mothers, were introduced into a family who believed in bloodlines.

Hints of the many problems that lay ahead can be seen on film. The first shots of Shelton clearly show his distress: he sits in a pram with Lael, his eyes closed and his head pressed against a wooden toy. He rocks back and forth. In later footage Valerie films him alone, crying in a corner of the backyard rather than stop filming to offer him comfort. Instead, the film is a record of the complaints she would make to Travancore.

Valerie would always assert that the adopted children were different—not *real Leas*, as they would be told—although able to share what the name offered in terms of comfort and opportunity. And for that they should have been grateful.

As in other aspects of her life, Valerie was an uncompromising film director. She was the boss. In years to come, the children would remember their mother's call to arms for photographs and movies: 'Stand in line, stand in order.' She wanted the children in order of height, standing ramrod straight against a wall. It was as if she needed the sequence of ascending height and order to tell the story.

What is more striking is the transformation of babies to adults; Valerie's film is a virtual time machine that not only tracks the physical development of the children, and the ageing of Valerie and Monty, but also the consistency of the character traits repeated over the years—the long-limbed Lael, with his goofy grin and clowning antics; the brooding Jason, asserting his elder son 'bully' status; and Gaela, the physical embodiment of her mother with the gentle spirit of her father, always filmed washing the family dog.

Brett's ever-present squint betrays a boy who is eager to please but not quite sure where he belongs, while Shelton's infrequent appearances highlight how much he was ignored and how young he was—twelve—when he began to drift free of the family, often disappearing for days at a time to roam the streets.

The one on-screen relationship that seems to work is the one between Honey and Charryce, although as they become adolescents their differences become more pronounced. Honey is taller; her hair is cropped and she favours jeans and shorts. Charryce has her long hair in plaits and is invariably in a dress. As the years pass, Honey appears less and less as Charryce becomes the focus of her mother's attention, highlighted by a fifteen-minute sequence of her ballet skills, a demonstration on the back lawn in her black tutu.

As the children grow up, the family home, The Lodge, evolves, expanding from a modest three bedrooms to a virtual boarding house, with a series of box-like rooms to accommodate children and staff and, later, ageing relatives and eventually paying tenants. The backyard is transformed from an ugly collection of broken concrete slabs and mismatched play equipment into a lovingly planted garden, gradually enclosed by ever higher walls that screen the family from the developing neighbourhood.

By contrast, the ornamental garden at the front remains virtually untouched, although the gate appears and disappears and reappears again, depending on the age of the Lea children and grandchildren. On the street outside, the family car, a Volkswagen Microbus, remains a constant for many years. It began its life as a workhorse, ferrying the family around town and on long road trips as far north as Sydney.

In the midst of it all, Valerie can never resist presenting herself in front of the camera. For example, at one time she is a curvaceous, middle-aged Madonna, swanning around in her swimming costume alongside pre-pubescent Honey and Charryce. At other times she is a huntress, lopping the heads off chickens for family dinners, and then a mother hen, forcing her hand, wrapped in a handkerchief, into the mouths of her children to wrench free teeth that would have fallen out naturally, then beaming at the camera and forcing her crying victims to display bloodied mouths.

Her removal of Lael's two front teeth when he was eight years old was one of the rare times she mentioned the movies in her diary, complaining that Monty was reluctant to film the event and then accusing the boy of being overly dramatic and shedding 'outraged tears'. The film shows her reaching into his mouth with grimacing intent while Lael yells out in pain and cries as his mother pulls his lips back to show the hole.

Valerie even had herself filmed when she underwent a facelift in her mid-fifties. Her face is swathed in bandages and her eyes are bruised, as if she has been beaten. She is unashamed in her desire to preserve the looks with which she had been blessed. She clearly had no desire to hide the surgical intervention that had re-smoothed her cheeks and tucked her turkey neck. Instead, she wanted Monty to film her as she proudly modelled her revitalised appearance before him.

ᘔ

Valerie's home movies were intended to present a wholesome image of a complex family, and some of it *was* a true reflection, as the three adopted children would always have fond memories of some aspects of their childhood, particularly the carefree summer holidays.

But the movies also underlined Valerie's belief that the children who were not of her blood were different. As far as she was concerned, Shelton, Brett and Honey were of lesser stock—physically, intellectually and emotionally. As time passed, she was less able to hide her misgivings; she was quick to praise her thoroughbreds and ever eager to blame the adopted children for any problems. Punishments meted out to her children were rarely equal.

Examples of her ambivalent attitude are littered throughout her diary. At the end of the 1953 school year Gaela and Lael received certificates for completing their year's work: 'There is not a mother prouder than me', she wrote, adding, 'I think Shelton managed a credit too, I'm not sure.'

She would record Jason's appointment as class head boy, Gaela's flailing attempts at gymnastics and Charryce's frequent 'honours' ribbons in ballet, but very little about the others. When there were exceptions, such as Shelton's pleasant singing voice in a choir, it was from surprise rather than delight.

Valerie's annoyance seemed to be aggravated by the reality that she could bear no more children. But despite her numerous miscarriages and operations, she had not lost her desire for them. She briefly considered adopting another staff member's unwanted baby. When, a few months after Honey's arrival, another employee announced she was having her fifth child, Valerie responded: 'I'm so jealous, I could spit!'

For more than a year after her adoption, Honey—or Kestin, as Valerie usually called her—was almost invisible. The first substantial mention of her came at the end of 1954, when Valerie noted: 'Kestin seems quite settled in now and seems to be as much our little girl as any of the others.' But these words sound hollow when compared to the sentiments she expressed over the following years: Valerie's pride, at least in her diary, was reserved almost entirely for her four natural children.

Jason was her male pride and joy, and he could do no wrong. When he abused an elderly neighbour, it was harmless skylarking; when he was caned at school, she wrote adoringly about his mature leadership; when his grades dropped, she blamed the teaching staff.

Charryce was her 'mini-me' who, she decided, needed an 'extra birthday' in September, because it was unfair that hers was too close to Christmas. In her diary Valerie listed the present—including a clarinet, telephone, paint set and a tea service—showered on her daughter,.

As far as Valerie was concerned, the adopted children were rebellious and led her 'placid' children astray. When Lael, Shelton and Brett were caught taking money from a moneybox kept beside the hallway telephone, they were docked their Christmas and birthday presents, and ordered to repay the stolen funds by helping on an early morning milk round. Lael received his presents three months later, Brett had to wait six months, and Shelton was finally given his presents in August the following year.

'I spent four nights a week sitting up until 11 o'clock at night writing page after page of what I shouldn't do,' Brett would recall. 'Eventually I'd fall asleep at the table.'

Shelton and Brett were the only children who were sent to a punishment room where the strap was kept. It was located behind the kitchen, under the staircase. As he sat alone in the darkness, Shelton would remember the smell of food being prepared as well as the sound of the family eating dinner.

One night Honey was woken by a storm. She drew back the curtains and could see a figure in the garden. A flash of lightening illuminated Shelton, and he was digging a hole.

She ran into Valerie's bedroom, only to be told to go back to bed. Shelton was being punished. 'It broke my heart. I felt powerless. Shelton wore such steel armour that you wouldn't have thought that love mattered, but it did. That image never left me.'

Lael had also watched the punishment unfold: 'I saw what happened that night and wished I could have done something to stop it. But I was a kid.'

◌

Honey was no stranger to Valerie's wrath. One night when she was ten, Valerie dragged her down the stairs by her hair for swearing; at other times she whipped her with the strap for discarding sandwiches at school in favour of tuckshop fare. She recalls being frequently hit with Valerie's metal walking stick for misdemeanours.

It reached a serious level one Sunday morning when Valerie called for a room inspection just as the children were preparing to go to church. As Valerie walked down the stairs, Honey whispered, 'Thank God she's gone down.' Her mother heard the comment and stormed back up the stairs, then pushed Honey into the corner of the room and began beating her. The attack was so loud and violent that Gaela came running, dragged Valerie off Honey and threatened to call the police if she didn't stop.

Later, as the family walked towards the church, Valerie came up behind Honey and brought her metal walking stick down on her shoulder before hissing at Gaela: 'Don't you dare talk about going to the police.'

The abuse of Honey wasn't only physical; just as damaging were the insults. One in particular—'Your nature is showing'— became a cruel refrain Valerie used to remind Honey of who she was—an unwanted child from North Fitzroy who would never amount to anything. It would remain embedded in Honey's mind, even in adulthood: 'It meant that I may have looked good on the outside, but I was bad on the inside.'

The older she got, the more she was regarded as a rival to her sister rather than a playmate. They had different friends, and their personalities were developing differently: Honey was an extrovert who loved fashion, art and music; Charryce was more subdued, with a passion for ballet.

Charryce too felt the changes. As young children she and Honey had been close, as dozens of happy photographs of them dressed in homemade costumes would attest, but as the girls approached puberty their differences became more obvious. Charryce was jealous of Honey's beauty and outgoing personality just as Honey felt the sting of a mother who, despite her best intentions, was drawn to her natural child at the expense of her adopted sibling.

Despite her adulation of Charryce's ballet talent and her pride in her frequent award ribbons, Valerie secretly hoped it would not amount to anything beyond childhood, certainly not a career: 'I'd rather she be a happy housewife with the THOUGHT that she COULD have become a great ballerina rather than become an unhappy great ballerina with all the hard work and jealousies and unrealness attached to the theatrical life,' she wrote.

Charryce was also realistic about her chances of a life as a professional ballerina: 'I loved my ballet but don't think I was ever quite good enough. Besides, nature got in the way when I began to grow up—and out.'

The social engineering experiment failed not because the children weren't capable of living harmoniously but because the adult in charge wasn't capable of loving equally, at least as far as the adopted children were concerned. As Honey recalls:

From the outside at least it looked as if she cared. She thought she was doing the right thing, at least initially. We went to good schools, were dressed well, went on nice holidays and ate well.

But the rest of it was terrible. Her anger would flare like a bonfire. You never knew when and where it would happen. I didn't know then of course because I was a child but now, as an adult, I can go back and look at it and understand it better. With age and time, I understand her better.

The pictures I've seen of her when she was young showed she was beautiful, fabulous and energetic. She was this amazing woman who married the boss, inherited money and has this dream of having a big family and then, before she achieves it, she loses her biggest asset—her body.

She was thrown from a car and when she stood up she lost [control of] her bladder, so for the rest of her life she had to wear a corset and pads and walk with a stick. She was in pain every day. All of a sudden, her physical life is hell. She wants all these kids so she literally stayed on her back and had twelve miscarriages trying to get those four shining children of hers.

I can understand that. I feel there was a rage in her, an anger, and we adoptees gave her an outlet for that. Her own children didn't. They looked like her, they smelled like her, they sounded like her. They were clones.

I don't know. Maybe she was on some drug for the pain that made her act like a mad woman. That's what she acted like; like somebody coming down off Valium. It was a roller coaster. You never knew when to be terrified of her. She had the energy of the mad. If she wasn't in the office designing things, she was making nighties and plucking chickens.

9

THE CHOCOLATE FACTORY

In 1941 Monty had spied a bargain. The old Royal Theatre in Chapel Street, Windsor, one of the first cinemas built in Melbourne, was on the market. Closed as World War II began, it was now being used for storage; its upper floors were filled with army surplus supplies and its yard with timber and old cars and buses.

Monty could get the place for £1800—a ridiculously cheap price, he realised, considering the furniture stacked inside alone was probably worth the price. He was right, and he quickly recouped his money by selling off its contents before purchasing the machinery he needed on the black market, created by the vacuum of war.

It was a moment of triumph that would inspire misplaced confidence in his own abilities, and come back to bite him many times over the next thirty years. But for the moment Monty was a genius, having effectively paid nothing for premises that would give Darrell Lea a solid manufacturing base in the southern capital. For his children it was a place with a sense of magic.

One of the family's favourite stories concerns a lost cargo of lollies. During the war effort in the 1940s the factory made hard-boiled candies and packed them in plastic-lined kerosene tins for the troops. One of the supply ships carrying these tins was sunk on its way from Melbourne to Sydney. Nobody ever found out whether it was destroyed by Japanese submarines or friendly fire, but somewhere off the Sydney Heads there is a wrecked ship with a cargo hold full of tins of Darrell Lea lollies.

A decade later, with the war over and the factory humming, Monty and Valerie began introducing their children to the family business. At various times they would all work on the window displays and at the front counters of the Darrell Lea shops now scattered throughout Melbourne's CBD. But mostly they would work at the factory, often on weekends and in the holidays, as well as during peak production, such as Easter, when the company ran three shifts, twenty-four hours a day, to meet demand.

Although automation had taken over some tasks, making chocolates and lollies in their various forms remained a mostly hands-on process. Coconut ice, for example, required workers to boil the coloured layers of sugar syrup in separate copper pots over an open gas fire. The pink layer would then be poured by hand onto a steel cooling table, followed by the white layer over the top, finished with a dusting of desiccated coconut, before the mixture was allowed to set and be cut up, again by hand.

Likewise, nougat bars were cooled and roughly shaped, then dipped in vats of chocolate and tossed onto a tabletop of crushed nuts where, still warm, they were rolled by half a dozen factory hands into sausage shapes. Finally the nougat was packed by hand—each portion weighed, tagged and bagged—and then stacked into boxes for distribution.

Caramel Snows, one of the company's first products, required a 'qualified dipper', who plunged each of the two-toned fudges into dark chocolate to a precise point a third of the way up the sides of each piece. To make Bo Peeps, or Wee Folk, hard candy in different colours was heated and pulled and stretched and folded into thin lines that would create a striped effect, before being fed into a roller and then chopped by hand into pillow shapes.

Toasted marshmallows were cooked in a steam-jacketed pan, an industrial version of the domestic pressure cooker, then cooled and aerated in a high-speed beater before being spread on a bed of toasted coconut and diced into cubes.

Liquorice, introduced in the 1950s and one of their biggest sellers, was mixed into a slurry, then cooked in a steam jacket to produce a jelly-like mass that was flavoured with aniseed before being extruded in long ropes onto metal trays and finished in a hot room.

The company sold their own version of Rocky Road, a recipe that Harry Levy probably stumbled across during his days in the goldfields, where it was said to have been a dessert named after the rocky road the miners endured. The Darrell Lea version of marshmallow, toasted peanuts and milk chocolate was hand-mixed and cooled before being chopped into mouth-sized squares and sold in half-pound bags as Rocklea Road. The name endures.

Even the Christmas 'puddings' were handmade. The base mixture of egg white and sugar was beaten to the texture of meringue before coconut, honey and fruit were folded in. Once set, the mixture was then shaped by wooden rollers into a 'pudding', which was robed with chocolate, decorated with icing and a sprig of holly, placed on a plate with a spoon and then boxed.

Honey's earliest memories of the Chapel Street factory are from the age of seven, when she began to work on weekends. Armed with a wide spatula, her first task was to perch on a box and clean up any excess chocolate that had spilled onto the table. This was akin to being given a spoon to scrape chocolate cake mix from a giant mixing bowl.

She loved the noise and activity of the factory, with its whirring and churning and staff scurrying around like scientists in white coats, inhabiting the magical world of Willy Wonka years before Roald Dahl penned his famous children's book. She was a female Charlie Bucket and the factory was her salvation, giving her freedom from the oppression of Lambert Road.

'I loved the factory,' she recalls. 'We kids sat on boxes at the end of the enrober belt, watching as crèmes and caramels were fed through a sheet of chocolate. It would [make] such a great film, this gorgeous 1950s era. It was magical.'

But her greatest joy, after the workers went home, was to roam the factory floor, poking her fingers into all the chocolate and caramel mixes, and bouncing the coconut on the marshmallow racks:

I knew every inch of the building. There was an upstairs room filled with patterned silver foil for wrapping. It was beautiful and the smells were delicious. There were other rooms filled with peanuts and toffees.

Charryce and I once found an x-ray machine that was used to inspect the coconut brought in from overseas. We kept putting our hands underneath it to watch the glow, completely exposing ourselves to the radiation. When Valerie found out, we were rushed off to the doctor, who made us wear gloves for the rest of the summer.

Honey adored the workers, particularly the woman she called the Coconut Rough Lady, who expertly hand-rolled the sausages of coconut-covered delight: 'The workers were my sort of people, unlike Lambert Road, where the only person who was ever kind was a housekeeper who visited me when I was sick and gave me balls of butter and sugar.'

Shelton was friends with Bill, 'The Pan Man', a tired-looking bloke with a squinty eye who was in charge of stirring the chocolate almonds mixture. After watching Bill pour sack loads of almonds into the vat, Shelton stuck his head over the side so he could breathe in the steaming hot vapours and heady smell of chocolate. Typically, Shelton wanted to know more about Bill and learned he had a son who was having trouble learning to read. Shelton offered to go to the family cottage in Prahran and teach the boy, but Valerie refused to allow it—a decision that would have unfortunate repercussions for him.

Unlike his adopted siblings, Brett found little joy in working in the factory and shops because it only emphasised the unfairness of his situation. He, Honey and Lael were the only serious workers, as he recalled; the other children were just interested in playing around. But it was the miserly pay that riled him.

This was the beginning of what became his life of crime. As he would recall years later: 'Our pocket money was threepence per week. A week! My peers at school had two shillings a day. I took to thieving and swapping and trading things just to get enough money to keep up with them.'

Lael watched from a different perspective, fascinated by the dynamics of his parents at work: 'What Mum did, Dad didn't do.' Monty operated from a front office where he conducted his various business activities and was mainly responsible for property and leases: 'All you ever heard from that room was laughter.'

By contrast, his mother worked from an office at the back of the ground floor, in a room filled with bolts of brightly coloured cloth and cardboard for shopfront tickets. Her desk was cluttered with designs scrawled on pieces of paper. In her world of frantic, creative energy, nothing was in order.

But Valerie was more than just a marketing force. She was also the factory drill sergeant, frequently emerging from her domain to conduct time-and-motion studies on unsuspecting workers, standing over them with a stopwatch, then instructing them how to tweak things to carve valuable seconds off menial tasks.

'We can do it better,' she would tell staff. In awe of his mother's presence, but aware that her dominance could also have an overpowering, negative effect, Lael watched with mixed feelings: 'There was simply no line with her, and there was a point at which she became confronting. But you didn't want to piss her off.'

Lael's fondest memories were of taking a tram into the city on a Saturday morning and working in the Swanston Street shop until late afternoon: 'We were expected to do it and I don't ever remember getting paid. Whenever I asked, Dad would say: "Oh, you'll get it in the long run." Honey was always working at the shop or the factory, but Bubbie [Charryce] was rarely there. She was off doing ballet.'

10

THE PINAFORE MATRIARCH

November 1953

If Valerie Trix Everitt ever harboured niggling doubts about the validity of her rise from anonymous teenage ticket writer to businesswoman and matriarch, then the events and media attention of 25 November 1953 would dispel them once and for all.

The venue was the wood-panelled Victorian pomp of the Supreme Court in William Street, the occasion a hearing into compensation for her back injuries sustained in the car accident two years earlier. She had suffered unrelenting pain ever since. It reduced her to lying in the back seat of the car when travelling with Monty, partly to ease her discomfort and partly from a residual fear she could never really shake. She doubted the pain could be resolved, but financial compensation, ever the driving force in her life, would relieve some of the discomfort.

The court was new to her. In her own environment she was a woman of great composure and self-confidence, but now she was being thrust into the public spotlight by courtesy of a published court list, eagerly read by members of the press who were well aware of her family and its fortune.

It all turned out to be good newspaper copy: a wealthy, good-looking couple with a successful, if odd, story combined with some pure courtroom theatre when her lawyer, a veteran QC named Reginald Smithers, resorted to dramatics by declaring the accident had all but ended a business career that was 'like that of a character from a Gilbert and Sullivan musical'. To highlight Valerie's rise from obscurity, he was referring to 'When I Was a Lad, I Served a Term', the popular patter song from *HMAS Pinafore*.

It was a long bow to draw, considering he was comparing her rise from salesgirl to company director with the comic opera's fictional Sir Joseph Porter's rise from cabin boy—'polishing the handle on the big front door'—to First Lord of the Admiralty, but it was a memorable parallel Smithers hoped would impress the jury determining the extent of the damages claim.

The insurance company, Norwich Union, was contesting neither the accident nor who was at fault, but it disagreed with her claim, in Mr Smithers' account, that she was confined to a life of 'boundless frustration', restricted and no longer able to indulge her ambition to see Darrell Lea 'grow greater and greater'.

Smithers, who would go on to become a Supreme Court judge and sit in judgment on performances such as his own, played up her virtual superwoman status as a mother of four natural and three adopted children. As well as running the manufacturing arm of Darrell Lea in Victoria for five years, her director's fee of

£600 a year went straight back into the running of her complicated household. She was a director of two companies—Montague Bernard Pty Ltd, which made the chocolates for Darrell Lea, and a second entity that was responsible for the merchandising. There were now a dozen shops in Sydney and four in Melbourne.

It was revealed that Valerie had not publicly declared that she and Monty were married until 1943, eight years after their wedding, and only after Jason's birth. The only explanation they gave was unspecified 'business reasons'.

The newspapers, tipped off that a Toorak matriarch was going to give evidence in court, lapped up the colourful testimony and published their coverage the next morning. 'There were double column articles and pictures of Monty and myself in all the papers,' Valerie wrote with some pride of the coverage, which included *The Argus* picking up Smithers' line and exclaiming '*HMS Pinafore* sketched her life'.

The Truth trumpeted 'He found the perfect wife. Sweets king says she's sweet', and quoted Monty's evidence, in which he recounted meeting the young salesgirl, who turned into a 'wonder wife' and whom he credited with the company's success. She was an organiser, saleswoman, display artist, staff tutor and inventor. He also revealed the carefully constructed web of private companies through which the profits were distributed. His wife was the sole director, although not a shareholder, of the main trading arm, but she could now only work one third of the time.

It had also changed their home life, he told the court. In the two years since the accident, she had only managed to climb the stairs to the second floor, where all seven children slept, on a dozen occasions. He added that she looked after the 'cultural and finer training' of the children by telling them Sunday school stories, looking after their Christian outlook, teaching them manners and reading them bedtime stories.

Valerie, wide-eyed and demure on the stand, was asked by Mr Revelman, the insurance company's patronising lawyer, how she spent her £29 weekly wage and director's fee.

'What becomes of the money from Darrell Lea?'

'It all goes on the home,' Valerie replied succinctly.

His follow-up question was even more condescending: 'And what happens to the money your husband gives you?'

Valerie held her cool in front of the all-male jury: 'My goodness, that goes too.'

The lawyer persisted: 'Is your husband a wealthy man?'

'Yes, he would be.'

'For reasons of finance and to avoid taxation your husband puts income into your name?'

'No, I think for all the work I did, I should receive some money.'

The tactic was clear. The plaintiff's lawyer wanted to paint her as a rich, entitled woman who fibbed about her role in the company and took money as a tax dodge. He couldn't have been more wrong in assuming that Valerie was a traditional mother. He appeared to have no idea about the staff she hired to look after her children, evidence that would have completed the portrait nicely.

However, the jury would never hear the rest of her evidence. After the lunch break Darrell Lea staff member James Gilligan, the manager of the Swanston Street shop, revealed he had been approached outside the court by a man who clearly had skulduggery on his mind.

'He said that I should see one of the jury men,' Gilligan said. 'The last words the man said to me were: "Well, what about a few chocolates to go on with?" I said it would be better not to do that, but that I would see him later. He then left.'

Mr Justice Martin had no choice but to dismiss the jury. With the day wasted, Valerie felt disheartened by the prospect of having to go through the whole process again in a few months' time. The culprit, a fifty-year-old caretaker named McLeod, was later arrested and then let off. He claimed he had been drunk and 'letting off hot air'; he said that he held no malicious intent and he had no friends on the jury. But Valerie wasn't buying it; she was convinced a member of the jury had seen an opportunity to enrich himself.

Even though she had been confident on the stand for the first trial, Valerie was tired and cynical as she prepared for the retrial three months later, in February 1954. Her resolve was shattered when she was forced to undergo an examination by two doctors hired by the insurance company; they claimed she had imagined the pain and even tried to manipulate her back: 'Back was very bad and in constant pain,' she wrote afterwards in her diary. 'Had a gruelling time with Smithers for three days preparing for the case again and decided I couldn't go through with it so settled out of court. Anyway, why would any jury want to give a "RICH" woman any more dough.'

The back pain was real and debilitating enough, although Valerie's claim in court that it had hampered her career was exaggerated to some degree, as she would continue to be a driving force in the business for years to come. Contrary to her evidence, Valerie was already back at work, eager to take advantage of the visit of the young Queen Elizabeth, who had just arrived in Australia on her first tour of the Commonwealth. Valerie was keen to cash in on the public adoration by designing patriotic lollypops in red, white and blue before turning her attention to creating the new range of shell-shaped and crème-filled chocolate eggs for Easter. Ducks and flowers would be the year's motifs.

Her lawyer had led her to expect a payout of as much as £50,000 from a sympathetic jury, but in the end she settled for just £2000 (minus expenses): 'Of course, £50 million would not have compensated me for what I've lost,' she complained.

11

SEVEN CHILDREN, SEVEN SCHOOLS

The summer of 1956/57 was a joyous one for the Lea family.

It was a holiday that drew them together. The formality of Lambert Road and the Chapel Street factory were put aside as they packed up the microbus and drove three hours south-east of the city to Wilsons Promontory, the national park forming the southernmost tip of the Australian mainland.

The getaway to 'the Prom', as it was affectionately known, was Monty's idea. He had taken Jason and some other boys there for a week the previous year and, much to the delight of his wife, had come back fitter, trimmer and full of enthusiasm for a proper family holiday. He was still keen at the end of the year, forking out £110 on equipment and borrowing a large tent to serve as a sort of campsite family room. He went down there a week ahead of the others to set up everything in time for Christmas, then drove back to Lambert Road to collect Valerie and the kids.

They had originally intended being away for three weeks but stayed at the Prom for five, Valerie declared in triumph, waxing lyrical in her diary about the holiday. She revelled in their freedom and the lack of boundaries.

The campsite was set between the Tidal River, which opens onto Norman Bay, and a broad stretch of white quartz sand known as Squeaky Beach, named for the sound it makes as you walk along it. More than a kilometre long, the beach boasts clean, shallow water and modest waves. Behind the beach rises a range of granite hilltops, where you can see across Bass Strait towards Tasmania.

The children slept in either the back of the microbus or in the tent, which was divided by canvas walls, and they showered away the salt in cold water. They explored the coast with its strange rock formations and tidal pools, and followed bush trails into the wild windswept greenery of Mount Oberon, often returning with stories of their adventures only at dusk. They reddened in the sun, then browned and finally tanned. They swatted away sandflies and mosquitoes, and ran barefoot along sandy tracks alive with lizards, snakes and bull ants.

When she wasn't filming, Valerie did the cooking, often stripping to her corset and petticoats to keep cool as she toiled over a Vulcan stove. She seemed more relaxed here, and even forgave them for dropping their names in favour of nicknames that sounded as if they were living an Enid Blyton adventure. Jason, cruelly, had called Gaela 'Fatso', which seemed to stick. Lael, who never stopped talking, was 'Yacky'; likewise 'Peanut' seemed to suit Brett's freckled countenance. Shelton's locks cast him as 'Curly'. Kestin and Charryce had long been 'Honey' and 'Bubbie', respectively, except when Valerie called them to order.

Friends and relatives joined them for weekends. There were fifteen of them when Harris and Sheila drove down to the Prom with their kids—Michael, from Sheila's first marriage, and Robert, Charon and Brenda, who had all been adopted. Others came for a few days—mostly senior Darrell Lea managers and their families, who made up most, if not all, of Valerie and Monty's small circle of friends.

Valerie captured the fun with her camera and for once did not try to control the vision. She was content to observe Honey and Bubbie as they practised using a skimming board at the river's entrance, drawing back to pan across the scenery as their guests waterskied across the bay. She filmed the children at play rather than insisted they act to the camera.

It was a welcome distraction from the rigid routine of home and business life. Valerie, normally anxious about safety, seeing danger at every turn, casually dismissed the fact that the children had to contend with a tiger snake near the tent and that a lad had drowned while spearfishing just after they'd arrived, events that would normally make her lecture the children about safety at the dinner table. She even turned a blind eye one night when Shelton swept the kids' uneaten vegetables into a brown paper bag so it looked as if they had clean plates.

This holiday joy was different from the excitement they had experienced a few months earlier, when they'd watched the first television broadcast in Melbourne. The Leas were among the five per cent of the population who could afford a television set, which cost ten times the average weekly wage. Valerie had watched the broadcast with mixed feelings. The variety show was quite good, as was the US sit-com, and there was a funny quiz show called *I've Got a Secret*, but she was concerned about the news of Russian tanks mowing down rebels in Hungary. It was confronting to actually see pictures of the fighting rather than just read about it in the newspapers. The splendid isolation of 'the Prom' was far more comfortable.

But amid the delight there was acrimony.

There was only one store in the area, open in the summer months and stocked with a modest range of goods. Naturally, it was a honey pot for the children, who spent their pocket money on ice creams and lollies. At some point the Lea kids noticed that the owner of the store had stacked the returned empty soft-drink bottles in the backyard to be collected later. The temptation was too much. Shelton, Brett, Honey and Charryce grabbed a handful and took them around the front to claim the three pence offered for each returned bottle. They did it again the next day and the next until, predictably, they were caught.

Honey's punishment was being ordered to sit in the back of the Kombi van during the day for the next three days, despite the heat—'jailed' in effect, with nothing but bread and water. Shelton, Brett and Charryce, who says she was coerced by Shelton and unaware they were stealing, were confined to their tents.

ভ

> We've decided to separate Kestin and Charryce. They were
> in the same class at Toorak Central but were getting rather
> cheeky . . .

No sooner had the family settled back into city life than
Valerie changed direction. Whether the soft-drink shenanigans
had anything to do with it or not, she and Monty had decided
that Honey and Charryce, 'twin' sisters and playmates for half
their lives, should be sent to different schools. Her reasoning, she
would say later, was that she didn't want them to be compared
with each other. Charryce would be enrolled at the independent
non-denominational Lauriston Girls' School in Armadale and
Honey at St Catherine's School in Toorak.

Melbourne in the 1960s was conservative, a bastion of class
and allegiance to the British Crown; its private schools mimicked
the old British system, along them Lauriston which considered
itself academic. St Catherine's was somewhat different, attracting
a more cosmopolitan crowd. 'Foreign' surnames—many Jewish
names among them—filled the class rolls because there was no
distinction made on the basis of race or religion; no prejudice, no
Christian dogma.

The boarding house at St Catherine's mainly comprised
the daughters of wealthy Western District farmers. They were
a conservative but earthy mob; sometimes, during a drought,
they had to be withdrawn from the school, unless their fees were
waived by a sympathetic school board. There were also some
international students, even a Thai princess in Honey's class.

The school motto is *Nil Magnum Nisi Bonum*—'Nothing is

great unless it is good'. However, the emphasis in those days was less on strict adherence to society's rules about how young women as a group should behave, and more on how they could grow and develop as individuals.

Val had unleashed Honey into an environment of privilege, where girls faced the world with a candid self-possession and a distinctive style, their hats abandoned and their skirts hiked up as far as they could go. They were intent on having fun.

As Shelton put it: 'St Cath's girls walked to a different beat, good-looking girls, a cut above the rest.' His sister fitted in perfectly.

'MURDER,' Valerie screamed in her diary. She had estimated that it would cost her £1000 a year in fees, clothing and fares for Honey. She knew that her brother-in-law Harris was sending his four children to a Catholic school, where the total fees were much less than she was about to spend on Honey's education.

The boys and Gaela would be treated the same way. Jason was in his second year at Caulfield Grammar, and Gaela was attending Shelford Girls' Grammar. Shelton was enrolled at Carey Baptist Grammar School, and Lael got into Wesley College, despite lounging over the principal's desk at his interview, much to his mother's annoyance. Brett would be accepted into Brighton Grammar and later transferred to Caulfield after Jason had left.

Valerie's choice of separate schools for each child seemed to undermine her policy of matching abandoned children to her offspring, but now that her biological children were going to schools that could provide dozens of friends, their need for play-mates suddenly evaporated. Shelton, Brett and Honey had served their purpose, it seemed, but their education was now costing a huge sum. Not once did she mention the cost of her natural children's education. After all, she was their mother; they were her blood.

It would also signal the end of any sense of unity between Honey and Charryce, and eventually lead to bitterness and separation. Valerie's diary would make it clear that she was focused on her daughter, while Honey was increasingly a source of annoyance.

Charryce could feel the growing tension in the relationship with her sister: 'I don't think she really liked me and thought I was favoured in the family. If I was [favoured] then I was, and she might have suffered, but it's something that I couldn't help. She has probably harboured those feelings over the years, which is sad.'

The boys, too, would drift apart. Shelton and Brett forged their own special bond, but Lael invariably went to friends' houses after school, rather than bringing them home to his. He acknowledged there were occasions when the adopted kids were treated differently, but there were also consequences for him as the forgotten middle child in a complex family structure who was constantly having to compete for his mother's attention.

As if life hadn't been complicated enough, the seven children were now going to seven different schools, each with a different uniform, scattered across four suburbs. Valerie recorded the daily routine one morning: the children, prim and proper in their carefully pressed uniforms, grinning on cue while Lael leapt with enthusiasm and galloped down the road, as she filmed them leaving the house one by one, the endless retakes ensuring that several would be late for class.

Valerie had done Honey a favour in many ways. She was no longer overshadowed by Charryce, if only during school hours.

And, by chance, Valerie had chosen a school that was not only among the elite schools in the state but also threw Honey into a milieu of liberal teachers, students and parents. Her friends and classmates were the daughters of theatre impresarios, actors, artists, leading businessmen, company directors, diplomats and politicians, and they would become career women—judges, academics, social workers, journalists, publishers and actors.

Diana Georgeff joined St Catherine's a couple of years later. Her first memory of Honey was at Miss Challingsworth's Dancing Class, known colloquially as 'Challs'. Traditionally, girls from private schools like St Catherine's would mingle with boys from other private schools at weekly classes, ostensibly to learn the classic ballroom dances such as the Pride of Erin waltz but in reality to launch their social lives. Girls and boys would cluster in segregated groups in the dance hall. But not Honey—she would make her way across the floor to join the boys as if they were her brothers: 'Well, I've grown up in a big family with boys and girls,' she shrugged later.

'Honey was one of those people who was self-contained', Diana recalls. 'Being with boys socially was a new adventure. It was a bit like learning to ice-skate—you knew it was going to be fun once you learned how, but Honey could already skate. She had great style. We all had little bows on our heads, the standard

Little Pattie look, and Honey had angular hair, the Mod look, like Carnaby Street. She was out there, funny and lively and the vanguard of everything new but she was never the mean girl, never conceited. A trendsetter. She was an organiser.'

At first Honey's academic marks were good, acceptable even to Valerie. 'Bubbie and Honey excellent,' she wrote in June 1957. But as time went on and the relationships in the family deteriorated, so did Honey's marks. And Valerie would be unforgiving.

Diana, who would later write *Delinquent Angel*, an acclaimed biography of Shelton, saw this behaviour in action on one of the few occasions she ventured to the Lea home. One Saturday morning a group of friends on their way to the Melbourne Royal Show called in at Lambert Road to collect Honey. But instead of Honey appearing at the front door, Valerie poked her head out the window of an upstairs room: 'Off you go, girls!' she shouted, waving her hands. 'Honey's not allowed to go, because she is being punished.'

Jackie Bing was another close friend. She had moved to the school from Brighton and foundered until Honey 'took a liking to me'. As she remembers: 'Honey was out there, always ahead of the trend, even wearing the school uniform which required grey stockings. Honey, of course, insisted on wearing black.'

For the next few years Honey and Jackie were almost inseparable, constantly at each other's houses after school and at weekends. Jackie visited the chocolate factory, and even worked one year at the show-bag stall at the Royal Melbourne Show.

The second storey of the Lea house was divided into a series of box-like rooms, each containing a fixed wooden bed. Here Jackie and Honey would lie around, talking about fashion and boys; sometimes they would be interrupted by Valerie's steely voice warning them: 'I can hear everything you're saying.' She was still using The Pixies speakers to spy on her children.

'I came from a traditional family but this was very different, confronting and strange,' Jackie recalls. 'Valerie was an authoritarian who would bang her stick on the ground when she got annoyed. On the day that Honey gave me a tour of the chocolate factory we stuffed ourselves silly, so I wasn't hungry when we got back to the house for dinner. Valerie had a red-hot go at me about the starving children of Africa but she backed off when I asked her why she didn't send off food parcels to help them.'

Despite their close friendship at school, Honey and Jackie would lose track of each other as their lives changed and adulthood beckoned. When they were reunited two decades later, Jackie was shocked: 'I knew she was struggling financially and that the family had refused to help. It made me angry to think that the Leas had taken Honey in, but then abandoned her when she needed them most.'

12

TWISTIES

Monty Lea might have been a largely silent figure in the family home, content to be the benevolent male beside his sergeant-major wife, but his business persona was very different.

Monty's chief role in the company involved financing and deals. Outside his office at the front of the Chapel Street factory there was a constant line of men arriving for closed-door meetings. The sound of their laughter could occasionally be heard on the factory floor. It contrasted sharply with Valerie's cluttered dominion at the back of the factory, where the door was always open and the room filled with ideas, raised voices and interactions about the day-to-day operation.

Ever since they arrived in Melbourne in 1940, still smarting from Maurice's rebuttal of their ideas, Valerie had been keen for her husband to break away from the Sydney operation so they could strike out on their own. She was loyal to the Darrell Lea brand, but she wanted to be in control of their destiny, rather than at the whim of Sydney's decisions.

She seemed happy, even keen, for Monty to diversify, despite this being at odds with her mother's dire words of warning about being careful, and not taking loans—not even for educational purposes. Preparing for a rainy day. But Valerie had a blind faith in her husband's ability, particularly after he negotiated the purchase of the Chapel Street factory.

Rather than just concentrate on what the family did best—making and selling confectionery for the masses—Monty wanted to build a multi-faceted empire; he was always exploring the possibility of another deal.

This search seemed to reach its peak in the mid-1950s when, according to Valerie's diaries, the company was doing well and Australian society in general was buoyant. Interest rates were low, employment levels high, and the country had witnessed two major events that brought with them a sense of international recognition—the 1954 Royal Tour and the 1956 Olympic Games.

In 1957 Monty bought a financially troubled confectionery firm called Glenvern Novelty Sweet Co. and brought its production into an expanded Chapel Street operation. The year before he had invested in a manufacturing company called Silverstream and its share of an operation called Burnley Ale. Neither would last long.

Monty had negotiated to buy two more central CBD properties and converted an old bond store into a depot for confectionery that he planned to distribute under licence, including product from rival firms like Hoadley's, Wrigley's, Nestlé and MasterCraft. He had also started a wholesale company, Victoria Nut Supplies, to sell chocolates and sweets into hotel chains.

Valerie never once asked where the money was coming from. Instead, she crowed about the wealth he promised: 'He'll be the richest man in the cemetery yet. It's going like a bomb. All I hope is the stock is going in the right direction.'

It was clear from her diary references that Valerie didn't fully understand what her husband was up to, not because she wasn't capable of understanding but because Monty was sketchy on the details, particularly financing, and even more so on planning. He was a kind-hearted man, who preferred to believe what he was told by others; he lacked the cynical soul of a successful businessman. But his biggest problem was his cavalier attitude towards money.

Time and failures did not dim his enthusiasm either. In later years Monty would grow mushrooms in storehouses he couldn't rent, sell frozen food and even trade in second-hand freezers.

ᥴჳ

Typical of Monty's deals was his relationship with businessman Isador Magid, a wool merchant who migrated to Australia from China in 1948. Magid would go on to become a wealthy and successful property developer in Melbourne, but one of his early business ventures was to try to create a new snack food using a machine called a rotary head extruder he had imported from America. It proved as awkward as its name.

Magid experimented with corn, which was ground and then cooked under high pressure before emerging from the machine in curled, gnarled shapes. But he struggled to make the extruder work; in 1955 he gave up and agreed to sell the machine to Monty Lea for £12,000.

Monty and his brother Harris experimented with the machine by using a combination of milled corn, rice, wheat and water, which was baked and then seasoned with cheese flavouring. The snack food, Twisties, was born and, thanks largely to the new medium of television and the popularity of early stars like Graham Kennedy and Bert Newton, who advertised it, it became popular by the end of the decade.

Valerie made a brief, excited mention of the success in her diary in October 1959, noting: 'Twisties are going madly since we've had them on TV. £80 per night for 30 seconds and four nights per week on *Melbourne Tonight*.' But she was being overly enthusiastic; the truth was far more complicated. Sales may have been solid in Melbourne, where the advertising was concentrated, but Sydney was a different market and struggled by comparison. It was the same story in other cities.

Within a few years Monty was searching for overseas markets to help prop up the disappointing domestic market results; the operation was now bundled into a new company called General Foods. It was yet another financial risk, but Monty seemed oblivious. He convinced family friend Ted Delbridge, who managed one of the Darrell Lea shops, to not only head up the British operation but to make his son Jason Lea his Number Two.

Despite his mother's glowing diary references, Jason had struggled in his final years at school, managing to pass his Leaving Certificate but with no desire to pursue further education. He had once dreamed of becoming a forest ranger, but he really had only one option—the family company—and in March 1960, aged seventeen, he left for London with Delbridge to try to resurrect the fortunes of the Twisties experiment.

They travelled via the United States, zigzagging across the country in search of new machinery options for production before arriving in London. Ted reported back that he had found a factory site, and he and Jason would live in a rundown flat upstairs. It all seemed a bit haphazard, unplanned and still experimental, yet Monty was prepared to raise loans to cover the rising costs of turning Twisties into a commercial success.

Within a year the problems became obvious. Valerie noted in her diary that they had sent over another manager to attempt to sort out the mess: 'Twisties are having a very rough time. Cheese went off, money was short. The distribution company was not doing its job and now [staff manager] Berger is over there trying to get it on its feet. If he can't we'll really be in the soup.'

CB

There was an unforeseen repercussion of Jason's departure. Despite his reputation as the bullying older brother, Jason had made one positive contribution inside the family—he had connected with Shelton. And with his friend gone from the house, Shelton, now aged thirteen, was beginning to run wild.

Jason would fondly remember Shelton as a boy who, despite being smaller and four years younger, was game enough to spar with him in backyard boxing matches. They would also skylark together around the neighbourhood, Jason 'dinking' Shelton on the handlebars of his bike as he rode to a nearby convent, where they would climb over the wall to prank the nuns.

But Jason's biggest contribution, according to Shelton, was music.

'Jason introduced me to jazz,' he would explain to Diana Georgeff years later.

I loved him for that because I recognised in jazz something close to my heart. He spent his nights after school in his room playing Duke Ellington, and I sat on the stairs outside and listened. He let me read his books on jazz and I remember pictures of black saxophonists, and I got lost in those books and with the music coming from Jason's room, and I wanted to feel what they were feeling. I missed Jason a lot when he left.

From the age of nine or ten, Shelton ran away from home on numerous occasions, usually in anger after an argument, like the day he found out that Monty had sacked Bill, 'The Pan Man', simply because he had invited Shelton to his home to help his son learn to read.

Shelton would later recount the confrontation:

His son was behind with reading, and I gave him a couple of lessons, and the old man sacked the bloke. When he came up to my room I said, 'You sacked him, didn't you?' and he said 'Yes' and I just jumped up—I was a little feller at the time—and I—bang—straight into him.

Lael remembers that fight: 'They were brawling in the hallway and Dad, who was a pretty good boxer, came off second best.'

Shelton would often hide in a neighbour's garden down the street where he could hear Valerie calling for him. It gave him some satisfaction that she was upset, and he also hoped that she actually wanted him to come home. At other times police would find him wandering the streets and bring him home.

The arguments and disappearances had become more frequent, but in the months after Jason's departure things would completely unravel: 'Have had a spot of trouble with our jewel Shelton,' Valerie noted sarcastically in her diary in May 1960 before detailing several incidents in which he took an overdose of sleeping pills. The first time it happened Shelton was hospitalised; the second time a doctor was called to the house, but he dismissed it as attention seeking. Clearly something was amiss when, a few days later, Shelton went missing in the city and was found collapsed in the street. But Valerie dismissed it as an act— lies and deceit to get out of school exams.

There was nothing she could do for him, she insisted, ignoring all the Travancore advice that he needed love and affection. Shelton had been trouble since he arrived as a baby and she wished she'd had him tested more fully. She tried to find reasons to praise him but she couldn't; she felt that what he really needed was a hell of a good belting from Monty, particularly as his behaviour was starting to have an impact on Brett, who was also acting up and had to change schools midway through the year.

But there had been at least one reason to praise Shelton—he had been a tower of strength in caring for her father-in-law, who had come to live with the family in 1956. Harry Levy, the former Cockney salesman, was now in his early eighties and slowly losing his mind. He was given a room under the stairs and staff took care of him during the day. Shelton would sit with the old man in the backyard on sunny afternoons and keep him company in the evenings, even bringing him a pan when he wanted to pee.

Valerie acknowledged his contribution in her diary: 'It's funny but Shelton is just wonderful with Grandpa, helping, so obliging and willing with him as indeed he is with all adults, teachers included. He's always ready and anxious to help do anything where Lael & Jason & Bretton say "Aw, what do you want NOW" most ungraciously.'

This act of kindness gives an insight into the character of the young boy, misunderstood and troubled by circumstance. Yet Valerie couldn't see it.

But Harry could. He promised Shelton his gold watch as a memento. But when the old man finally died in mid-1957, back in a Sydney sanatorium, his wishes were ignored. Shelton never saw the watch. Jason thought that Charryce might have inherited it.

In early 1960 Valerie again turned to the medical profession, seeking help to manage Shelton. Child psychologist Dr Leo Murphy immediately identified the boy's attachment to Jason and advised that Monty should take more interest in Shelton, because he needed male influences rather than what Dr Murphy called 'female domination'.

Valerie remained unconvinced. She decided that Shelton needed discipline and despaired that Monty was not firm enough to deal with the boy. The last six months had been hell, she said.

He was constantly argumentative and she was at the end of her tether. Then he ran away.

In June Valerie received a letter from the family GP, John Colebatch, who had referred Shelton to Dr Murphy. He was worried that the Leas had stopped taking Shelton to the appointments:

> It is of course for you to decide what you want to do with and for Shelton. However, having been consulted about him, I must in fairness tell you that Shelton's problems are already rather serious and could easily become magnified over the stressful period of puberty and adolescence in the next couple of years. I have seen so many cases of real delinquency develop unnecessarily that I feel you would not be wise to discontinue the type of program which Dr Murphy had commenced on Shelton's behalf. Such a program needs not only full cooperation from the family but continuous supervision and guidance from someone like Dr Murphy for several months at least and generally longer than this. I am not anxious to interfere in any way and I am sending copies of this letter to Dr Murphy who is quite able in collaboration to help you achieve good results with this boy, and I am sure you feel that Shelton is worth the trouble.

Dr Colebatch's fears were well founded.

13

CHICKEN MEAT

Shelton Lea stood at the top of Lambert Road. Watchful, yet easy, a rebel with a swagger.

Peering from the small window in his upstairs bedroom, Brett had already spotted him. He could feel a tingle of excitement up his spine in anticipation that something was about to happen, something outrageous. Shelton was like that—unpredictable, a mutinous spirit striking out to establish his identity in a world he didn't quite fit.

Every day after school for the past week, Brett had kept a vigil from his window, waiting expectantly for his older brother to show up. This time Shelton had run away because of a fight with Dad and hadn't come back. But Brett knew he would, if only to sleep and grab something to eat while his parents were at work.

None of the other children knew Shelton like he did, not even Lael who was supposed to be his 'twin'. They were only one day apart in age, yet Shelton and Lael could not be more different. Unlike Brett and Shelton, who were brothers in every sense—except blood.

And there he was, dressed as a bikie, for heaven's sake. The black leather jacket was way too big for him, sloping over his shoulders and trailing to his knees. Stolen most likely. The belt was wrapped twice around his skinny waist, its stainless steel studs flashing like a disco ball in the afternoon sun. To anyone else he was a ludicrous figure, but to Brett, Shelton was the anti-hero, a suburban Huck Finn without the fishing pole and freckles.

Shelton had moved closer. He was standing across the road from the Radcliff house. Max Radcliff lived there, or had until recently; his parents had sold up and moved away. Both Shelton and Brett liked Max, although the boys' boisterous play would often end up in an argument and a fight, with Shelton at the centre of it, of course. Maybe that was why the Radcliffs had moved; at least that's what his mother thought. Shelton's fault. Bloody Shelton.

It was true, at least in part. Shelton loved fighting, even though he wasn't much good at it. Plenty of heart and not much else. Getting punched in the face seemed to liberate him. Brett had watched it time and again. Shelton wanted to prove that he could take what the world threw at him—laugh at it and take some more.

He loved stirring things up, especially down at the takeaway chicken shop in Toorak Village where they would hang out with other local boys on weekends. This old bloke named Geoff used to run the place. He drank port and sherry when things got quiet, as they often did in the afternoons, after the lunchtime rush. If Shelton pestered enough, Geoff would give them some of the booze and they'd sit out the back, swigging from the warm bottle.

But trouble was never far away. Like the day a bunch of yobbos from Caulfield turned up, driving past the shop, back and forth, shouting foul-mouthed challenges at Brett, Shelton and a group of mates. Their opponents were clearly older and bigger, but that didn't stop Shelton, who started giving it back to them: 'Go on, ya wankers. Come here and I'll bash your head in.' Blah blah blah. On he'd go.

It went on for a few minutes, then the car stopped and the yobs piled out, confirming their size advantage. It didn't faze Shelton for a moment. While Brett and the other boys prepared to scatter, he stood his ground, looking them up and down before picking the biggest. The two boys agreed to fight out the back of the shop.

Brett and the others raced back inside the shop to arm themselves, grabbing the metal skewers used for roasting chickens. Then they marched back out, swords drawn in a guard of honour for their foolhardy general. It was to no avail. Shelton didn't want help, although he needed it.

The other kid was twice Shelton's size and proceeded to belt the shit out of him, but he refused to give in, even when the kid kept bashing his head against the bitumen. 'Get fucked! Get fucked!' Shelton yelled as his head hit the ground and blood started matting his hair, as if the sound of his own voice hid the obvious pain. In the end, the kid gave up and left the bloodied boy on the ground, still hurling abuse. It was no fun when the victim refused to be a victim.

Shelton had moved closer to the Lea house now, stopping by the fence next door. He could only be waiting for one thing— to make sure that his mother wasn't home before climbing the drainpipe he often used for his exits and entries. He needn't have worried. His parents were still at the factory and wouldn't be home for hours. Shelton would be long gone before they turned into the driveway and settled at the dinner table by themselves, the kids having been packed off to their rooms after their earlier meal.

But he wasn't coming home. Shelton was here to cadge a meal, grab some clothes and scoop up any money he could find lying about the place before disappearing again. But Brett wanted his brother back in the house, worried that he was living on the streets by himself. He went downstairs to surprise his brother as he came through the first-floor window.

∝

Valerie arrived home that evening to find Shelton in bed. Instead of letting him sleep, she woke him up and began lecturing him about making her anxious over his welfare. She was angry rather than concerned, and intent on punishing him rather than trying to understand what was wrong. Shelton's anguished response just made it worse: 'I want to get away. I don't want to stay here. Why should I be good? If I'm good you'll want to keep me.'

Despite his angst, Shelton agreed to stay and returned to school. But in early August, after finishing a training session in Carey Grammar's gymnasium where he had become gymnastics champion, Shelton stole a bike and rode out of the city, heading for Adelaide.

It was a spur of the moment decision, but the destination was significant because it was the city where Harry and Esther Levy had been married. The old man had told him stories as they sat together in the backyard three years before, leaving an impression on the troubled boy.

Shelton would detail his sad and lonely trip in great detail many years later in a conversation with Diana Georgeff: how he rode until dark and found a barn where he slept under a tarpaulin. The next day he pushed the bike along the road until he heard a truck approach from behind. He flagged it down and told the truck driver that his grandmother was ill and his parents couldn't afford the fare. The story worked and he caught a lift as far as the outskirts of Adelaide, where he got back on the bike and rode into town.

No one back in Toorak could have guessed how far the distraught but determined thirteen-year-old boy had managed to travel, or where he had gone. Shelton, still in his now sodden school uniform, mooched around Adelaide and its beaches for five days. He slept rough and begged or stole food, unsure why he was there or what to do next. He wandered through the city's great parks for hours and rode his bike down to the beach at Glenelg, where he scrounged his only hot meal for a week—a portion of chips wrapped in newspaper, bought with a sixpence he had cadged from a passer-by.

He contemplated hurling himself from a bridge into the Torrens River, but changed his mind when he 'saw all the duck shit'. Eventually, reported to police by a suspicious woman and threatened with arrest, he hitched a ride back to Lambert Road, where he shinnied up the drainpipe into his room to change his clothes and find food. Brett told him that some neighbours were away on holidays, so he broke into their house and spent the next week catching up on sleep and raiding their pantry.

When the neighbours returned, they called the police. Shelton was arrested and charged with breaking and entering, and stealing goods amounting to little more than £14, including a pair of binoculars he had used to keep an eye on the comings and goings at home.

This would be a defining moment in Shelton's life, when a troubled boy who should have been protected and counselled was, instead, carted off in a paddy wagon in front of the neighbours to Prahran Police Station where, unable to keep his mouth shut, he was roughed up and threatened. It was just as Dr Colebatch had feared—Shelton had embarked on a life of delinquency.

He was sent off to Turana, the state's juvenile detention centre, where he was held on remand with 500 other boys in a cramped, spare and threatening environment for ten days before his court appearance on 24 August. He wet his bed for the first time in years and was tormented by his fellow inmates.

Although he never spoke about the experience in detail, it is almost certain that Shelton was raped within the first two days. Diana Georgeff believes so, after watching him cry while she discussed these events with him. If Shelton had been lucky, he would merely have witnessed the atrocities of initiation in which new inmates—'chicken meat'—had their heads covered with a pillow. Then their pants were pulled down around their ankles and they were buggered again and again.

Valerie would have known nothing of the sexual abuse; her only diary entry on all this upheaval focused on how she had been wronged. They had been blind all along, tricked by the system into taking a boy who could not conform. There was no blame on her part. Now she felt justified and empowered.

Although the legal system had still not dealt with him, Valerie was prepared to cast her own judgment. Guilty. She wanted to be rid of Shelton, something she had threatened many times.

While Shelton waited for the courts to deal with him, she sought the help of the local Anglican minister to ensure the boy would not be returned to Lambert Road. Instead, he would be sent to a home, the St John's Home for Boys, and she signed a form giving them permission to keep him there, regardless of the verdict.

Her answers to a questionnaire were curt and confirmed her belief that she had done her best for him. He had been brought up with six siblings in the comfort of a home with seventeen rooms; he had been regularly immunised and was in excellent health; he had been sent to the best schools and was, both she and Monty believed, of above average intelligence. The only question she answered with more than a few words was—had she any complaints about his behaviour? 'Yes,' she wrote. 'He steals, lies and cannot get on with the others.'

With that she left.

CB

Henceforth Valerie moved on with family life. Her diary detailed her delight at Lael growing taller; he had received an average school report and now had his first girlfriend, a 'tomboy type' who had even made her own billycart. Charryce, of course, carried off honours *again* for her ballet exams and at school had been judged Most Likely To Succeed.

That summer Valerie and Monty loaded the other six kids into the family wagon and drove more than 1000 kilometres to Sydney. If the trip wasn't difficult enough, Valerie, still wary of car journeys, insisted on lying down so she couldn't see where she was going. The memory still makes Honey cringe: 'I couldn't stand it. I'd escape by climbing onto the back shelf, curl up and watch the countryside go by.'

In Sydney they rented a cottage at Balgowlah, near Manly in the city's north. There were the usual holiday glitches: Honey was stung by a bluebottle, and Gaela, now aged seventeen, was too shy to appear in public in her swimming costume. But it was clearly a joyful family time—hosting barbecues, visiting the zoo, taking a harbour cruise and swimming at local beaches.

Yet Valerie was obsessed with its cost: 'I am NOT EXTRAVAGANT at all,' she protested in her diary. 'I have spent £20-30-150-18-30 = £248 and am now broke.' Mungah had stepped in to help pay the rent and provide another £100 in spending money—the price she had to pay to see her grand-children. It wasn't the first time she had chipped in or sent money.

And with Shelton gone, Valerie's criticism had moved to the other two 'orphans'. She despaired at Brett's school report and the fact he was playing the class clown, particularly when a psychiatric assessment had concluded that, far from struggling intellectually, Brett was of above average intelligence and simply loafing. Rather than finding out why he was misbehaving, Valerie was angry.

On his thirteenth birthday that year, Brett had been allowed to have a party at which twenty of his school friends saw Valerie present him with a watch and a pair of sunglasses. They were easily the best presents he'd ever received and he proudly wore them all day in front of his friends. But later that night, after the guests had gone, Valerie took them back.

The presentation had been a deliberate gambit to make their confiscation sting him as painfully as possible: 'You'll get these back at the end of the year if you get in the top three in your class,' she told him. Brett never saw them again.

For a moment he had owned something important, but it had been taken away just as quickly. If she had wanted to punish him, Valerie should not have given the gifts in the first place and certainly not in front of other people. Rather than inspire Brett to do better, Valerie's punishment had only served to embarrass him in front of his friends, who wanted to know why he wasn't wearing the watch at school. He would never forget it.

Honey, aged eleven, had been in trouble too—not for her school results, which were good, but for her 'poor attitude' when she was farmed out to elderly relatives in Sydney for the school holidays so Valerie and Monty could go away for their twenty-fifth wedding anniversary. She stayed in Stanmore with Monty's mother, Esther, now aged seventy-four, and his spinster sister, Nona. She was alone, with no friends, and stood accused of being untidy and offering no help around the house. Valerie was also angry that Honey hadn't shown enough enthusiasm when her Uncle Darrell paid £18 to buy her 'correct fitting' socks, a cardigan and a car coat.

CƆ

The day after he arrived at St John's Home for Boys, Shelton turned fourteen. He celebrated by sneaking off with two other boys as they were being led to the chapel for evening prayers; they broke into the wine cellar of the nearby masonic temple where they made themselves sick on bottles of sherry. It took two days for him to recover from alcoholic poisoning.

He would continue to misbehave in protest against his treatment, running away several times over the next month and going on a stealing rampage in shops and homes in the area. When his case finally came back to court, there were another six counts of stealing against him and he was placed on a three-year good behaviour bond, removed from St John's and sent to Sale, a four-hour drive from Melbourne, where he was placed at Kilmany Park, a juvenile prison farm owned by the Presbyterian Church.

Kilmany Park Boys Home was a working farm run by Eric and Edna Frith, whose belief system matched Valerie Lea's. Eric Frith was an ex-sergeant major and believed in discipline and punishment. There were school, homework, chores and night-time hobbies for the 30 or so inmates. Misbehaviour was punished with a strap or a dose of Epsom salts. Shelton may as well have been back at Lambert Road.

It was inevitable that he would escape. Sometimes he headed into Sale, where he would go shoplifting, treating it as an art to learn as one would learn to play the piano. At other times he hitched back to the city, where he would drift for a few days before being picked up and handed back to the Friths for punishment. When he wasn't running away, Shelton would find other ways to rebel, on one occasion taking the tractor for a joyride.

He would remain at the home for five months before the Friths finally had enough. They contacted Shelton's probation officer, a young man named Bill Bainbridge, who found Shelton standing silently to attention in the hallway, his packed bags beside him.

Bainbridge had arranged for a new place, the Menzies Home for Boys in Frankston. This time it was Monty who dealt with the paperwork. The last question on the form asked how long they wanted Shelton to remain inside the home.

'Three years,' Monty wrote. The rest of Shelton's childhood.

14

A WARD OF THE STATE

At first glance the Menzies Home for Boys or 'The Home on the Hill', as it was commonly called—seems a place of benevolence and hope. The building is set high on Oliver's Hill at Frankston above Port Phillip Bay. Oliver had been a local fisherman who, in the mid-1800s, had erected a rough cottage among the eucalypts so he could keep watch for shoals of fish in the waters below.

Long after the fisherman and his cottage had gone, the land was cleared and levelled for a new house for the Melbourne Ragged Boys Home, which had been established in the late nineteenth century to house the huge numbers of unwanted children abandoned on the city's streets in the wake of the Victorian Gold Rush.

The Frankston home, with its wide, lush lawns, carefully arranged gardens and even an orchard with rows of apple and citrus trees, was opened in 1924. Its exterior was meant to convey homeliness and care, although it was always what happened inside the walls that had the biggest impact on the troubled lives of its young residents. One can imagine the easy walk down the sandy path to the beach and the relative freedom of the children, who attended local schools and lived under tight supervision in timber cottages scattered around the grounds.

But the sense of displacement of these children could not be glossed over with pretty pictures of grass and trees. Close inspection of the promotional photos reveals a wariness in the eyes of the boys ordered to smile for the camera. It is almost as though they expected failure at some point in their fractured lives.

When Shelton Lea arrived at Menzies in February 1961, the home was going through an identity change of its own: it was about to become a facility for both boys and girls.

He swaggered in like James Dean, sure of himself in a home largely filled with orphans with no, or petty, criminal records. It was a place where he could be king, and that's how he was treated by the others; larger than life, with a shield of bravado that hid his confusion and resentment. In research for her biography of Shelton, Diana Georgeff managed to track down one of his cohorts, Johnny Truscott, who summed up his old friend succinctly: 'He exploded the joint. He was awesome. He was bigger than Ned Kelly.'

Shelton slipped easily into the outlaw role. He adopted the leather dress code and the mandatory cigarette, and was soon initiating the high jinx and petty thefts of a boy with nowhere else to go, nothing else to do. He joined forces with a local gang whose members drove endlessly up and down the beachfront, whistling at girls and stirring. Shelton, sometimes with other boys like Johnny Truscott in tow, frequently went AWOL to steal milk money from doorsteps or nick beer left out for garbos. They pilfered from local shops and one night threw an octopus and stingrays into the swimming pool of TV star Graham Kennedy, who lived nearby.

But behind the bravado was a sad teenager, hoping each weekend for a visit from Bill Bainbridge. As Shelton told Diana Georgeff: 'I always thought the orphans were luckier because they never expected visits, and they couldn't be disappointed. Bainbridge was the only person I thought was really batting for me. I can only remember one visit from Monty.'

His memory was fairly accurate. Valerie's first mention of Shelton's move was almost seven months later, in a diary note on 24 September that began with a boast about the number of show bags that had been sold at the Royal Show—'3,500 UP':

Monty visited Shelton a few weeks back and said he was the same old Shelton. A couple of months ago Lael went to see his school and had a chat with him. Apparently, he does not have to do any jobs as at home, can come and go as he likes, as he couldn't do at home, and is relatively happy. I was very thrilled that he passed in all four subjects the mid-year test for the Intermediate. Mr Bainbridge is Shelton's probation officer and he took Shelton and another boy he had to Jenolan Caves for the school holidays fortnight and footed the complete bill. I send £5 a week and clothes to the home and none of the children went away for holidays. Bainbridge says he smokes like a chimney . . . and he told him he'd like to be a schoolteacher.

Although there are signs of sympathy here, and even a semblance of pride in his academic achievement, the overriding impression is one of Valerie's resentment—her other children had suffered because of the financial commitment to Shelton's care, and there was no sign that he was changing.

When she wrote about Shelton in her diary, Valerie's mentions were piecemeal and scattered, reflecting her own confusion and doubts. They were always surrounded by comforting references to Gaela, Jason, Lael and Charryce—rarely Honey or Bretton— as if she was seeking reassurance of her performance as a mother: Gaela adored her pet corgi, Lael was a smasher with the girls. And, of course, Charryce had received her fourth honours certificate for ballet with glowing remarks and had been chosen to dance with a partner at a function for star pupils held at Her Majesty's Theatre in Exhibition Street.

⅓

The contrast between Valerie's adoration of her natural children and her frustration with her social experiments was never more evident than in her diary entries in March 1962.

Gaela, now almost eighteen, had become a physical triumph, thanks to a diet consisting mainly of salad—a transformation orchestrated and encouraged by her mother. According to Valerie's scales, her oldest daughter had lost almost four stone in three months: 'She is now eight stone and looks like a swan,' she cooed. Valerie had also approved cosmetic surgery to remove an unsightly pear-shaped mark and to shorten her nose. The combination, she reckoned, was 'a beaut': 'She is quite the soigné young lady now and isn't so inclined to fool and amuse people and make outlandish faces.'

There were also positive signs at school for Gaela. Hopes that she might gain entry to university had now been replaced by plans to enrol her at Swinburne Tech, where she would study a combination of commerce, art, ticket writing and arithmetic. It sounded grandiose but it was clear that, behind the upbeat tone, Gaela's future lay with the family business—a secretarial job perhaps, and then marriage and children. Grandchildren for Valerie.

Sixteen-year-old Lael was blossoming. Now almost six feet tall and wearing a size 10½ shoe, he towered over his father, who didn't like the idea of having to look up to his son. 'He is long and skinny and positively delicious,' Valerie crowed, adding with some pride that he was good at remembering his household chores—putting out the milk bottles and garbage. '. . . but Bretton, oh my, he's just so lazy and doesn't remember a thing.'

Shelton was another matter entirely. In a three-page rant, she detailed his misdemeanours and crimes at Menzies, from smoking in bed and stealing money from the smaller boys to ransacking the office. There were even allegations of Shelton behaving badly on a beach with a local girl. When the girl's father threatened to horsewhip him, Shelton had fled back to the city and jumped a goods train to Sydney, which pulled into the wharves near the seamen's hotels, the Royal George and the Welcome Inn.

These pubs were two of the haunts of the Sydney Push, an anarchist libertarian circle that attracted philosophers, writers, musicians, poets, artists and academics. Germaine Greer, Eva Cox, Clive James and Frank Moorhouse were among its members.

The woman who ran the Royal George, known as Mrs G, gave Shelton a bed and board in return for clearing dirty glasses. He stayed for a fortnight and listened to the boisterous conversations of the Push before heading back to Melbourne. But he would return: 'It opened my eyes,' he said years later of this fleeting but significant experience.

At Menzies he fell back into bad habits and refused to perform chores, such as scrubbing floors and cleaning the kitchen. Then, in February 1962, he and two other boys were convicted of breaking and entering, and stealing beer and £130 in cash.

In his police statement, Shelton freely admitted to his crime; he was a fifteen-year-old boy, lost and alienated by a system in which he had no identity. He succinctly detailed how he and the two boys—David and Geoff—had walked out of Menzies and wandered down to the local beachfront a few hundred metres away, where they spent the afternoon loitering among the strip of shops there, looking for opportunities to break in under the cover of darkness.

They had targeted a supermarket, which on inspection they realised they could enter by raising a rear window with a nail. They were attracted by its stock of beer, but there was no point stealing cartons of beer without transport. That problem was solved when they met two other young men driving a green Holden who agreed to take the cartons and hide them until the heat had died down. The naivety of Shelton and his accomplices was highlighted when, after they'd made arrangements to meet later, they watched the men drive off with the stolen beer, never to be seen again: 'I haven't drunk any of that beer or received any money for it,' Shelton wrote in his police statement, as if it lessened his crime.

They also broke into a chemist shop by using fence palings to bash in a section of masonite. That yielded cash stuffed into a locked leather bag, which they cut open with scissors. Shelton hid his share inside a shoe and later stashed it in his locker back at the home.

He told the police in a statement that he knew any words of regret would sound hollow: 'I knew that it was wrong to break into those places and steal things [but] it is too late to say that I am sorry and I'll just have to take what is coming to me.'

When the matter came to court in the outer suburbs of the city, Valerie and Monty sat there, listening silently. They had been forced to attend the proceedings—'we had to be there'—while the magistrate issued an order, making Shelton a ward of the state. The only indication of Val's concern was a fleeting reference in her diary to 'poor old Shelton', as she rattled off details of a post-hearing conversation with the secretary of the boys' home, who reported that Shelton had run amok in the year he had lived there.

To make matters worse, Shelton had been bad-mouthing the Lea family: 'They said it was wicked how he was dragging down our good name and that he spoke foully of me,' Valerie wrote.

In Valerie's mind this was the final straw. Yet, as she fumed about Shelton's failure, there remained a desperate hope for her troubled adopted son's future: 'I am not really worried about how his actions will affect us and our name, but mostly that my main desire for every one of the children was that they should be HAPPY, irrespective as to whether they worked in the business or not, and that is what really hurts, that he is ruining his chances of happiness for the future.'

The comment is telling. It was at this moment that Valerie decided he should be written out of her and Monty's wills.

og

While he waited for the court to decide his future, Shelton was tossed back into the rat hole of Turana, in a section called Quamby, where a prison guard told him he was about to be taught a lesson he would never forget. 'We don't want you to come back,' Shelton later remembered him saying.

He would spend only nine days there—beaten by guards and inmates, sleeping on a stone floor and eating food covered in rat droppings—until Bill Bainbridge arranged to have him transferred to yet another boys' home, the Tally Ho Boys' Village run by the Methodists in the far eastern Melbourne suburb of Mount Waverley. This home would later become infamous for its institutionalised abuse of residents.

It did not take Shelton long to get into trouble again. He and two other boys left the home after dinner one evening and were caught four days later in Apollo Bay, a coastal holiday town 200 kilometres south-west of Melbourne. They had stolen a Ford Mercury in the city and robbed a supermarket. Shelton had then driven off, sitting on a stolen crate of tomato sauce bottles from the store so he could see over the steering wheel.

As they headed out along the Great Ocean Road there was another problem: Shelton couldn't see clearly because of dust on the road. In a moment of madness, he stood up while the

138

other boys tried to push a pillow underneath him. But he lost control and rolled the car, which crashed through a safety fence and tumbled onto an embankment, the only protection from a 120-metre drop into the Southern Ocean below.

There was tomato sauce all over the place but no blood. Incredibly, the three boys walked away without a scratch, unperturbed by their miraculous escape and intent on continuing their adventure by stealing another car, which they intended to drive across the Nullarbor to Perth. When the police finally caught up with them a few days later, they found £200 of groceries in the boot of the car, along with a stolen rifle, ammunition and two transistors. The boys had broken into five shops and as many as fifteen holiday homes, apparently just for the thrill of it.

Bainbridge rang Valerie to tell her about Shelton's latest crimes, and that the charges were too serious for Shelton to be returned to Tally Ho. She rang the police at Apollo Bay.

'How long since you've seen your son?' the officer inquired.

Valerie thought for a moment. 'Three weeks ago at Frankston Court, and his father spent three hours with him at Tally Ho last Saturday.'

Shelton had told the officer a different story, that he'd been kicked out of home more than two years before and hadn't seen either Valerie or Monty since. He boasted that he had burgled the family home a couple of times. Valerie was flabbergasted and angry, as she would later write:

It's quite impossible to really believe that all this is happening to us. He always makes sure he tells people who he is and then elicits their sympathy with the most outrageous lies which naturally people believe until they meet us which, of course, then spoils the picture he has built up in people's minds and then he is discredited in their eyes which he does not appreciate at all.

It was obvious, said the officer, that Shelton was intelligent; in fact he was in awe of his IQ. But he was worried that, if the boy kept on his path of crime, he would become a burden to law enforcement. As far as the police were concerned, there was no room for compassion. What Shelton Lea needed was discipline.

'They all said the same thing; that there had been too much talking and not enough firmness,' Valerie wrote. 'I wonder what the future holds in store for both us and Shelton.'

15

A BREACH OF TRUST

Mungah was selling up. After a lifetime of buying, renovating and renting property in the inner west of Sydney, she had finally decided that, at the age of almost 80, she was getting too old. It was someone else's turn to take responsibility for the Bulwark Against Disaster.

'Selling all her troubles' was how Valerie described it in her diary in July 1962. It was a description an outsider might find ludicrous. Troubles? Surely it was something of which to be proud. In a society where the purchase of a family home was an achievement to be treasured and protected, her mother had, from modest beginnings in the 1920s, built a mini property empire stretching from Haberfield to Paddington.

It had been no simple matter to acquire these properties, or to handle their ongoing management. Many of the houses had had to be restored or reconfigured before they could be let out to tenants. When they were all added together, they gave Mungah a wealth that her hoarding nature could not fully appreciate.

She was of a generation who had felt the need to prepare for the worst. This had been drilled into their consciousness and fed by the bitter reality of war, followed by recession, followed by another war. It was understandable then that Mungah had built and sandbagged a financial wall—not for pleasure and enjoyment, but out of fear of impending disaster. Consequently, she never demonstrated her wealth. No travel or jewellery. Not even a car. She lived frugally and mostly wore second-hand clothes.

Even her nickname, an innocent attempt by a child to say 'Grandma', conjured images of a hunched, largely unhappy figure trudging the streets of Petersham—walking, rather than wasting money on a bus, and retrieving pennies from electricity meters in darkened hallways.

Her oldest daughter was no different. Valerie had grown up in her mother's thrall, in total admiration of her work ethic and view of life. The money earned was sacred, to be used carefully and without deviation from the grand plan.

In mid-1962, as Mungah began to gradually sell the individual chess pieces of her empire, Valerie was busy recreating her mother's model in the southern capital. Three months earlier she had forced Monty to have the family home at 22 Lambert Road transferred into the names of their four natural children. It was no coincidence that he did so on the same day they watched Shelton convicted in court and sent to Turana.

Likewise, she arranged to have the neighbouring houses,

numbers 24 and 26 that she had bought a few years before, put into a deed of trust, divided into equal portions for Jason, Gaela, Lael and Charryce. There was no mention of Shelton, Brett or Honey.

Just like her mother, Valerie was obsessed with detail. While Monty took the children away for the day, she finalised letting number 24 and number 26—one to a mother and her 'four very nice boys' for £15 per week and the other, at £16 per week, to four young men with decent jobs.

A month later she went on a buying spree, flush with the money Mungah had raised from selling the first of her properties, a canny bank manager named Speedie by her side. On 15 April she paid £7500 for a four-bedroom house in Moore Street, Hawthorn, paying roughly half in cash and borrowing the rest. Three days later she paid £8000 in cash for a three-bedroom house in Orrong Road, Toorak, and a week later outlayed another £8550 to buy a huge five-bedroom house in Mary Street, Hawthorn.

The strategy was different for each property. Moore Street was a straightforward rental to a family and should return £24 per week. But the Orrong Road house would be turned into a five-bedroom house by utilising a rear sleep-out and a small study; it would be rented room by room. Mary Street would be different again—divided into two flats.

Valerie was, quite rightly, well pleased with her purchases. She had spent just over £24,000 buying three houses, using £16,000 of her mother's money and raising the rest in loans. The rentals would easily cover the cost of the mortgages, so much so that the bank had offered a £9000 overdraft 'in case I see anything else'.

Mungah would have been well pleased.

ɕɜ

19 July 1962

Valerie was angry, angrier than she could ever remember. The rejigging of the family finances had exposed Monty's embezzling and she did not know if she could forgive her husband. Their marriage was in crisis.

The bank had told her that Monty had secretly borrowed £8000 on the Lambert Road mortgage, which would make it difficult for her to increase the overdraft as she had planned. Worse still, Monty had taken £5000 that Mungah had sent them the previous year to be invested in a house and, instead, put it into his own business ventures, including the Twisties experiment, which was struggling in the UK.

In Valerie's words, for the past decade the Darrell Lea company in Melbourne had been 'using Mungah's money' to either prop up shortfalls or fund some of her husband's wild business schemes. To make matters worse, Monty had always promised her that any money borrowed would be formally noted and a healthy interest rate of 12.5 per cent paid.

But there was no record of any money borrowed and no reference to either an agreement or interest payments. Although the couple would not show it, Monty's breach of faith had caused a major rift in their marriage and, with Mungah selling her assets, the issue had come to a head:

> I never, until this last six months, ever allowed money to affect our relationship but it just couldn't keep on going when it's . . . [money] that has come from Mungah down to Melbourne to be invested for the four natural children, her real grandchildren, and to date there is nothing on paper to show for it.

Valerie's sense of debt to her mother made her husband's carelessness even more galling. She felt ashamed; she had let Mungah down. She now had to find a way to make things right again.

Despite Monty's promise of a healthy interest rate, the company accountant, a man named Honen, told her otherwise: 'Oh, I understood they were interest-free loans.'

The revelation couldn't have come at a worse time for Valerie. She was in the process of finalising the purchase and rental of the new properties and Mungah had now sold everything except a handful of houses, including the first two she ever bought— numbers 17 and 24 John Street, Petersham. They were an important reminder of both her mother's single-mindedness and Monty's breach of trust.

The diary rage that followed revealed Valerie's deepest fears. She would probably never have uttered such unfiltered comments aloud, but somehow she felt comfortable making them in print:

> How completely insane I was in the first place to jeopardise our marriage by letting him get his paws on any of the money that my

poor mother has worked so hard for, and is still slaving for when loaning to the business leads to this. How stupid I have been to have trusted him when money was concerned when the whole world knows that a Jew has no conscience and cannot ever be trusted. It is very hard to wipe all this sort of thing out of one's mind and I cannot look at him without feeling I would like to ground my boot into his face. I have never ever felt so hopelessly vicious before. I sincerely hope it will wear off. I would hate to spend the rest of my life like this.

The parlous state of their real financial situation was slowly being revealed—a house of cards on the brink of collapse. Valerie and Monty could never be accused of enjoying a lavish lifestyle, beyond paying for their seven children's expensive education. Yes, they employed staff to keep the home managed, but at the time labour was cheap and plentiful. The younger kids lived mostly in hand-me-downs, as did Valerie, who was not averse to wearing second-hand dresses. And they didn't have a wonderful social life either.

Their excesses were Monty's forays into new business ventures—whims that had not been analysed for their cost, potential risk and likely income. The most obvious of these businesses was the Twisties gamble, which, according to Monty's latest estimate, was close to going under with debts of at least £40,000. To compound matters further, in one of their city buildings a tenant had lagged behind with his rent payments for years; not only did he now owe £14,000 but Monty had let him get away with it.

Two other tenants were about to end their leases and there was an impending bill for refurbishments to other properties. The Leas' financial position was perilous yet Monty was embarking on a new project—growing mushrooms in the basement of an otherwise empty grain storehouse somewhere in Melbourne's outer suburbs. This too would fail.

Valerie had always known that Monty liked to take risks, but she'd chosen to believe his assurances. She stopped short of blaming herself for her husband's mistakes, even though she had always been aware of his shortcomings in business. Monty was not known, she wrote, for 'over-researching'; rather he was wedded to the creed that he should follow his own instincts and never allow others to talk him out of what he wanted to do. The problem was that he was too willing to allow others to talk him *into* ideas:

> So he's done exactly that, and life is not pleasant anymore. It's an effort and I've lost all my 'go'. Can't stand for long, eyes have gone, can't sew. I'm just useless and I've lost my heart in just about everything. I can't be bothered trying any more.

ଓ

For once, Valerie was not consumed by the problems of her adopted children. In fact, there were kind words for Shelton, who was inside Turana: 'We are visiting Shelton every Sunday and his attitude is excellent,' she wrote. 'We'll have him home for Christmas for good, we hope, and we hope it WILL be for GOOD and not bad again.'

Brett was still wafting through life, she noted, although she was content to pay £40 for some coaching classes through the school holidays. Honey also received rare praise for a reading she'd done at the Christmas Eve service at St John's, their local church, the previous year—'She did it beautifully [and] could be heard quite clearly through the church'—although Valerie could not help noting that Charryce was 'the best and clearest of all'.

Her biggest concern was Jason. He had been in London for almost two years now and been chilled by a particularly cold winter. On the positive side, he had almost topped his class in a business management course and, much to her delight, was ready to come home, although it seemed he would not be alone.

Jason had fallen for a girl he had met at business school. Her name was Hilke (pronounced Hilka) Murphy and it sounded serious as he detailed a romantic driving holiday 'on the Continent' in an open-topped red coupe. But Valerie was having doubts: 'She's Irish and Norwegian,' she wrote, as if attempting to explain the name, a strange response given her own predilection for unusual names.

Hilke—who was actually German and raised by her German mother and English stepfather—was eighteen years old and Jason had turned nineteen: 'I can't really look on this as bad news because, if she's the right girl for him, I'm really tickled pink,' Valerie wrote, privately unconvinced that it would work.

A few months later Jason wrote again, this time to tell his parents he wanted to marry Hilke and that she was pregnant. Given their ages, Jason needed parental consent before they could marry in either the United Kingdom or Australia. Valerie and Monty were unwilling to grant it.

They were too young to really know if their infatuation was the real thing, Valerie argued, ignoring her own life experience of beginning a relationship with Monty when she was aged just seventeen. She also assumed that Hilke was Catholic and, although she did not pursue that thought, it hinted that she had reservations about the religious mix.

It was all the more remarkable given her own problems with Mungah about her marriage to Monty, and the great kerfuffle when she and Monty travelled to the United States. It also emphasised her mother's influence.

Her sister-in-law, Sheila, initially supported Valerie's hard-line position but then, on reflection, decided that marriage was better 'for the baby's sake'. It seemed a remarkably shortsighted statement to Valerie, who reminded herself that only one of Sheila's four children was 'natural'; the others were adopted.

Instead, Valerie proposed a convoluted and bizarre plan under which Hilke would come to Australia and have the baby which Valerie and Monty would 'adopt' to ensure it was 'still a Lea'. Jason and Hilke would then live together, but wait until Jason turned twenty-one 'when they are quite sure about each other' before getting married: 'I can't wait to get my clutches on the baby,' she wrote, without mentioning when or even *if* the child would be returned to its parents.

Valerie was even prepared to fund the airfare—£450— although it would have to come from Mungah's pot, because Monty's financial shenanigans had left them almost skint.

Although she had not mentioned this to her mother, Valerie felt it was a legitimate way to spend the money, because it was for the benefit of her children.

The uncomfortable stalemate continued for months, with the company's UK manager Ted Delbridge eventually weighing into the discussion, sending a telegram in which he begged them to allow the wedding to go ahead.

Monty, still in the bad books for his misuse of Mungah's money, had softened his stance by this stage, but that only seemed to make Valerie more determined. When Jason threatened to get a court order, she became even more forceful: now she was describing the union as a forced marriage that couldn't be lived down if it went wrong.

Jason made one last attempt. If they didn't give their consent, he and Hilke would travel across the border to Scotland, where they did not need their permission to marry. Still Valerie would not budge, arguing that the decision would have consequences if the couple had other children and later divorced. True to their word, in September 1962 Jason and Hilke drove across the border and were married without fanfare in the famed 'runaway marriage' village of Gretna Green. Hilke was six months pregnant.

Valerie's belligerent opposition was all for nought, but her prediction about the longevity of the marriage would prove accurate, as would her fears that the children from the marriage would suffer because of it.

16

THE REVELATION

The court had no compassion for Shelton and his rampage through Apollo Bay. Yet he only seemed to worry whether Val and Monty had been in court to watch the sentencing.

'Has a Volkswagen bus turned up?' he asked a detective, who shook his head.

'Oh, that's good,' he responded.

He had been sentenced to eighteen months' prison; a return to minimum-security farm life was no longer an option. Instead, Shelton Lea would have to serve his time inside Turana—among the screws and rats and slime, where the inmates sat around an empty gymnasium for hours each day, bragging about their criminal lives.

Shelton had a tough persona but it was just a facade, a suit of armour to help him survive his childhood battles. He did not belong in Turana. He was the only inmate who read from the stack of books in the prison library; the only one who loved gymnastics and sang in a choir. His posh Toorak accent stuck out like dog's balls in a sea of squalid ignorance.

'It felt so barren to appear on earth and to find that nobody wanted you,' he later told Diana Georgeff. 'I did not belong to the Leas and no one could belong to Turana, so where would I go at the end of all this? I was alone, fractious and as bewildered as the wind.'

A ward of the state. The ramifications of these words began to bite: it was a life sentence, and someone had thrown away the key. At least that's the way it felt for a fifteen-year-old boy who couldn't see a light at the end of the tunnel. Years later, Shelton would call it 'bestial'.

'You never know when you're getting out. The maddies are what they give that to. Those poor bastards—I mean, whether they deserve it or not, it's a terrible way to treat another human being, given *no* time, because they just go berko. They just get progressively fucking madder,' he told fellow poet and friend Michael Sharkey. 'They made me a ward of the state . . . so I kept hitting the frog.'

Shelton bragged that he kept 'hitting the frog and toad'— hitting the road. On seven occasions he broke out of Turana with a mate named Stevie Stovell, who had been locked up since the age of ten for the murder of a man from whom he had stolen twelve shillings. He reckoned it was a record number of escapes: 'Some people escape because they've got nothing to lose. I escaped because I had everything to gain.'

Their first attempt—through the boiler room, across a

courtyard, and up and over a roof—lasted less than half an hour while the sirens sounded and the warders simply waited for them at the bottom of a park beside the prison. The boys found several other routes over the next few months, but they were always caught soon afterwards. The warders particularly delighted in returning Shelton to the cells: 'Still here, Lea?' one smirked.

But one breakout was memorable. One afternoon Shelton and Stevie grabbed a bench in the gymnasium and rammed it through giant opaque windows at the end of the room. This time Shelton had caught the screws by surprise, and he managed to find a bike and ride off before the posse was organised. He was given a lift over the Grampians by a passing truck driver and later told stories about living with gypsies. But wherever he ended up, Shelton was eventually discovered and hauled back to the prison.

ೞ

For all its horrors, Turana was the place that would change Shelton's life for the better. One night, as he lay on his thin mattress, reading by the light of a security beam outside, poetry came into Shelton Lea's life. He had always read widely, amassing 300 books by the time he ran away from home. He had admired the works of English cleric and poet John Donne from his early teens and had found comfort in the soothing rhythms and 'perfect words' of Henry Lawson while at Kilmany Park, but on this night—he could never date it specifically—his imagination was sparked by the rhyming couplet at the beginning of a poem.

Forewarned by legends of my youth
I trust not an associate's truth.

The words seemed to strike a chord as he played them over in his head. Rather than keep reading, he sat up and began composing his own lines to follow the 'borrowed' opening ones.

Shelton would keep writing furiously through the night, verse after verse until there were thirty or more. The resulting poem, 'Forewarned by Legends of My Youth', would always be among his favourites, at the heart of many performances he would give as an adult, but at this moment it gave him, for the first time, the means to express his anger and fears.

In his later years Shelton would rail against poetry being used as therapy—'it's an art, it's not therapy'—but as a teenager who had been made a ward of the state, it was his means of escaping without physically breaking out of Turana.

The revelations would continue over the next year while he was imprisoned in this most forbidding of places. As he read his way through the prison library, he discovered the work of the American poet and modernist Ezra Pound, whose economy of language and musical balance was 'fucken equisite'. In particular he came to adore a three-verse poem, 'The Garden', which defied the conventions of rhyme and meter and told of a man watching a beautiful woman walk through Kensington Gardens, in London, surrounded by a group of ragged children. Ezra Pound was describing him 'and those like me', Shelton decided as he read the poem. And he was *unkillable*, as he told Diana Georgeff.

It was such a hopeful line. I saw us there in Turana—notwith-standing all the misery and mysteries of why we were there, we were still alive and laughing! I felt as if I was conscious for the first time. I saw something extraordinary—poetry contains keys, keys to the meanings. I realised that words don't have to mean exactly what they say.

In his excitement, Shelton would ask his sister Honey to search for more Ezra Pound books. She remembers it vividly, and the delight on his face when she visited him. Valerie and Monty visited too, every Sunday according to Val's diary. Despite Shelton being made a ward of the state, they had stopped short of abandoning him.

Valerie even revisited her decision to adopt him, writing at length in her diary about Shelton's mother, Gwyneth Roberts, and dissecting her background, as if searching for clues to Shelton's problems. He had been a puny baby compared to chubby, healthy Lael; he had dribbled and moaned as he banged his head back and forth, night after night. But it would have been so difficult to reject him back then because he was so young.

Whether it was the poetry or the arrival of a new super-intendent named Ian Cox, towards the end of 1962 Shelton began to settle down. Cox introduced a change in what Shelton would describe as the ambience of the place. He even listened to the boys' complaints, something Valerie dismissed as airing griev-ances about conditions, as if it were inconsequential.

Cox believed Shelton was intelligent and needed time to mature. He also needed a mother figure rather than a disciplinarian, something experts had been telling Valerie since she took him to Travancore more than a decade before.

Her observation that Shelton's attitude had improved would be borne out when he was released in early December 1962 with a prison report card that revealed he had passed his Leaving Certificate: 'Shelton uses his intelligence and has been able to adjust his behaviour, gradually improving. He is now happy, relaxed and keen to make a new start at home,' the report concluded. 'His family have been concerned and prepared to co-operate with the institutional program. He has enough ability to accept work and cope with slight setbacks he may meet.'

The setbacks ahead would be far from slight. But when he looked back on his time at Turana, Shelton would later say that it marked 'the beginning of my life'.

Although he had a certificate, it was not formal education that would carry Shelton through life. It was the survival skills he'd learned inside: how to read people and talk to them, how to make a buck and, of course, how to write and perform his poetry.

17

DODGEM

Jason was finally home from England.

All seemed to have been forgiven between mother and son. The marriage to Hilke was now not only sanctioned but welcomed, and Valerie and Monty drove down to the Melbourne docks to greet their son and his heavily pregnant wife. 'Jason couldn't get over our dreadful Aussie voices', she laughed, delighted he was back after almost three years.

The birth a few weeks later of their first grandchild, Jason Jnr, added to the joyous clump of family birthdays in mid-December, with Monty and Charryce on the fifteenth and baby Jason the following day.

The birth was celebrated in style, with Valerie devoting hours of film to the baby and his mother, whose ash-blonde hair and blue eyes denoted her German roots. Hilke, eager to please, joined in the video pantomime and obeyed her mother-in-law's commands as she showed off her baby, who managed to smile as he was tickled and jiggled and tossed.

Even Shelton was home a few months later for the christening, hardened by his experiences yet still boyish with his wide, soft eyes and mouthful of crooked teeth. His casual clothes and rocker haircut were in stark contrast to Lael's and Brett's short back and sides and schoolboy uniforms. The family warmth seemed to have washed away the shadows cast by financial woes and Shelton's misdeeds.

But the good feelings would be fleeting.

Shelton had emerged from Turana proud of his Leaving Certificate, and with a head and heart full of poetry. But neither impressed Valerie, who refused to consider letting him continue his education. Instead, there was a factory job on offer.

The hopeful suggestions Ian Cox had expressed were ignored. Shelton would come and go from Lambert Road during the first half of 1963; he would return home but leave again as soon as the inevitable fight erupted. By mid-year, he had left for the last time, leaving his beloved books behind.

Valerie, ever worried about money, had decided that she had spent enough on the children who called themselves 'We Orphans Three'. She threatened to remove Honey from St Catherine's and 'scoot' her back to the local public school, even though her grades were 'always good' and her teachers acknowledged that her carefree attitude was improving. Valerie also noted that Honey had started smoking and was interested in a boy. As always, she could not help making a comparison with Charryce, whose results were 'almost always suitable for framing, they are always so good'.

Brett too was under fire, 'wafting through life in a dream', his time at Caulfield Grammar clearly limited. By the end of 1963 he would not only drop out of school, at which he had struggled so much, but also follow Shelton by walking out of the family home. The education system gave him permission to leave in the year he turned sixteen and, given his increasing unhappiness at home, escaping the Leas seemed the logical thing to do. Brett may have regarded Valerie as his mother, but that didn't mean he wanted to live with her, even if he had nowhere else to go.

Shelton needed to leave not only home but also Melbourne. He headed for Sydney, initially working as an assistant window dresser in a Darrell Lea store until he was involved in a dispute over his shifts. He left in protest and spent the next nine months living on his wits, splitting his time between the dark vibe of Kings Cross and the artistic politics of the waterfront hotels to which he'd been introduced in his earlier visit to the harbour city.

He contacted Mrs G and got a job at the Royal George. But this time he was not a boy picking up dirty glasses—he was a young man delivering drinks, often accompanied by lines of verse. Shelton had found his spiritual home. He recited poetry in exchange for food in the Cross, wrangled free beer in exchange for verses at the New Zealand Hotel in William Street, recited with jazz musos at the El Rocco in Potts Point and posted his creations on the walls of the soup kitchen at Ted Noffs' Wayside Chapel. He was befriended by the famous and the bohemian, by poets like Gavin Greenlees and Kenneth Slessor, but he was also in awe of less well known poets, like the Hungarian taxi-driver-turned-writer Sandor Berger.

Suddenly poetry was not just words on a piece of paper but something to be performed. The rowdier the audience the better, as he told fellow poet Michael Sharkey in a 1988 interview: 'Sandor and I would be just sitting on fruit boxes in Darlo Road, getting spat on, and getting yobbos trying to fight us. Sandor was a tough little nut, and I knew how to handle myself, and we used to give as much as we got. It wasn't until I came across Sandor that I knew that that *extra* was there, that poetry was about *giving*.'

CB

After nine months in Sydney, Shelton heard that his brother Brett had followed his lead and left Lambert Road. He took it as a prompt to head back to Melbourne.

One day, on Valerie's orders, Brett had gone down the street to buy a pint of milk from the local shop—and simply never returned. Still six months shy of his sixteenth birthday, Brett was sleeping rough in empty rooms and under staircases, seemingly drifting without intent. It was unsurprising that the police picked him up twice by for vagrancy, a crime in those days.

Valerie and Monty only confirmed Brett's view of them when they turned up to court on one occasion, not to support their 'son' but to seek an explanation from him, through the magistrate, as to why he was on the street and stealing. They left empty-handed, and without speaking up in support of the boy they had taken as their own at birth.

In an interview with Diana Georgeff, Brett gave an insight into the relationship:

The Leas never tried to help. When I got into strife the first time I was only a kid. They appeared in court and said: 'Make him tell us why he does these things. Why he steals stuff.' The basic reason was that I never got anything. I was never given any pocket money to be myself. Other kids had plenty of money. I'd sell friends something to get money. The other kids were allowed to go out with their girls. They were given special money to go out with them, but we never did. They didn't think we had a reason to get any extra. Real second-class citizens. And we got hand-me-downs as well. That gets you after a while; the shoes are never the same when you get them off another person. Really tight. Just amazing. I lived under stairways. I was homeless. It was an offence to be homeless and there weren't many of us then. I was arrested twice and went to jail. I got six weeks for vagrancy. I was fifteen-and-a-half.

Brett had been heavily influenced by what had happened to his older brother. They reconnected one night in late 1963 during a stand-off outside the Malvern Town Hall between rival gangs, the Jazzers and the Rockers. Brett, who hung around jazz clubs, was squaring off, ready for a fight, when he saw Shelton standing in no-man's land: 'Still causing trouble, Shelton Lea?' he called out.

The brothers would form a duo as Batman and Robin in a fantasy world of derring-do: 'We did heaps together,' Brett would recall with some glee. Sometimes they were in a posse of untamed youths, like the day they decided to rob an Armadale petrol station in a quick grab for cash and cigarettes. On other occasions it was just the two of them.

Shelton was keeping himself alive by nicking milk money left on front doorsteps, but he was never after a big payday: 'I'd take just enough to keep me going for the day. Ten bob or so. I wasn't greedy. This was about survival, not profit.' Then he found a part-time job working in a shop in Prahran. For a teenager in his precarious position, this might have been an opportunity to make his mark, perhaps to get a promotion or more hours, but for Shelton it was an opportunity for a quick score.

Somehow he got to know where the keys to the office safe were kept. One night, in the summer of 1964, he convinced Brett to go with him. Brett waited outside while his older brother climbed up the side of the building and snuck in through a side window.

Shelton was only inside for a few minutes before he reappeared in triumph, waving a fistful of notes. He dropped back down to the ground via a drainpipe. Brett couldn't believe it. Until now they had mainly pilfered—a packet of cigarettes from a service station, a few bottles of booze, small stuff in the main. But this was different. Shelton had just grabbed £400 from a locked safe; in the early 1960s this was a small fortune for anyone, let alone a couple of teenagers.

And that's what they were. Children, albeit out of control. The brothers managed to hail a taxi, which dropped them in St Kilda. It was now late at night and they stood out as innocents in streets lined with brothels and nightclubs. When they tried to book into one of the hotels along the strip, they were rebuffed by suspicious staff because they were so young and had no belongings with them.

In the end, with their pockets full of notes, Shelton and Brett walked down to Luna Park, the seaside amusement park on the foreshore of Port Phillip Bay, where the rides were closing for the night. They wandered about for a while, wondering what to do next, when they noticed an attendant not much older than themselves managing the dodgem cars. He looked like a knockabout kind of guy; a cigarette dangled from his lip. Would he keep the ride open for them? Shelton asked. The guy's eyes widened when Shelton peeled off £100.

The amount meant nothing to Shelton, but the attendant was looking at several months' wages: 'He was as happy as Larry,' Brett said years later. The rest of the park closed soon afterwards. Save for the dodgems, where Shelton and Brett drove around and around for hours, laughing with piratical glee at their surreal adventure.

The next morning they took a cab back to the city, where they bought riding boots and spurs, big army belts and some large daggers. They looked ridiculous, but still managed to get yet another cab and head to a pub that Shelton knew, the Red Bluff at Sandringham, which was usually full of the beatniks the two boys tended to admire and copy.

Shelton was refused service in the bar, so he bought beer from the bottle shop and the brothers went down to the beach opposite the hotel, where they drank and practised throwing their knives into tree trunks. Now drunk, Shelton headed back to the pub; here he got into a fight and was accused of threatening someone with his knife. The police were called and the boys, their pockets still half full of stolen money, were arrested.

Shelton was held for three days and charged with two counts

of assault and offensive behaviour. He paid the £6 fine from what was left of his ill-gotten gains. Brett was released without charge.

Worse was to follow. A week later they were in a group of four who broke into the Armadale railway station, only to be caught red-handed. The police drove them to Prahran Police Station, with Shelton sitting on Brett's lap the whole way. Then the cops bashed Shelton with a truncheon and a phone book because he wouldn't stop being cheeky.

'Prahran cop shop was terrible,' Brett recalled. 'They'd put telephone books over your chest and hit you with truncheons. You didn't get bruises but the whole area would be sore. Shelton was cheeky. Nothing worried him. They put him in a metal box and threw it down a short flight of stairs, letting him tumble around inside. He wouldn't stop telling them to 'Get stuffed' so they hung him upside down out of the top window. I saw that.'

Shelton later claimed that he pulled out a pencil and wrote his name upside down on the station wall. Given his love of the dramatic, it was just as likely a fabrication as the truth, but alongside Brett's first-hand account of his brother's behaviour, it clearly demonstrated that Shelton was a seventeen-year-old who had already given up on the world and the consequences of his own actions.

Three days later, subdued by tea laced with bromide—which the police gave him to make him docile—and sporting the bruises of more beatings, Shelton was sentenced to three months in the forbidding adults' prison, Pentridge.

CB

Shelton only served two months of his sentence, but the experience was something that a man normally unafraid of telling his stories rarely discussed. He was sent to C-Division, where the bushranger Ned Kelly had waited to be hanged.

There was no sewage system. Each morning the prisoners would remove their buckets from their cells and empty them into a central cesspit. The stench was overpowering. The cells were overcrowded and the prisoners tossed in together, regardless of their crimes. Violence was constant, sexual assault frequent and safety only possible through vigilance.

Diana Georgeff was convinced that Shelton would have been raped at some point but she never pressed the issue in their conversations, during which he revealed the horror of daily life at Pentridge. As he told her one day:

It's not like being on an aircraft. You can't change your seat. You're there, and with them. Someone who describes in detail what it's like to bite off a girl's ear. These people terrified me. You see men die in the yards. Bashed. Shot with a zip gun. Someone moves in quickly, there's a sudden eruption of extreme violence. You get your back to the wall very rapidly. It's finished in two or three seconds. One moment they're all over a guy, the next moment they are away from him, leaving him on the ground, slashed up, with the weapons beside him. The screws don't even see it.

He later summed up the experience in an unpublished poem called 'A Day in the Life of Shelton Yabelnovic'.

Six months after Shelton's release, Brett followed his brother into Pentridge. Barely seventeen years old, he was sentenced to one month behind bars after being convicted of housebreaking and pawning stolen goods. It was Brett's first conviction as an adult and he might have been spared the brutal experience had his parents paid the fine on his behalf. But Val and Monty refused, apparently hoping that a month in an adult prison would teach him a lesson.

It didn't, of course, serving only to alienate him further, and ensure his departure from the family and mainstream society. A year later he was back in court for possession and smoking cannabis, resulting in another month behind bars in Pentridge because he couldn't afford to pay the small fine.

This time, on his release, Brett kept going to Sydney to hook up with Shelton once more. Although he would return to Melbourne from time to time, Brett would never live there again.

18

THE BARGAIN

22 May 1965

How can I possibly have left this book for so long, especially
as such a lot has happened in these last two years?

Valerie was admonishing herself. She hadn't written in her diary
since March 1963, when she'd recorded the arrival of Jason and
Hilke from Europe the previous November, then the birth of
Jason Jnr, her first grandchild, a month later.

Then nothing.

Valerie didn't say what prompted her return to the diary
but there was certainly plenty to tell. Jason Jnr was now two
and a half, and he had a sister, Angeline Suzette, who was now
fifteen months old, with eyebrows like her father's and her Aunt
Charryce's, and a mouth and eyes (albeit light brown) like her
mother, Hilke.

Life was good for Valerie's oldest son, who was learning the
ropes at the new Sydney factory at Kogarah where he would soon

assume a senior management position. He and Hilke had moved into a house in front of the factory with 'a nice little yard for the babies'. Val had delighted in looking after her grandchildren at Lambert Road for nine weeks while they took a holiday in Surfers Paradise and then concentrated on getting the house ready for their young family. The cost of their extensive renovations were presumably paid by the family company, which owned the property. Walls were knocked down to make way for a 'lovely' kitchen and new living room, complete with a 'beautiful' lounge suite and all the mod cons, such as a new fridge and stove.

Valerie admired Hilke's eye for design. Although taking care of her grandchildren had tired her, she delighted in her contribution to the family's future. Any previous doubts had been erased, or so it seemed: 'I can only hope that I get as good [an] "in-law" for Lael, Gaela, Bubbie and Kestin as Hilke is,' she concluded, ignoring the fact that Shelton and Brett might also marry some day.

But her claim that she 'loved every second of it' was disingenuous. A few pages further on—seemingly inserted as an afterthought—Valerie describes in great, angry detail the physical sacrifices she had made, with callouses and aching limbs from chasing her errant grandchildren around the Lambert Road house and yelling at Jason Jnr to 'SHUT YOUR EYES' when he refused to go down for a nap. Not to mention the items that had been lost, broken, pulled, pushed, hidden, opened, tugged, twisted, emptied and ruined by their endless mischief.

The tirade spills over two pages, beneath the capitalised heading 'DAMAGE TO BE RECOMPENSED IN THE FUTURE', as if she expected Hilke to pay a damages bill for her own grand-children. It began with the torment of the family cat and dog, and an inventory of chipped and broken crockery and glassware, before descending into a list of ills and spills, including a flooded bathroom and unrolled toilet paper, baby powder rubbed into a rug, plants stripped of their leaves, sticky sweets taken from a cupboard, a bag of hair rollers scattered, the worn edge of a bassinet dragged across the floor, a sleeping bag soiled, bath plugs missing and 'very good dirt removed from plant boxes and transferred into mouths'.

The rant might be dismissed as attempted humour for the audience of family members, whom she expected to read her diary some day, but the anguished detail suggests otherwise. The bathroom scales used to weigh her own children for twenty years had been shattered; a treasured bottle of perfume, only used on special occasions, had been opened and tested; a 'very expensive stick with a rubber flap and plastic scraper' was broken. She counted the number of vinyl records used by 'Jacie' to create a playground of stepping stones (120), the fringes pulled from a cow-hide suite (eighteen), light bulbs taken from a storage cupboard (fifteen) and the number of pieces into which the aforementioned stick had been broken (eight).

Despite her catalogue of complaints, Valerie insisted that she wanted more grandchildren. Angeline's birth had been easy, unlike her own experiences of labour, and Hilke had put on hardly any weight. Yet she had now gone on the pill; grand-children were on hold until Jason Jnr started school.

'I'm heartbroken,' Valerie lamented. 'I was so looking forward to a never-ending succession of little Hilke-Jasons. But if course it isn't good to have one's own way ALL the time!!!!'

Her last comment was a portent of the disaster to come.

☙

Life had settled down since the trauma three years earlier, when Valerie was confronted by her husband's dishonesty. They had stemmed the tide of woes by selling off General Foods. 'So that's it for Twisties,' Valerie noted with some regret, even though, despite the losses, Monty was able to pay back some of his debts to Mungah's pot.

Even with the huge marketing campaign, Twisties simply hadn't taken off the way they'd hoped in either England or Australia although, inexplicably, they would become popular in other countries, such as Italy, where the snack was produced by another company in a slightly paler—almost buttercup yellow—colour and sold as Fonzies. They were also popular in Malta and some of the Pacific Islands, but it would take the change of ownership for them to finally succeed throughout Australia. The loss of this product would remain a personal regret for Monty.

The sale of General Foods had refilled the coffers, at least temporarily. The family still had significant property holdings, largely purchased with Mungah's savings, which had somehow survived the crisis of Monty's failed experiments and expansions. There were also three shops in Melbourne's CBD, a wool store and a seed and grain store.

There were also some new acquisitions. Mungah's remaining

funds had been placed into a private company, strangely named Atlantic Steel Corporation, which now owned an increasing number of houses in Richmond and St Kilda.

And there was a new venture, a twenty-three-room motel on the beachfront at Brighton. At £100,000, Monty reckoned they had bought a bargain. Valerie was not so sure.

೮ङ

Life in the Lea family appeared to be following a similar roller-coaster trend. Concerns about her children had subsided and new opportunities beckoned, although, once again, Valerie could not help but draw a distinction between her natural-born offspring and the adopted trio.

The biggest relief was Gaela who, like her father, had always been shy although she hated any comment being made about it, even more than half a century later as she recalls hiding in her bedroom when Jason brought his friends over because she thought she was ashamed about the size of her bottom: 'I was just a plump, lazy little girl,' she says. 'Mum didn't write very nice things about me in her diary.'

It was true. Valerie had long worried that her oldest daughter would become 'another Nona', a reference to Monty's older sister, who had never married and still lived at home. It irked Valerie that a daughter of hers would show no interest in boys, blaming her weight for her lack of self-esteem.

After finishing high school and bombing out of an accountancy course she regarded as a waste of time, Gaela had spent a couple of years working in the family shops, where she was 'quite good'; but there was no real change in her social habits, even after having surgery on her nose and losing weight.

The turning point had been her twentieth birthday, in August 1964, when Val and Monty presented Gaela with a ticket to Europe. The world had suddenly opened up, and six months later her parents were receiving ecstatic letters about the wonderful time she was having. Gaela went on a three-week walking tour with two friends, worked as a telephonist, then as a waitress and a chambermaid in the Swiss Alps for four months. After a holiday in Basel, she was now back in England.

Valerie expressed hopes that she would enrol in an Italian university, possibly Perugia, which welcomed the children of wealthy British parents. Gaela had not yet committed, her mother wrote in her diary, although she was not keen to come back to Australia.

Lael, by contrast, was having a hard time. He had struggled at Wesley College, needing two attempts to pass his Intermediate Certificate. Then, at the age of eighteen, he failed to pass his Leaving exams. (It only became clear years later that he battled an undiagnosed attention deficit disorder.)

It was here that Valerie's maternal love shone through, as did her true feelings about her adopted sons: 'I must admit he did try so hard that I do feel sorry for him. I just wish Shelton and Bretton had tried as hard as Lael did.'

With no desire to go on to tertiary study, Lael was sent to Sydney to work in the Kogarah factory under the watchful eye of his uncle, Darrell. It wasn't working. Lael was unhappy and out of his depth, living with relatives and with an interest in shooting that frightened his mother: 'He seems most unhappy and fights with Darrell and just can't seem to do the right thing.'

Despite her disappointment, Valerie had advanced Lael the hefty sum of £300 to buy a Land Rover and drive around Australia. But even this hadn't worked. Lael had purchased the car but then abandoned it—unregistered, with its engine removed—in the car park outside the Kogarah factory. Valerie was not angry, just worried and perplexed: 'We don't quite know what we can put him to and yet I'd love to have him back here with us. He is lovely.'

In contrast, there were few words and less comfort, let alone financial help, for Brett or Shelton. Unlike Lael, Shelton had passed his Leaving exams and clearly had intellectual capacity. Instead, Valerie focused on their problems. Brett had spent the previous Christmas in Pentridge before moving to Sydney. Shelton, who'd joined his brother in the harbour city, had been arrested for 'thieving' and was now in Long Bay Gaol.

She had little sympathy for either of them, although Brett was at least earning a living selling newspapers: 'Bretton says he is on the upgrade when he rang me the other night,' she wrote. 'It is very difficult to truly believe what he says. Shelton is supposed to be on drugs but he may be merely using that pretext as an excuse for his behaviour.'

Honey was in the same boat as her 'orphan' brothers, as far as Valerie was concerned. Not only did she have information that Honey had been involved in some skylarking but she appeared to accuse of her adopted daughter of loose moral behaviour, writing: 'A very advanced young lady who constantly went to the village after school instead of coming home.'

19

BRIGHTON SAVOY

Mungah had few rules about investing, but she expected them to be followed. There were to be no loans to family members and no money used on business ventures. The other rule of significance was Mungah's insistence that her money only be invested in residential property, not shops or factories. Her reasoning was as simple and logical as her doomsday strategy: 'All shops and factories were vacant during the 1930 Depression but people still had to live in houses or flats.'

Valerie had already broken the first two commandments, having been led astray by Monty's unshakable confidence in his own ideas and duped by his secrecy in misappropriating his mother-in-law's generous contributions. It seemed highly improbable that Valerie would blindly follow Monty again, but she did.

What ultimately became the Brighton Savoy Hotel was initially built in 1909 as a luxurious mansion for one of Melbourne's wealthy businessmen; it then became a boarding house for an exclusive girls school. In the 1940s it was transformed into a private hotel and in the fifties extended to include a motel with a function room.

It was Melbourne's only beachfront hotel, perched above Brighton Beach and its brightly coloured bathing boxes. It offered views across Port Phillip Bay back to the city, and had been chosen to host the Logie Awards in 1960, when Graham Kennedy, the Lea family's Twisties spruiker, won the Gold Logie for the most popular television personality.

And now Monty had bought it, his eyes shining at the prospect of turning the building into a showplace for artists like Welsh singer Shirley Bassey and Liberace, the American pianist, actor and showman.

Monty insisted it was a bargain: he reckoned the building alone was worth the price tag of $200,000, which meant the furniture came for nothing. He had been right once before when the company bought Chapel Street, so Valerie decided to back her husband.

She never recorded Mungah's reaction, even though the funds would come directly from her mother's Bulwark and breach all of its investment rules.

But the deal turned sour in a matter of months. As usual, Monty had not been thorough and there was no due diligence performed on the income figures provided by the previous owners. The business was struggling, and the building itself was in need of repairs and refurbishment.

Monty's grand plan—to put Ted and Cecile Delbridge in charge, with the aim of quickly building up the business and then selling at a big profit—proved way off the mark. Ted may have been a good manager for Darrell Lea, but neither he nor his wife knew anything about hotel management. What had been proposed as a bargain had turned into a money pit and a management disaster, and Val felt she had only herself to blame.

Even the free publicity created by the strange case of the 'Giveaway Girl' failed to boost interest in the hotel, although it must have left a mark on Valerie. It was an episode that was disturbingly similar to the stories of Shelton, Brett and Honey.

 C҉

In May 1965, not long after Monty and Valerie purchased the hotel, a young Adelaide mother advertised her three-year-old daughter for adoption in a city newspaper because she couldn't make ends meet: 'Would some kind couple like to adopt a pretty three-year-old,' the woman wrote, explaining that she had another child to support on only £12 a week and was unable to cope. 'They must be able to give her a better life than I can.'

Susy's story sparked national interest and sympathy, with dozens of couples around the country offering to take the little girl. Eventually the mother agreed to give her child to a Melbourne couple, who paid for the mother and daughter to fly to Melbourne, where they checked into the Brighton Savoy.

Cecile Delbridge, who was interviewed by a number of newspapers, watched them arrive on the evening of 28 May but in the morning they were gone. The mother had changed her mind and returned to Adelaide with her child. Unlike the mothers of Shelton, Brett and Honey, she would find a way to cope and raise her child.

ᚼ

By the end of the 1966 financial year the Brighton Savoy had lost £11,000. Valerie fired the Delbridges and tried another manager, but things went from bad to worse, and they lost another £25,000. The money was all coming from the precious Atlantic Corporation fund. Her children's money. Mungah's sweat.

In desperation, Valerie moved herself, Monty and Charryce from Lambert Road into the hotel. She left a staff member to manage the Toorak house and, not wanting to miss an opportunity, she rented out individual rooms there. She then took over the day-to-day operations at the Savoy and ordered Gaela back home from Europe to help out. Any dreams her daughter had of a university education were now put aside for the sake of the family business.

As Gaela was coming home, Lael was leaving Australia. He'd saved enough money to pay for his own ticket to Europe, and it was time to explore the world. His parents weren't happy. Typically, one of the first things he did in London was buy a couple of cars—a Renault and a Fiat.

He then made the mistake of writing to his mother about the cars, asking if she would send him some money, as he recalled: 'She rang the British consulate in Melbourne and asked them: "My son is in England. He owns two cars. What would you class him as?"' he later recalled, laughing at the memory. 'They told her I was "affluent", so she wrote back and told me I was affluent, so I could piss off. It made me realise that I told her too much.'

It was little wonder Valerie was peeved. The Kogarah factory in Sydney's south-west had centralised manufacturing for the company. Its recent opening meant not only the end of production at Chapel Street but also the need for Monty to spend more time in Sydney. It would leave Valerie and the girls to make a go of the Brighton Savoy operation, which had twenty-three motel suites and twenty-one hotel rooms, a restaurant and three reception rooms available for conventions, weddings and dinner dances. The prospect was ridiculous: 'I was frantic,' she would write. 'The place was costing £500 per week to run and there was only ONE guest in the hotel. I used to walk through the halls with my face streaming with tears.'

Under new management, declared an advertisement in *The Age* on 23 February 1966, offering accommodation at a motel/private hotel with elegant suites, excellent cuisine and easy transport into the city six miles away—'For that restful, pampered break'.

But everything behind the scenes was far from restful. Valerie, Gaela and Charryce were working sixteen-hour days while trying to fill staff vacancies and coax the function business into life.

Charryce, who worked mainly in the office and reception, recalled in an interview the dark days when her mother slept on a li-lo in the front office to answer late-night phone calls: 'In true Monty style he skedaddled back to Sydney, leaving Mum to pick up the pieces, and she did although there were days that she felt like walking across the road to Brighton Beach, walking into the sea and never coming back.'

And to complicate matters even further, Valerie had also moved Mungah down to Melbourne to live with her. After a lifetime of simple home-cooked meals, the old lady was struggling to cope with the oily hotel food.

By 1967 they began to make headway and, impressively, turned a small profit for the financial year. But it was too late. Valerie and Gaela had worn themselves ragged: 'I felt I couldn't face another mother and bride,' Valerie wrote.

Valerie was also under pressure from Darrell Lea management in Sydney. This was an important period for the company and they needed all family hands on deck. There was no longer a factory operation in Melbourne, and the company had also shut a number of the less profitable city shopfronts. The southern arm of the company they had so carefully built over twenty-six years had been reduced to a stub.

Managing director Darrell wanted his sister-in-law to sell the hotel—accept a low offer if necessary and swallow the loss—so that she and Monty could move north permanently to help full-time with the Kogarah factory. In fact, Monty had already been working there for more than three months. Valerie felt her marriage was under strain once more.

She was grateful when a decent offer was finally made towards the end of the year, although it was not without problems. A young real estate conman convinced Valerie that he had the funds to buy the property, then he moved into the hotel and began siphoning off the weekly takings before she realised he was a fraud.

It would take several years to reclaim those lost funds, but the drama opened the door to another buyer and in December 1967 the Brighton Savoy nightmare was finally over. A small capital gain had been made, but overall the early trading losses during this gruelling experience had cost the Atlantic Steel Corporation almost $100,000. Although the Bulwark Against Disaster had held up, it was sagging under the strain.

20

GO-SET

One morning towards the end of 1965, Honey Lea turned up at school in tears. Diana Georgeff describes the scene: 'I can still see her in the quadrangle, near the clock tower with girls huddled around her. She was standing, sobbing with her face in her hands. Monty had driven her to school that morning and told her they had decided to make her a ward of the state.'

More than eleven years after adopting Gayle Lesley Johns as a made-to-order playmate 'twin' for their natural daughter, Valerie and Monty had decided that the girl they had renamed Kestin Fearne Melani Lea was of no further use to the family; she was of bad blood like Shelton, so they would 'un-adopt' her.

The threat seemed to cool over the next few weeks. Then one morning Honey had to face Valerie and admit injuring herself while riding on the back of a motorbike at a friend's house. In doing so she had skipped a day of school. Honey recalls:

Valerie was furious. She said I should go to the doctor, but that I would not be going back to school. I had to go and get my things. I thought she was joking, but after the summer holidays everyone else except me got their school uniform.

That was it. Instead, I would work in one of the shops and be a window dresser on something ridiculous like £5 a week. Valerie then took board and insisted that I buy my own stockings, which left me with something like 10 shillings at the end of the week. It wasn't even enough for the bus fare.

The job didn't last. Valerie refused to increase Honey's wages, despite the fact that the company was paying salesgirls a minimum of £7 per week to work in their city shops, so Honey decided to take a live-in job at Brighton, helping a young couple with two young children.

'So, she's happy', Valerie concluded erroneously, unwilling to acknowledge the clear division that she had established between her natural and adopted children, in either understanding the problems of their early adulthood or providing them with financial stability. While Jason, Gaela and Lael were given money for overseas trips, expensive cars and even house renovations, Brett, Shelton and Honey were denied even basic support and, in Honey's case, paid less money than the company's employees.

Of all her children, Valerie seemed most preoccupied with Charryce. The departure of Honey from Lambert Road had been a blessing, she wrote. Honey was a vindictive young woman with a chip on her shoulder; she was arrogant to the staff, had started arguments and was capable of saying such nasty things to her sister that Charryce had often been trapped alone in her bedroom while Honey entertained friends downstairs. 'Everything has been so peaceful and enjoyable these last couple of months and it is so nice to see Charryce actually blooming and enjoying herself at last without Kestin's competition.'

Despite this new-found freedom, Charryce dropped out of school the following year and was packed off to Sydney, where she lived with an aunt and worked as a window dresser in one of the Darrell Lea stores before enrolling in a business course to learn typing and shorthand.

Valerie's natural children were praised for trying, and forgiven for failing. Love, care and hope for them were expressed—as one would hope for any child—but not when it came to the 'orphans'. Instead, hope was greeted with suspicion, problems with accusations and cries for help with rejection.

A little further on in the diary, Valerie offered this explanation: 'I suppose that basically the four natural ones have been so easy to bring up because they are all quite placid personalities, where the adopted ones are bound to be difficult because of their backgrounds . . . the adopted ones always made the natural ones look so good in comparison.'

ॐ

Honey scoured newspapers looking for alternative jobs, eventually finding a live-in nanny job in East Brighton. But that job went badly wrong very quickly when, one morning a few weeks after she moved in, the husband waited until his wife had left the house and then molested her, forcing the sixteen-year-old against a wall and rubbing his erection against her. She fled the house, found a phone box and asked to come home.

Despite her previously harsh attitude, Valerie relented, even offering to enrol Honey at a well-known modelling school and pay for the course if she came back and helped out.

Her enrolment at the Bambi Smith Model College would change the teenager's life almost immediately. In early February 1966 Honey was chosen as one of the contestants in a beauty contest at the International Motor Show held at the Royal Exhibition Hall where, dressed in a sash and ball gown, she would be photographed as Miss AMC alongside luxury cars.

Honey finished third in the contest, which was hosted by a television identity, and offered a $100 prize in the nation's new decimal currency. As she stood there, a bit awkwardly, while photographs were taken, a boy approached and asked if she would like to go to a party 'with the *Go-Set* people'.

Honey knew what he meant by *Go-Set*. It was a new magazine, focused on music and fashion. The previous week she had seen a copy in one of the hotel's bedrooms, left behind by the local pop singer Dinah Lee who had been staying there during a promotional visit. Honey had stopped cleaning for a moment and sat on the bed to read it, captivated by its photos and articles. It was the second edition, headlined by a backstage interview with the British band Herman's Hermits.

She happily agreed to go to the party; the idea of meeting the people behind the magazine was irresistible. She hurriedly changed into jeans and dumped the ball gown, her modelling career over in a moment.

The party was in one of the side streets at Toorak Village, at a club where the age of a young and pretty girl was never checked on the door. Although, given the layers of makeup she was still wearing from the beauty contest, Honey looked much older.

She knew none of the people sitting at a big round table, nor a tall man sucking on a pipe who walked in soon afterwards, a worried look on his face. Someone leaned over and told her it was Tony Schauble, the editor of *Go-Set*. And he had a problem.

'Can anyone here type?' Schauble asked, shouting over the music.

Honey looked around. No one had moved. 'I can,' she volunteered, raising her hand like the schoolgirl she was.

It was a lie.

Schauble looked down at her, trying to assess the young woman in front of him. 'Come with me,' he said simply and turned on his heel. Instead of partying, Honey spent the night in the back of a house in Drummond Street, Carlton, helping to get out the next edition of *Go-Set*—its name a marriage of the words 'go-go' and 'jetset'.

It was an atmosphere of frenzied creativity, and Honey revelled in the chaos. The night had changed her life, but two days later everything was thrown into turmoil again when Monty somehow found her and demanded that she go home immediately. She reluctantly obliged, believing it was because they were concerned about her being on the streets.

Instead, when Honey got back to the Brighton Savoy, she was confronted by her angry parents who had found and read her diary, including entries about catching Charryce with her boyfriend. Her sister, who says she doesn't recall the incident, had denied the accusation and Valerie was outraged.

Honey looked at the woman who had pretended to be her mother for the past twelve years.

I realised that Valerie had never cared at all. Her only concern was that I had maligned her daughter, her flesh and blood, and I was a lying, ungrateful guttersnipe. It just showed how much differently we were regarded. I called someone from *Go-Set*, and they came and got me. That was it. I never went back.

This moment would have far-reaching consequences for Honey's life because it gave the woman who adopted her when she four years old the justification to cut her off financially forever. In the mind of Valerie Lea, the adopted children had abandoned her and the family, and in doing so had forfeited any right to its benefits. The fact that they were still children, confused about their own identity and value, was irrelevant. None of them would receive any financial support of substance for the rest of their lives.

ଓ

Go-Set, a small weekly magazine published by Schauble and Phillip Frazer, a couple of broke nineteen-year-old Monash University students, would become the bible of Australian music. The first edition of *Go-Set* appeared on Melbourne's streets on 2 February 1966 with Welsh heart-throb Tom Jones on the cover and twenty pages of pop music interviews, 'mod fashions' and surfing news.

It was an immediate success, a publishing revelation in a society whose music and fashion trends had been sparked by Beatles hysteria and the sight of bare-legged Jean Shrimpton in a miniskirt at Flemington on Derby Day. It was targeted unashamedly at the teen-girl fan market—'A love child from the coupling of new youth oriented journalism and the growing beat and progressive music scene', as it was later described by pop culture historian Jeffrey Turnbull.

By the third edition, which featured the youthful Rolling Stones on the cover, sales had doubled. It was soon being printed in Sydney, and by the end of the year in every other capital city. *Go-Set* helped launch the careers of people such as music guru Ian 'Molly' Meldrum and fashion designer Prue Acton.

Reflecting on the early days of the magazine, the forerunner to the Australian edition of *Rolling Stone* magazine, Frazer would later write about the people behind the phenomenon that created the country's first national pop music chart. They included a suburban printer named Jim, a photographer with a Pentax but no flash, a university mate with the curious name of Doug Panther who offered to do interviews, an advertising salesman named Tez with great telephone banter 'and a sixteen-year-old fashion expert named Honey'.

The Carlton house in which they put together the first edition was rented by the magazine's photographer, Colin Beard, a blond lantern-jawed Englishman in his mid-twenties who gave up a well-paid engineering job to help create the magazine. He had only picked up a camera six weeks before photographing Tom Jones for the first edition and was reading how-to manuals as he and Doug Panther slipped past security at a Sydney hotel to take exclusive shots of the Rolling Stones; Mick Jagger was so impressed by them that he hugged Colin at a press conference.

Half a century later, Honey retains warm memories of Colin, who now lives in North Queensland after a career in fashion photography and academia. She had a relationship with him during the heady first months of the magazine. They slept together in a bedroom in the Carlton house, surrounded by drying photographic prints. He recalls trying to prevent any from dripping on her as she slept: 'I remember how sweet she looked lying there.'

Honey would often tag along with Colin while he covered city discos on Friday nights and suburban dance halls on Saturdays, where local bands like the Twilights and Masters Apprentices were discovered. The demanding pace of the work and their age difference meant the relationship wouldn't last and, sure enough, it ended after seven months. There was no acrimony and they continued to work together on the magazine.

By then Honey had been promoted to fashion editor—Prue Acton had dropped out—for a magazine that had now strongly established itself. The teenagers of Melbourne and Sydney were clamouring for its unique access and insight.

In September 1966 the ABC's *Four Corners* program recognised *Go-Set*'s importance by running a segment on the magazine as part of a feature on teenage culture. The Beatles' just-released classic 'Yellow Submarine' played in the background as the reporter explained that all the magazine's staff members were under twenty-one. Honey, the youngest, was among those interviewed. With her auburn hair cut in the bob style made famous by

Vidal Sassoon and her eyes heavily made up with eyeliner, she'd dressed in the classic sixties fashion of fitted jacket and turtle neck.

Asked how much power she had in influencing fashion, Honey grinned at the interviewer: 'I hope the kids will follow me and every word I say, and that if Honey says that a dress is hot then they're all going to rush out and buy it. I want the fashion houses to have faith in me. Already I've had hundreds of letters from kids saying how much they like the dresses.'

But behind the show of confidence, Honey remained fragile. When she was still with Beard, she occasionally confided in him about her life with the Leas. She needed reassurance, touch and smells 'like a little girl'. On occasion they would lie in bed, her head resting on his chest, and she would lament that he didn't 'smell of anything', as if she needed a touch-base fragrance. 'She was clearly affected. I couldn't understand why anyone would adopt three children and then treat them as second-rate,' he recalls.

On another occasion Charryce came to visit and stayed overnight. Honey insisted that her sister sleep in their bed, between them.

'It was very strange,' Colin recalls. 'I still don't know if Honey was testing Charryce or testing me.'

Honey would also venture back to Brighton, where the Leas were still living, mostly because she missed the family dog, whom she would take for walks through central Melbourne. One day, with Colin by her side, she asked Valerie and Monty for financial help. They refused. The memory still sparks strong emotion in Colin. 'I was really, really angry about it. I could not believe how detached and cruel these people could be.'

21

THE ORIGIN OF EVERYTHING

Cheverells was a stately three-storey mansion in Elizabeth Bay Road, just behind the El-Alamein Fountain in the heart of Sydney's Kings Cross. It was pulled down in the late sixties to make way for the Gazebo Hotel, which in turn became today's Gazebo Apartments. But until then it had been a prominent building in the modern story of The Cross, beginning in the 1940s, when it was used as an officers' club for American servicemen. By the 1950s it had been turned into a rambling guesthouse/private hotel, its cramped rooms filled with a bohemian collection of artists and musicians, hookers and drag queens.

As far as Valerie knew, this was where her two adopted sons were living by mid-1965. Brett had telephoned her from Cheverells one day to tell her he was doing okay, selling twenty-cent copies of *The Kings Cross Whisper*, a satirical tits-and-bums paper started by a couple of journalists who wanted to take the mickey out of the conservative politics of the day.

Although she clearly did not approve of the 'dirty joke paper', Brett seemed to be faring better than his brother. Shelton was back in jail—this time for breaking and entering; he had been initially sent to Long Bay Gaol but would serve most of his time at Goulburn Prison, emerging eighteen months later with a new set of teeth (his old ones had apparently been removed without anaesthetic). He vowed never to go back inside.

It was hardly surprising that Brett and Shelton had gravitated to The Cross, home of the disaffected and the afflicted, where they felt comfortable among the petty thieves, drug addicts and hucksters. They could always steal and deal to keep money in their pockets. They sold a bit of hash, mostly in places like the Piccolo Bar on Roslyn Street behind the main strip. Shelton even traded love poems for tobacco, just as a street artist might sketch a quick portrait for a bit of cash.

When he spoke to Diana Georgeff years later, Brett would proudly tell her how he and Shelton had helped to lay bricks for the drop-in centre at the Wayside Chapel in Hughes Street where Ted Noffs—who offered food in exchange for labour—founded the famed street organisation. Then, in the next breath, he'd reveal that he happily sold drugs to passing schoolgirls: 'It was always good around there.'

But Brett stuck mainly to what he knew. At one stage he was running what he called (perhaps ironically) a chocolate shop, where the real money was in cut-price cigarettes. This came about not because he had a good supplier but because he'd go out at night and steal from other stores. Then he'd line the shelves of his own shop and sell them at half price.

Like everything else he did, Brett was in it for the lark. But although he and Shelton were close, they did not live in each other's pockets. They were different; Brett admired Shelton's skills as a poet but didn't understand his work. In style at least, Brett was more of a beatnik, a member of the Jack Kerouac-inspired sub-culture of the 'beat generation', who had their own rebellious response to a world from which they felt disconnected. He had adopted this pose back in Melbourne; he now found a home among the patrons at one of Shelton's old haunts, the Royal George Hotel, where he convinced the manager to let him keep his clothes in the cellar.

Shelton was now in a relationship. There had never been a shortage of women in Shelton's life—his soulful features and maverick heart proved irresistible to many—but after a succession of girlfriends he had met and fallen in love with a young woman named Wendy Liddle. He expressed his devotion in a poem 'What Does It Matter'.

When he met Wendy, Shelton was living at Cheverells, earning his keep, he insisted, by looking out for the dozen or so prostitutes who had rooms where they took clients. 'I was time keeper for the Tim [brothel],' he told Michael Sharkey, whom he had also met at Cheverells. 'They were all half-hour tricks, and my job was to go and knock on the door: "You ready, are you, Marge? Everything sweet, love? Time's up."'

He seemed to invent jobs for himself, partly out of need but also in order to belong. When the great jazz artist Thelonius

Monk came to town, Shelton became his 'minder' at the Chevron Hotel. 'Thelonius taught me about timing. He said, "Shelton, it's the space between the notes."'

Sometimes it was hard to distinguish between Shelton's real adventures and those he loved to invent, such as his insistence that he met the American satirist and stand-up comic Lenny Bruce when he played at the Wintergarden in Sydney in 1964, then spent a week with him while he was under house arrest, again at the Chevron. The story sounds plausible until you realise that Bruce only toured Australia once—in September 1962, when Shelton was still serving time in Turana.

But life was about to change, for better and for worse. In early 1967 Shelton and Wendy decided to move in together and rented a cramped flat in Hartnett Street, Woolloomooloo. They were setting up house together because Wendy was pregnant and Shelton Lea, the orphan whose only male role model since the age of fourteen wore a uniform and beat him up, was about to become a father.

He and Wendy needed decent accommodation, or at least something better than the cell-like room with a sink at Cheverells, so they could not afford to continue living hand-to-mouth. After all, poetry paid for nothing more than beer and cigarettes.

Instead, they resorted to dealing drugs for their income—not just the small amounts of hash they were peddling, but also the hallucinogenic LSD that had begun to appear on Sydney streets. The drug was mostly brought in by US servicemen on leave but Shelton had also made contact with a university student named Robert Milne and a research scientist called Paul Taylor. They were manufacturing the drug in Milne's Bondi flat.

Shelton could see no problem with either drug. The dope made you mellow and LSD could change the world, setting off 'little bolts of lightning' in the brain: 'It expands meaning and produces parody.'

His daughter would be named Chaos—appropriate given the nature of the world in which she would begin her life—but Shelton's choice was based on his reading of Greek mythology in which Chaos was the origin of everything. She was born in mid-1967, around the same time Milne and Taylor were coming to the attention of police, who had also placed Shelton and Wendy under surveillance as they came and went from the flat, filming them from inside what looked like an outdoor toilet across the road.

In hindsight, Shelton would remember feeling odd about the 'latrine-like object', but he was so excited by the imminent arrival of his daughter that he ignored his instincts that something was amiss.

On the night of 25 September police followed Milne and Taylor as they drove to meet Shelton outside the flat in Harnett Street, where they handed him several packets before driving away. Shelton went back inside the flat and fifteen minutes later he and Wendy emerged with the pram; Chaos was swaddled inside and the packets of LSD hidden in a false bottom. Shelton headed in one direction and Wendy the other as she pushed the pram up Palmer Street and waited outside the Merryfield Hotel, hiding the packets in grass across the road.

In the meantime, Shelton had gone to a nearby motel to meet two men from Canberra who were willing to pay $4000 for 1500 LSD trips; he didn't realise they were undercover police. From the back seat of their car he directed them to where Wendy was waiting. As soon as she handed over the packets, the police pounced. Milne and Taylor were arrested soon afterwards. Shelton and Wendy had stood to make $500 from the deal.

The case caused huge excitement in the Sydney media when the police announced they had cracked down on a major drug ring. But their claims were as fanciful as the occupations listed on the charge sheet for Shelton (a printer) and Wendy (a process worker).

The court was packed as the events were described, but there was little the magistrate Walter Lewer could do, as legislation covering the manufacture and sale of LSD was not due to come into effect for another five weeks. 'If I were dealing with you under the *Police Offences Act* I would sentence you to 18 months hard labour,' he thundered as he fined each of them $100 for the sale of a restricted drug.

Shelton and Wendy dashed out of the court. But they could not escape the media, who chased them through the city streets while Shelton chanted that 'everyone is gee'd on speed'. When they reached their flat, they discovered they'd been evicted.

Shelton was more concerned about the head of the CIB, Detective-Sergeant Cec Abbott, who had sidled up to him in court and whispered: 'You'd better get out of town, Shelton, coz your shadow won't be able to piss without us knowing.'

He left town two days later and headed back to Melbourne.

22

A SPECIAL SOMEBODY

The *Go-Set* office in St Kilda was a vibrant place, where irregular pay cheques and meals of tinned spaghetti were offset by nights filled with the excitement of backstage passes and free entry into Melbourne's bars and discotheques with names like the Biting Eye, Sebastian's, Bertie's, the Garrison and Traffic, which all opened in the mid-1960s as music took hold.

But their favourite was the Thumpin' Tum in Little La Trobe Street. It was here in late 1966 that Honey met seventeen-year-old Geoffrey Hales, a dresser at the Princess Theatre, in Spring Street, who hankered for a career in photography. And he could dance.

Honey, barely seventeen herself, was at the club with friends one night, sitting upstairs at the 'Go-Set Table', where she could see Geoffrey dancing below. 'He was beautiful,' she recalls. 'I said to one of the others to go down and get that man to come up here and sit with us. He did; there was an instant connection and we went home together that night, and two weeks later we were living together in St Kilda.'

As laidback as Colin Beard was intense, Geoffrey was experimenting with life—from the theatre and ballet to rock bands and fashion—fuelled by readily available drugs and the 'free love' of the 1960s. Late one night he opened the door to be greeted by two strangers.

'Are you Geoffrey Hales?' they asked. 'Are you with Honey?'

'Yes', he nodded.

'Thank God,' one of them said. 'Here, this is from Shelton.'

Inside the envelope were several sheets of blotting paper containing what was probably one of Melbourne's first batches of LSD. Shelton, who had been selling it on Sydney streets, had sent the package down to Melbourne with two mates, telling them that Geoffrey was a musician and living with his sister. They thought he meant Geoff Hales, the well-known bandleader, and turned up where he was staying, but left quickly when it became obvious they had the wrong man. Somehow they then found Geoffrey and Honey at St Kilda, probably through Brett, who had visited them a few weeks before.

'We didn't even know what LSD was, let alone ever used it,' Geoffrey recalls. 'I decided to try it one morning after Honey went to work. I remember putting one tab on my tongue and nothing seemed to happen. I then went into town to see Honey. By the time I got into the city I thought I was on Planet of the Apes and was going around trying to touch everyone on the nose.'

Life was impulsive. There was little money, just energy and ideas. Geoffrey had played in bands, danced, helped start a flea market and even designed leather jackets. But his great love was photography. Many of his shots were forgotten for decades, only to be rediscovered and printed, now providing an income half a century after being shot: 'The younger me supporting the older me,' he reflects.

Geoffrey's relationship with Honey epitomised their youth. She got him a gig at *Go-Set*, taking photos for her fashion page. Then they brought in Geoffrey's younger half-sister, Lyndall Hobbs, as a fresh-faced model and created a comic book-like strip called 'Lindy: The Girl Who Could Be You', following her with a camera as she explored the fashion, music and band scene in Melbourne.

On one memorable day, they took the British band The Yardbirds shopping with Lyndall. As they were returning the band members to the Southern Cross Hotel, Roy Orbison stepped into the foyer on his way back from buying cigarettes. Spying Lyndall, the singer issued a low growl and started to sing his hit, 'Pretty Woman'. Seizing the opportunity, Geoffrey and Honey quickly persuaded Orbison to agree to some promotional photos.

The pair frequently acted on the spur of the moment, like the day they heard that the fashion designer Pierre Cardin was at a gallery in Toorak. They raced there and took pictures of Honey with the designer and his entourage in the background. 'Honey was pretty much the heart and soul of *Go-Set*,' Geoffrey remembers. 'She wasn't just doing fashion, she was a powerhouse of energy around the office and I guess that was what was so attractive about her. Everything seemed so easy in the sixties. We didn't stop to decide if something could be done. You just did it. That was Honey.'

Geoffrey is thoughtful when he speaks about a woman he seems to regret not having spent his life with: 'You don't realise just how special somebody is when you're young, because you think everyone is special. And they're not. We only lasted about two years, because I was young and stupid; but of all my old girl-friends, she is the only one that I've stayed friends with.'

Yet behind the exuberance, Geoffrey could sense the conflict within Honey. There were even times when she spoke about it— the confusion of being given away and then being regarded as second-rate by her new mother: 'I knew she was tormented by what Valerie had put her through. The line about her "true nature showing" was particularly damaging. She told me about it at the time. I remember it clearly because it left such a mark on me.'

CƷ

Geoffrey is a book of stories all on his own, particularly about the mid-1960s when he was photographing musicians such as the Rolling Stones and Bob Dylan as they passed through Melbourne.

It was April 1966, not long after he moved in with Honey, that Geoffrey met Dylan. He'd been at the Thumpin' Tum with two American musicians who wanted to score 'some smoke', so he took them to South Yarra and bought 'some nice Lebanese red hash'. They were back in a Spring Street hotel—'cool guys with a gaggle of local chicks'—when the door opened and Adrian Rawlins, a poet, performer and promoter, walked in with Dylan, who promptly broke off some hash and summoned a few of them, including Geoffrey, to his room. Dylan agreed to try him out as a tour photographer.

The next day Geoffrey went back with a borrowed camera and took a series of shots backstage. Dylan was happy to play along, but when Geoffrey got home, he realised he hadn't loaded the film canister properly. He'd screwed up the opportunity. He heard later that police had raided the hotel after one of the girls in the room told her mother she'd been smoking drugs with the members of Dylan's band. He was told they spent most of their east coast concert earnings keeping the scandal out of court and out of the newspapers.

Geoffrey had met the Stones the previous year when they toured as Roy Orbison's support act. They had the top floor of the John Batman Motor Inn to themselves and Geoffrey knew Suzette, the daughter of the owner. He managed to get past the crowd of screaming girls and inside through the kitchen, where he drank tea with the band and watched Bill Wyman directing security staff to pluck girls from the crowd below: 'That bird there, no, not that one, her friend with the blonde hair.'

He hit it off with Brian Jones, then a member of the band, but when he too went off 'to comfort a girl', he found Mick Jagger alone in a bedroom playing records on a portable plastic record player: 'I swear this is true. He was playing a Motown record on 33 instead of 45 rpm. It was very funky, slowed right down.' He was singing his own words to it and told Geoffrey: 'I'm going to write my own songs now and this is a good way to learn song arranging.' He then started prancing around the room, singing with a pretend microphone.

The Stones stayed at the Batman again in 1966. Geoffrey decided to try his luck with a camera and snuck in through the same kitchen entrance. Brian Jones answered the door to the band's apartment and invited him in to show them his work. The Stones were talking about drugs, and amyl nitrite poppers were mentioned. Geoffrey casually dropped into the conversation that the drug, used as a vasodilator to treat heart disease and angina, was legal in Australia and could be bought at any chemist. Jones grabbed him by the hand and dragged him back into the main room where Keith Richards was sitting.

'Tell Keith what you told me. Tell him what you just said,' Jones said excitedly.

'Amyl nitrite is legal in Australia,' Geoffrey repeated, confused.

A few minutes later Geoffrey found himself wedged between Jones and Richards in the back seat of a taxi. 'We visited every chemist between St Kilda and Ripponlea,' Geoffrey laughs. 'I would go in and explain that my father was going away and needed five boxes to tide him over with his heart condition. I can still clearly see two Stones grinning maniacally at me from the back seat of the cab as I came out of the chemists.'

That night Geoffrey accompanied the Stones to see local band The Wild Cherries at the Garrison Nightclub in Prahran. 'Out came the amyl nitrite poppers. Brian broke one too many under my nose and I fainted dead away. I woke up hours later and everyone was gone, the evening over.'

cs

The first time Jenny Ham walked into the *Go-Set* office, Honey hid. Jenny, a successful former model and television personality, could be a prickly goddess of beauty and style—'on another planet'—but it was her personality that Honey found overwhelming.

Jenny was a public relations powerhouse in Melbourne, often quoted for her views on Australian men, whom she found largely tiresome and unable to show 'love, tenderness and emotion'. She had quickly recognised the influence of *Go-Set* on the music scene, and she wanted to ensure that her own clients were inside the tent.

Despite Honey's initial misgivings, it seems she had made an impression on the businesswoman, who decided that the now eighteen-year-old would be an asset in her growing agency. In mid-1967, with the encouragement of Geoffrey Hales, Honey decided to accept Jenny's offer and leave the magazine.

It was a decision she never regretted. Life was moving so swiftly that it was difficult to keep track of time passing, let alone the significance of what was happening. The handcuffs of the Leas had been removed; she was no longer a 'guttersnipe from Fitzroy', as Valerie believed, rather a young woman who was sought after and valued. She was soon running Jenny's office on the first floor of the Southern Cross building, and their clients included Roy Orbison, hair stylist Vidal Sassoon and many of Melbourne's fashion houses.

It also became obvious that Jenny was having a secret affair. She was a single woman and entitled to form a relationship, but the man she was seeing regularly was not only much older but also married. Jenny only said that he treated her well—to him she was more than just a beautiful woman; she had brains. She insisted that, unlike her lover, the typical Australian male was only interested in football, punting and drinking with his mates.

Honey saw the mystery man on the back steps of the office several times, but she paid no attention when he lowered his head and passed by. She decided that it was a private matter. All she knew was his Christian name—Harold—because there was a phone on Jenny's desk that was 'just for Harold'.

It was only on 18 December 1967 that she realised the identity of her boss's lover. She arrived at work to find Jenny crying at her desk: 'He's dead, he's dead. They say he drowned.' She was talking about the prime minister, Harold Holt, who the previous day had gone missing, presumed drowned, at Cheviot Beach, at Portsea. They had been lovers for several years, possibly since Melbourne Cup Day in 1964, when they were photographed together in the members' enclosure.

Again encouraged by Geoffrey Hales, Honey would move on in 1968 when she was offered a job writing fashion for the *Australian Women's Weekly*. It would be the last time she reverted to using her 'Toorak name'. Writing under the by-line 'Kestin Lea', she was responsible for the magazine's centre-page spread on fashion trends, and she also covered society events, first nights, visiting celebs and royal tours, just as she had covered bands at *Go-Set*.

But there was no rock'n'roll at the *Weekly*. It was all so very grown-up in the offices in Collins Street. Honey had traded her jeans and T-shirts for gloves and hats, moving from a chaotic student house in the suburbs to an office building in central Melbourne, not far from the doctor's surgery where she had once been handed over to Valerie Lea.

It also spelt the end for her relationship with Geoffrey, who one night told her they were finished as they sat in a car outside a pub in South Yarra called Maisie's, considered the new place to be. He was interested in someone else, he said.

Honey said nothing. She got out of the car and walked into the pub, intent on finding the best-looking man at the bar. Life was about moving on. This way you avoided the regret of looking back.

23

A GYPSY MIND

In 1965 Darrell Lea had become chairman and managing director of the company named after him. At 38 years old, Darrell was much younger than his brothers and business partners. Monty, thickset, with a greying beard, had turned 56; Harris, 50, was balding; and his older brother Maurice at almost 60 was old enough to be Darrell's father.

Darrell was different from his siblings in many other ways, beginning with his sexual preferences. 'Candy', as he was known around the gay haunts of Sydney, did not publicly declare his homosexuality; neither did he hide it.

He was tall and handsome, taking after his mother rather than his father, and at times his flamboyancy created embarrassment for the rest of the family, such as the night he was found wandering drunkenly through the streets of St Kilda, dressed in women's clothing. He was subsequently rescued by Monty. On one occasion he even turned up at the Chapel Street factory in drag.

He was also extravagant, at least in comparison to the others. He lived in a large house on the banks of the Georges River, in southern Sydney, and had expensive taste in clothes and friends. He loved attending society openings, collected expensive art and travelled widely, often returning home from overseas trips bearing expensive gifts of jewellery and clothes for his mother and sister. According to the family history, this caused some consternation among his thrifty brothers and their wives, who had grown up during the recession of the 1930s and been involved in the initial graft of establishing the business. Valerie, in particular, was angered by her brother-in-law's profligacy.

In later years Darrell would become involved in some wild investment schemes. Although he was not the only brother to stray from the chocolate business mould, his investments in experimental items—such as interchangeable plastic shoe covers, fibreglass chairs and tables, and dog kennels, among others—made Monty's investments seem conservative. Needless to say, Darrell's ventures all failed.

But his steerage of the family firm was more assured, or so it seemed. The company sought to evolve and expand during the 1960s, embracing the advent of shopping malls by opening a storefront in Sydney's first mall at Roselands, then new branches in cities such as Brisbane, Adelaide and Perth. The threat to the corner store was clear and in many ways an anathema to the company's marketing traditions, but turning their back on the future could be disastrous.

The appointment of Darrell to chairman and MD made sense as a step between the generations, before the inevitable handover to Harry Levy's grandsons, Jason and Lael, and their cousins, Michael and Robert, the sons of Harris and Sheila. All four of these young men would start working for the company in the 1960s, an era in which the male line was still considered of greater importance. But unlike Valerie and Monty, who insisted that 'blood' was important, Harris and Sheila seemed to make no distinction between Michael, Sheila's son from a previous marriage, and Robert, who was adopted.

Charon, another of Harris and Sheila's adopted children, would also have a series of jobs in the company over the years. The childless Maurice and his wife, Sharpe, would move to Brisbane to manage the Queensland operation while Sheila would be responsible for Adelaide, which she and her son Robert would manage remotely from Melbourne.

While the company was expanding its sales presence—even opening Darrell Lea 'agencies' in rural areas, with cut-down displays and product ranges where a full shop would not have made financial sense—Darrell had centralised management and production in Sydney. It was this Sydney-centric move, with the new Kogarah factory, that had so outraged Valerie because it effectively reduced Valerie and Monty to the role of storekeepers.

Valerie had railed against the move, furious that 'Sydney would take control', and pleaded with Monty to keep Chapel Street open and begin their own operation, complete with the five city shops. But Monty refused. Valerie, Sheila and Sharpe had always been strong voices within the family business but when it came to the future of the company, the brothers' view would always hold sway.

There was one famous family story that typified these relationships. To escape 'the wives' and make a unified decision, the brothers once held a late-night meeting inside a locked car in the darkened car park of the Kogarah factory.

Times were changing and the technology improving, and it had been hard to argue against modernising an operation that was using machinery long out of date in factories that desperately needed maintenance. Chapel Street would now be leased, reverting the building to its original purpose—a place of entertainment. But rather than a cinema, it was to be a theatre restaurant that would soon host singing stars like Shirley Bassey.

But Darrell wanted to go further. There was an untapped wealth in the value of the company's financial success, its physical assets and its future. Almost forty years after its creation, he wanted the family to partly relinquish its grip on the business and float one-third of the business on the public stock exchange, in the belief that it would place a much-needed value on the confectionery business and also help fund its evolution and expansion.

There would be an important caveat to the deal. The family would retain ownership of its property holdings, including fifty shops across New South Wales, Victoria and South Australia, and only float the two arms of its operating business—the retail business, Darrell Lea Chocolates, and the wholesale company, Ricci Remond.

The prospectus showed that Darrell Lea was a company on the

rise, with 'substantial increases' in profits over recent years and a forecast dividend of more than twelve per cent six months after the float. That forecast would prove accurate as the company produced a string of good results over the next five years.

The future for the Darrell Lea empire looked bright but, in Melbourne, Valerie was contemplating a future that probably meant moving back to Sydney. At least she had a new grandchild to look forward to, with the birth in October 1966 of Jason and Hilke's third child, a little boy named Lincoln.

There was a poignant moment in the midst of the huge upheaval when a classified ad appeared in the *Sydney Morning Herald*:

Volkswagen Micro Bus de Luxe. 1 owner, 1959 large motor. Seats 9 persons. Excellent condition. 10 months rego. You must see it. Darrell Lea Chocolate Co.

The children had all left home, and Valerie and Monty were selling the family car.

ധ

By this time Shelton was back in Melbourne, settling into the city's inner northern suburb of Carlton, next to Fitzroy, where he had been born to Gwyneth Roberts two decades before. Unbeknown to him, his biological mother was living a few suburbs away in respectable, middle-class Hawthorn.

The Carlton culture was not unlike inner-city Sydney, where drugs, alcohol and art all sat comfortably together, each feeding the other. So too did the mix of race and language, from the clumps of European migrants who would ultimately turn Carlton into 'Little Italy' to the urban Aboriginal families with whom Shelton had developed a connection.

Most of all, there was a mix of politics and the arts—writers and artists, musos and painters—he had embraced in Sydney. If only he could keep out of prison. He took a job as a barman to help make ends meet for Wendy, who would soon be pregnant again, but his real love was poetry.

There was no shortage of venues in which to be inspired, socialise and perform. Pubs like the Albion in Lygon Street, which was nondescript, even plain, on the outside but a riot of colour and character in its beer-sodden interior, where everyone had an opinion but little money.

Across the road was La Mama, an old shirt factory turned into an experimental performance theatre by its feisty director, Betty Burstall. It was 'an old living room', inspired by the New York experimental theatre movement, which hosted folk music and poetry readings, and staged plays and even late-night cabaret performances.

In his 2008 autobiography *The Naked Truth*, the writer and actor Graeme Blundell described La Mama as a workshop of ideas: 'A theatrical and literary laboratory. Writers were able to fail—as indeed they must—in order to improve; directors could play to their heart's content; and actors stretched, and sometimes discovered themselves.'

The 1960s was an era ready-made for poets, a time of radical social change and political upheaval, like the repercussions of the Vietnam War. But Shelton, unafraid to be different, was more interested in exploring life experiences in his work: 'You have to write what's in you,' he told one journalist. The actor and prolific writer Barry Dickins met Shelton around this time; he recalls a performer whose controlled delivery marked him as 'the best reader of poetry in Australia'.

It seemed only a matter of time before Shelton's verse found its way into print. In 1968 the poet Michael Dugan first published his literary journal *Crosscurrents Magazine,* which championed the voice of 'new poetry'; he published Shelton Lea, as did Kris Hemensley, a young British immigrant who launched another magazine, *Our Glass.*

Shelton came to wider public attention in 1969 when *The Age* published a glowing tribute headlined 'Beauty in a gypsy mind'. Shelton had just published his first book of poems: 'It's called *Corners in Cans* and it's very beautiful,' wrote journalist Mary Craig, clearly in awe of her subject, with his 'marvellous mind and sleepy brown eyes and soft hair'.

Asked how he wrote, Shelton shook his head:

A poem just pops into your head, a series of words that start happening in your head and they seem to make a line, and they seem to make a verse. I get a thought in my head, and I know it's a poem, it just suddenly arrives, it's like walking down Swanston Street and a poem sort of comes bouncing along the street . . . like some sort of balloon bouncing down the street. You've got to be pretty quick to try and get it down otherwise it bounces past.

If he was unsure about *how* he wrote, Shelton was far more certain about *what* he wrote: 'I like to think of things in rather grandiose terms ... to explode little things into big things—not emotive things, but things you see on the street. I like to see things softly ... chiffony thoughts wafting and dreaming ... a sense of lightness in poetry.'

He railed against 'caustic, cryptic and cynical stuff', insisting on writing what he felt, rather than what might be popular: 'So then we're all supposed to agree and write beaut poems and slap each other on the back about it. That's all rubbish.'

Shelton mentioned his childhood—'adopted son, unhappy scene caper'—but did not dwell on it: 'The way I look at life and approach it, you know, is a sort of gypsy mind that can pick up and wander ... I think I am very lucky to have this.'

Mary Craig agreed: 'Shelton Lea is a loner. He goes his own way, lives by his own code, loves in his own way and exists for something he can't really describe but wholly understands. He's a very special person.'

છ

When Honey met Charlie Vodicka in 1968 he was running a bohemian shop on the ground floor of the Southern Cross Hotel building. Charlie was Geoffrey Hale's mate really—six years older, with a cool magnetism. The trio would hang out and eat Chinese food—not the Chiko Roll and buttered-bread experience of the suburbs but yum cha and dishes like whole fish in black bean sauce at the King Wah restaurant. Charlie in his trademark jeans and T-shirt, and Honey in office clothes.

Charlie was a long-haired entrepreneur who had tapped into the zeitgeist of the sixties, importing clothes, beads, bags, incense and all the paraphernalia associated with the US hippy culture. There was nothing like it in Melbourne, and Charlie prospered.

When the Tivoli Theatre in Bourke Street was gutted by fire, Charlie saw an opportunity in the blackened ruins. He offered to pay a peppercorn weekly rent and turned the site into Australia's first flea market and a huge money-spinner for himself as a landlord.

And he ventured beyond Melbourne. Fascinated by cinéma vérité, he transformed the Odeon Theatre in Sydney's Taylor Square into a rainbow-coloured cinema called the Mandala, where he showed arthouse movies like Yoko Ono's *Bottoms* and Federico Fellini's *8½*.

He also bought the rights to films by the famed documentary maker D.A. Pennebaker, including *Don't Look Back,* the 1967 documentary on Bob Dylan, which played to packed houses.

Charlie's ambitions didn't stop there, as he told *The Age* in a 1970 interview under the heading 'What is Charlie Vodicka?', a reference to his reluctance to be classified. He eschewed tags like 'hippy' and 'businessman'; he was a will-o'-the-wisp character who cruised international rock concerts and wanted to get into the film business and produce documentaries like his hero, Pennebaker.

'Charlie is definitely going somewhere—probably to the top and fast,' the journalist concluded. 'Just how he's going about getting there is a matter for conjecture because he's about the only person who knows, and he's not about to tell anyone else. This dodginess has a certain charm. You can't help liking Charlie.'

Honey Lea could only concur. She agreed to throw in her job at the *Weekly* and work for him. She knew he was always surrounded by girls and vowed never to become one of them, but on a business trip to Sydney 'it just happened', and that was it.

'He seemed magnificent,' she recalls. 'I was young and it was the time of free love. I didn't think I needed to own him to have him. I was happy to go along with it because life was so exciting.'

Charlie was married and had children but it seemed to be an open relationship.

24

EIGHT, NINE AND TEN

November 1969

Hilke was gone. The almost seven-year marriage to Jason had ended and she was on her way back to England with a single suitcase and no money, except for the proceeds from the sale of her car and the cash her mother sent her.

She was only going for a few months, Hilke would say later, but her angry husband told her that she might as well stay there, and checked her bag on the way out the door to ensure she wasn't taking anything.

The marriage had fallen apart in a sea of loneliness for a woman who, with a workaholic husband, had been left to mind three young children with little time to herself and few friends. Even her home shackled her to the business—a weatherboard cottage across the road from the Darrell Lea factory, one of a number of properties owned by the family along the busy thoroughfare that followed the western shoreline of Botany

Bay. But it was too far back from the coast for her to see the sparkling waters.

Jason suspected she might be having an affair—she wasn't—and told his mother, who agreed to hire a private detective to spy on Hilke, even though he was already courting a new girlfriend as he showed his wife the door.

Valerie backed her son. A few years earlier she had written in wonderment at her daughter-in-law's ability to make a home in the cottage. But it had quickly turned into a nicely renovated prison; unlike her mother-in-law, who had been able to escape daily from the rigours of motherhood and leave the housework to paid staff, Hilke had simply watched her husband walk across the road to work every morning before turning back to her life of drudgery.

She and the children rarely saw Jason return before nightfall. His oldest son recalls with bitterness the chocolate stains on his father's shirt as he bent to kiss the boy goodnight in a darkened bedroom. Chocolate was the reason for his absence from their lives rather than a sweet family legacy.

Jason had been consumed by the business since his return from England; his priority, according to his mother's edict, was that business always came before family. It echoed his own childhood memories of Monty who, like him, was a chocolate-stained man coming home to say goodnight to his children.

As Jason told the ABC's *Dynasties* episode about the Leas in 2005: 'You've got to understand a very simple premise and that is that the business feeds the family. The bloody family don't feed the business. If the business isn't successful, the family don't have a roof over their head. So whatever is best for the business has to be the number one priority.'

It was a dogmatic ethos that would ultimately destroy his family and bring the cherished enterprise to its knees.

ෆ

Jason and Hilke's family planning had been perfect—a boy followed by a girl and then another boy, each two calendar years apart. Jason Cary had arrived in December 1962, a few weeks after his father had brought his new bride to Australia; Angeline Suzette was born in February 1964 in Hobart, where Jason had been sent to learn the business ropes; and little Lincoln Montgomery arrived in October 1966.

When the marriage broke up, the children lost both parents. Hilke's pleas to let her take the children with her to London fell on hard, deaf ears. Backed by Valerie, Jason refused, warning her that she would never see her children again if she tried to challenge his decision. He told her that this was the authority of a husband over a wife under Australian law.

In one last attempt, Hilke begged to be allowed to take the youngest, Lincoln, who was now aged three. The answer was no. The children were Leas and they would stay in Australia, Jason insisted. He was even more adamant after he had read a letter from her mother who managed a cafe in London; it revealed that Hilke intended to work once she returned to England and had arranged to pay a friend living in the same street to take care of Lincoln while her two went to school.

Of course Hilke had to work. She was now a single mother

and the Leas had no intention of providing her with financial support, even though the three children were family. It was the height of hypocrisy, given that Jason had no intention of parenting by himself. His own mother had stepped into that role.

Valerie Lea would eventually get herself a new family—children numbers eight, nine and ten.

෩

More than forty years after the trauma of his parents' divorce, Jason Lea Jnr remains confused about why he and his siblings ended up living with their paternal grandparents. He assumes that his mother was 'encouraged' to leave Australia and that there was a cramped, listless life waiting for them back in a North London council flat with a maternal grandmother they had never met.

The children had been told that life 'would not have been as nice in the UK' but, at the age of six, he wasn't in a position to argue with his father: 'I could have ended up back in the UK as a Cockney, ironically the same place that Harry Levy came from,' he reflects.

But behind the black humour there is sadness:

Even now I look back and wonder why it happened. My mother has always been evasive about it. She won't talk about some issues, which is understandable, but why didn't she stay in Australia and fight for us? Why did she succumb to the demands of Jason?

I blame my father in many ways. There are a lot of things that could have not happened if things hadn't been the way they were.

Outwardly you try to show a very happy family, and the whole lolly thing was great, but deep down there are a lot of bad memories in there.

The most vivid memory Jason has of this period is of his father, the man he was named after, almost immediately abandoning any notion of responsibility for his children while he pursued his career and a new relationship. For a short time, Jason, Angeline and Lincoln remained with their father at their bayside Sydney home, but in the care of paid staff, who would turn up in the morning to get the older two ready for school.

But their father was nowhere to be seen; all they knew was the smell of chocolate on his hands as he bent to kiss them goodnight long after they'd gone to bed. The hypocrisy of his own criticism of Monty was not lost on Jason Snr, as he told ABC's *Dynasties*:

> I'm not a fatherly father. I never have been. Monty was never a father to us and I'm sort of the same. So you're a product of your environment. Maybe if I hadn't been so all-involved with the business, I would have been a better daddy. I was just doing what I thought had to be done and what I thought was expected of me. And that was how it was.

It wasn't long before the children were packed off to Melbourne, to be raised by their grandparents. Valerie had initially wanted them to refer to her as 'Mummy' and Monty as 'Daddy', but she backed off after Charryce intervened and insisted it would not be appropriate. At least that's what Jason Jnr was later told.

His sister had a vastly different reaction to Hilke's departure. Almost 50 years later Angeline casts her mind back to the day she watched her mother leave the house carrying a suitcase: 'She told me that she was going out to dinner but she never came back.'

And yet for the next three years, until Hilke returned to Australia with a new husband, Angeline simply accepted that Valerie was her mother: 'I'm not sure what I thought really. I guess everything just melded together and I called my grandmother "Mummy" because I thought she was my mum. It was that simple.'

Her father, upon whom she doted, was still Daddy although the incongruity of the situation simply never occurred to the little girl: 'I just remember a loving childhood, raised by an elderly mother who brought us up with love and common sense. Valerie was protecting us from the things that happened. She took us on outings, even to an Abba concert. She didn't drive so we caught trams.'

It was only when Hilke returned to Melbourne three years later that Angeline realised Valerie was not her mother. She took it in her stride, telling her school friends that her 'other mother' was coming back. The reunion took place in a fast food restaurant called Red Barn, a 1960s precursor to the McDonald's chain: 'I remember asking my brother what we should call her [Hilke]. Valerie was walking ahead of us, like she always did, so I decided to call out her name to her to see how she reacted. "Valerie, wait for us!" I shouted, and she stopped and turned to look at me. So I started calling her Valerie from that moment.'

By the time they took the children to Melbourne, Val and Monty were living in rooms above the old Chapel Street factory. It was typical of them: a 'make-do' home that was less than perfect, despite their obvious success and wealth. Offices had been turned into bedrooms, a lounge room and kitchen. Monty had added a bedroom above the rear portico to accommodate the three children. It was a hasty job—a metal box with no insulation, which made the room boiling hot in summer and ice-cold when the rain hammered down in winter.

Unlike the Lambert Road house, there was no grassy backyard with playground equipment. Not that the old factory, with its rusting steel oddments and crumbling concrete surrounds, was boring. Quite the contrary. The back of the disused factory was filled with old car wrecks, in which homeless men often found a place to sleep. Jason and Angel would delight in throwing rocks out of their bedroom window; they'd ding against the old cars, disturbing the men, who searched in vain for the culprits.

The nights were frequently filled with noise as drunks staggered out of a hotel on the other side of a railway line behind the property, swinging fists at each other but mostly missing their mark. At other times the children were woken to the sound of gunfire as police chased thieves through the bushes.

But for all the excitement, this was not a home and an environment in which to raise young children, and Jason made his displeasure known. They would have been better off living with their mother.

Hilke sent her children cards and gifts from the UK, but these were intercepted by Valerie, who did not pass them on. Just like Honey's mother, as far as Valerie was concerned Hilke no longer had a role in their lives. Valerie alone was their mother and protector.

CB

Jason's marriage had ended in divorce, and the 'in-law' Valerie had once praised was now considered unworthy of raising her own children, but she was hoping for better as Charryce and Galea prepared to marry in the first half of 1970.

The sisters had been living together for the past two years in a flat bought with Mungah's money, a few doors down from the old family home in Lambert Road. Charryce, now almost 22, had an office job at Crawford Productions, which produced the hit television crime series *Homicide* and *Division 4*. She had started in the typing pool, then graduated to script assistant, and was now in the public relations office; this meant long hours, but it was 'lucrative', according to Valerie, who clearly approved.

Charryce had been in a steady relationship for almost four years with a young man named David Nixon-Luke, whom she'd met while they were living at the Brighton Savoy. They'd had an on-again-off-again relationship, partly because David had spent two years in Vietnam. But in February 1970, encouraged by Valerie, Charryce quit her job at Crawford's and secretly married David before the young couple flew off to Europe for a year. Only Valerie knew of the union.

Meanwhile, shy Gaela had been swept off her feet by a South African mining consultant named Charl Grobelaar, whom she'd met while working as a receptionist at the Royal Automobile Club. They would marry a few weeks after Charryce and David, although Charryce was unaware of her sister's marriage. Valerie's only disappointment was that Charl was going to take his new wife back to South Africa, because of its more lenient tax laws: 'He earns a great deal of money,' she sighed in print.

It was as if Valerie had orchestrated a repeat of her own secret marriage to Monty all those years before and the very public wedding of her sister, Lola, a few months later.

Lael was no closer to finding a wife. He was twenty-three years old, tall and handsome in his mother's eyes but apparently he could not find the right girl: 'He likes them for a while then turns cool,' Valerie wrote. 'Plenty of time for him though,' she concluded before launching into a commentary on the loose morals of modern women, and her gratitude that, compared to Honey, who was 'normally endowed', Charryce and Gaela had been 'very late starters as far as sex went'.

It also sparked a curious entry about her own marriage, revealing that she had threatened to cut off Monty's penis with pinking shears if she ever caught him having an affair:

I'd gently lift it, like this and k-k-k snip, right off at the root and all he'd have left would be an agitating serrated stump and I wouldn't worry one bit. I could quite happily do without it.

Maybe it's the thought that has kept him faithful to me (I think) . . . although I've always been petrified with terror that some little snip, maybe half Oriental or Indian or Maori would set her cap on him and steal him away. But, of course, I've never given him any cause for jealousy. I could have, of course, but have realised it's just not worth it.

25

THE COBRA

One day in 1970 Shelton walked out on Wendy Liddle without a word. He would say later that their relationship had been unravelling for a while, but the timing and the way he made his departure were, nonetheless, abrupt.

It would remain a pattern of his adult life—never marrying the women who bore his four children, always moving on until the last decade or so of his life. A man who craved the security of love yet turned his back on it when it was offered, because he was incapable of trusting it.

Wendy had asked him to find a kitchen implement but, instead of taking it to her, Shelton decided that this was the moment. He put it back in the drawer and walked out the back door.

There was no explanation. He left behind a woman who, in his own words, was 'not well'; one who'd shared his troubled years in Sydney and his breakthrough career as a poet in Melbourne.

The Darrell Lea stand at the Melbourne Show in 1954. Valerie, Monty, Sheila and Harris were all on hand.

All smiles. The seven children in their seven different school uniforms. Behind the smiles there was darkness for the adopted children.

Off to the Prom: the Lea family and friends in the late 1950s.

The family bus parked outside 22 Lambert Road, Toorak, 1949.

Honey, aged 16, had left home and helped start *Go-Set* Magazine. Photo by Colin Beard.

Harriet Everitt, known to her grandchildren as 'Mungah', early 1950s.

The Lea brothers and their wives (from left): Sheila, Harris, Valerie, Monty, Sharpe and Maurice.

Above: The grandchildren: Lincoln, Angeline and Jason Jnr.

Left: Photo booth photo of Valerie with her grandchildren, Jason Jnr, Angeline and Lincoln, 1970.

What was more, she now had two young children. Their son, Zero, named after the American actor Samuel 'Zero' Mostel, was still being breastfed and Chaos had not yet turned three.

Shelton was now twenty-three, with a growing reputation as a fearsome poetry warrior. He was known to leap onto pub tables in Collingwood and Carlton and deliver his poems like a striking cobra.

That's the way he would describe it to Diana Georgeff when he reminisced years later:

You've got to know how to deliver a poem. You've got to know, like a cobra, how to get the audience. That's the function of the word—to get people in and that's how I scratch a living from poetry. People are looking for chimes and resonances. Chimes leave echoes, and that's what rhyme is. Poetry is about leaving an echo imprint in somebody else's head, in the dark snow of their mind.

He also seemed irresistible to many women, and not just within his cohort. Mary Craig, the journalist from *The Age* who had written about him in almost lovelorn prose, was one who fell in love with him.

'Shelton Lea is a loner,' she had written. And now he was living with her in South Yarra, although the circumstances were traumatic. Not only had he ended the relationship with Wendy but he had also fallen out of a second-storey window of a house in Hawthorn and broken his ankle. Shattered it, in fact.

It was a serious injury and he would never walk again without the aid of a stick, but it also provided a prop and a storyline, or several as it turned out—he had been chased by an irate husband; taken LSD and tried to fly; slipped while robbing a house; or he'd simply tried to show how one simple act—such as stepping out of a window—can change your life.

Mary became his nurse as well as his lover. She was a society girl and interviewer of the stars who was harbouring in her bed a vagabond poet and small-time crim with a limp and a lip to match. She did it because she loved him and his ways, but it also answered her own need to rebel against a mother she detested. Berenice Craig, Melbourne editor of the *Australian Women's Weekly*, had crushed her daughter's dreams of becoming a dancer and tried to stifle her life.

Shelton Lea was Mary's reply. Where others saw darkness, she saw a soul full of goodness; to her, his rebelliousness was a middle-class survival mechanism and his criminal escapades a disguise for a man who craved respectability. When they dined at society restaurants like Tolarno, owned by the art patrons Georges and Mirka Mora, Mary would dress in chiffon and heels while Shelton puffed on a smoke and carried a flick-knife.

The affair was as intense as it was brief. It couldn't last because Mary was desperate for commitment and Shelton was unable to give it. He was the love of her life but she was only one of many of his loves. Mary went horse riding one day to think things over. When she got back, he was gone—off to Sydney, his leg still in plaster, with a girl named Loma Carey.

ം

Shelton was still with Wendy when he first met the writer Barrett Reid, a man who would have more influence on his poetry than anyone else—'the most important relationship of my life,' Shelton would say.

They were opposites in obvious ways: Barrett was gay, a career public servant and prominent member of the arts community, while Shelton was a womanising part-time barman and artistic buccaneer. Barrett recognised their differences the first time they met over lunch when Shelton, dressed in his latest persona as a gypsy, jibbered nervously and waved his cigarette around while Barrett assessed him.

'He carried on a treat and I let him,' Barrett told Diana Georgeff. 'He had earrings and God knows what. He had very long hair. What did I think? I thought he was a boy trying to be a gypsy. I thought he should be disabused of that as quickly as possible. And I said so.'

But they were also kindred souls—motherless from an early age, battling rejection and leading bohemian lives in early adulthood, although for vastly different reasons. As much as he wanted to straighten Shelton out, Barrett saw a creative spirit that required harnessing, not breaking: 'Undisciplined but real talent, most unusual.'

The lunch with Barrett had offered Shelton an invitation to the respectability that Mary Craig could sense he wanted. Barrett represented artistic royalty: he was chair of the periodical *Australian Book Review*, co-founder of the National Book Council Literary Awards and publisher of *Overland* magazine, among a myriad of other roles.

Not only was Barrett a mentor—although he would say that Shelton taught him as much as he taught Shelton—but he also opened the door to other friendships with people like John and Sunday Reed, the great patrons of Australian Modernism. At their property Heide in Bulleen, writers and artists such as Sidney Nolan, Albert Tucker, Joy Hester, Charles Blackman and Mirka Mora gathered and worked. When the Reeds both died within ten days of one another in 1981, they bequeathed the property to Barrett Reid for the term of his life.

In the early seventies Shelton would become a frequent visitor, delighting in Heide's history and tales—the couch where Danila Vassilieff died, the room where Nolan painted the Ned Kelly series. Shelton was not only accepted by the Reeds, he became great friends with their adopted son, Sweeney, who owned a contemporary gallery and the publishing house Still Earth Press. A rabblerouser himself, Sweeney made Shelton Lea one of his 'glam poets'.

Shelton's reputation as a poet was now as an artist of merit and depth, not just a pub warrior. His style would remain what others would regard as wild and undisciplined but for the city's art lovers that made him even more magnetic. By 1975 Shelton had published five books, the last three—*Chrysalis* (1972), *The Paradise Poems* (1973) and *Chockablock With Dawn* (1975)—in as many years.

But he could not shake his ways, nor stop drifting into darkness, frequently falling back on the comfort of a swig from a bottle, a pull from a cone and the sting of a needle. Shelton took off for Sydney once more, this time to be with Loma Carey.

26

LINCOLN

Valerie was well aware that the old Chapel Street factory was not an ideal home for raising small children. Worse still, she'd been told that it was dangerous. Jason visited his children so infrequently that he had become 'Daddy Jason', as if there was a need to distinguish between him and Monty. Apart from his busy working life, Jason was planning a wedding. Yet even Jason, with all these distractions, had noted the dangers around the factory and voiced his concerns several times.

Valerie mentioned her son's worries in her diary. Chapel Street was an industrial lot, not a home, Jason had complained, and he would rather that she and Monty take the children back to Lambert Road, which was being rented out in piecemeal lots to students: 'Jason wanted me to get away from the dangers here, the cars and trucks coming through, the railings in the theatre and the railway tracks along the side . . . that big gate leaning up against the wall.'

But Valerie did not listen.

At least Sundays were relatively quiet compared to the frenetic activities of weekdays, and Jacie, Angeline and Lincoln were allowed downstairs to play in the grounds behind the factory. Valerie thought they were safe.

Lincoln—a four-year-old boy of boundless energy, slightly naughty in the most delicious of ways, and oh, so affectionate— loved the freedom of the grounds. While his older brother and sister were usually content playing upstairs, Lincoln was often outside, rummaging and exploring as little boys do.

Sunday, 4 April 1971, was no different. It was the weekend before Easter and Melbourne was flooded with autumn sunshine. Chapel Street, a busy shopping strip during the week, was all but silent. Valerie and Monty were home, Charryce and David were visiting and, the last time Valerie had checked, the children were scattered in and around the house—Jason watching TV and the other two outside.

Then came the shrill and piercing scream as Angeline ran into the house. Something terrible had happened, an accident, and Lincoln had been hurt. There was blood, she shrieked. Valerie ran back down the stairs and round the side of the house. A huge wrought-iron gate, which had been propped up against a wall, was lying on the ground. Lincoln, poor little Lincoln, was beneath its bars, his head crushed between the gate and the concrete driveway. He was dead.

It looked from the position of his feet as if Lincoln had been trying to climb the gate, as was his wont; but how could it have tilted and tipped backwards? It didn't seem possible, particularly with his tiny weight. Valerie knelt beside her grandson and tried to lift the gate off him. She felt her back click as she attempted to move the weight, to no avail. Someone later said it weighed three hundred pounds.

I held it on my knees but I knew he was gone with his dear little face lying in a pool of blood. All I could feel was a terrible, terrible, uncontrollable rage that we'd lost him.

Unknown to Valerie, Jacie had not been watching television; he was outside with his siblings. And he saw what had happened. More than four decades later, the shadow of his little brother's death still weighed heavily.

It was pretty late in the afternoon, and Lincoln had climbed onto one of the heavy iron gates that were propped against a wall. He was about halfway up and was jiggling up and down. I turned away, doing something else and then the next thing you know, it fell. Angeline screamed, I turned around and saw Lincoln lying under the gate, his eyes open and blood coming out of his nose and ears. Valerie heard the scream and came, tried to lift the gate and drag Lincoln out. It was too late . . .

Jason paused, the vision of his dead brother too much. Tears welled: 'Strong memories, even now,' he croaked.

Valerie's world became a sea of flashing red and blue as police and then an ambulance arrived. Her world had been shattered; she was so distraught that Angeline watched a police officer slap her grandmother's face to try to calm her down. Valerie couldn't watch as they took poor Lincoln away, and retreated upstairs to quiz Angeline, who had been playing a game called Donkey with her little brother, bouncing a ball against a wall. Between turns, the ever-active boy had climbed onto the gate.

Angeline had watched as the great, heavy gate teetered and fell, pinning Lincoln beneath. Blood trickled from his eyes and ears: 'I knew he was dead,' she would recall in an interview, revealing that she still keeps her brother's ashes and clothes, even his toothbrush.

Valerie's thoughts and fears tumbled over themselves in her diary. She'd had nightmares for months beforehand about losing Lincoln, his death foretold down to the detail of Angeline delivering the news:

I have been so frightened that something would happen to spoil things and I've truly expected it and a half dozen times I've had semi-nightmares of having to phone Jason in Sydney to tell him that we'd lost Lincoln, always Lincoln—never the other two, and it's always been Angeline running up the stairs screaming that something had happened to Lincoln.

And the gate. Sometime last year Monty and some of the men had moved it from the front of the property and propped it up against the side wall, out of the way. They had jammed an old white hose underneath it, to make sure it couldn't slip—a bit shoddy perhaps but it worked, or so it had seemed. She'd had her doubts, she couldn't deny it, walking past it every day and wondering if it was safe, but assuring herself it couldn't be moved. It was too heavy.

Even burly police officers, who propped the gate upright again after Lincoln's body was taken away, couldn't make it fall again.

But it didn't change the fact that Lincoln was dead:

I'm so frightened that although Daddy [Monty] says he doesn't and can't blame himself for pulling the gate from the front and leaning it there against the wall I'm still frightened that inside himself he does feel that he was responsible, but I'd look at it day after day and never once did I ever consider that any child was capable of moving it. It was as much as two men could do to drag it from one spot to another.

'Thank God for Charryce.' Valerie's beloved youngest daughter had made the phone call to Jason that Valerie couldn't face. Jason would go into deep shock and, unlike his mother, accept the guilt that went with refusing to allow his former wife to take her own children back to England.

Charryce's sympathies lay with her mother:

It was indescribable what it did to Mum, and affected her for the rest of her life. She had done her level best to raise Jason's children. So long as they were loved, it didn't matter that they lived in a flat above a factory. You could have the most wonderful environment and a gate could still fall on a child. It was him [Lincoln] who was climbing up that gate.

And what of Hilke? The once perfect daughter-in-law was ignored in the murky mix of guilt and grief and was only told about her son's death days after the funeral.

Lincoln was cremated within three days, in a ceremony organised and driven by his grandmother. Jason, calmed by sedatives and consumed by guilt that his decision to separate his former wife from her children had contributed to his son's death, rushed down from Sydney, as did other members of the family.

There was no time for funeral or bereavement notices; instead Lincoln Lea's death was paraded in the tabloid press. *The Sun* asked for a photograph of the boy, which Valerie provided, handing over one of the two of them: 'I said "Don't put me in please" and he said "Alright" but next morning there is the big picture of Linky and me and so of course we've been inundated with cards and letters.' *The Truth* promised to use the story as a warning to other parents about dangers around the home, but in their coverage they ignored that angle.

ᘓ

From her back door Hilke can see over Station Pier, the ports suburb where she arrived more than half a century ago as a recently wed, pregnant eighteen-year-old. It is a memory she holds dear despite the trials of a difficult marriage breakup, the separation from her three children and the subsequent death of her youngest child.

Before she met Jason at business school, Hilke's life was already a bit of a rollercoaster. She was raised by her German mother and English stepfather, whose love affair was like something out of a romantic novel. Her real father was killed during the war before her mother, Edith, met an Allied soldier named Donald Murphy, who was so smitten with her that he returned to Germany after the war ended. They married even though neither spoke each other's language, and they tried living in England but Edith's German background made life there difficult. The family moved back and forth between England and Germany for several years and even lived for a while in Hong Kong before Hilke's schooling made them finally settle outside London.

'I was torn between the identities of being German or English until I came to Australia,' Hilke says, the round vowels of her English schooling smothering any hint of her German heritage. 'For the last thirty years I have felt Australian.'

Now in her seventies, Hilke speaks quietly and carefully about the breakup of her marriage to Jason and the subsequent events. She has long forgiven any mistakes that were made, insisting that the breakup was mutual. She wasn't aware that she had been spied upon or that false accusations had been made about her behaviour. Instead, she blamed the marriage problems on immaturity and work pressures.

'Jason and I were very young and I was dropped into a very busy family. We saw less and less of each other and eventually grew apart. I missed my mother terribly so I planned to go back to England for perhaps three months. Jason said I might as well stay there.'

At first she had fought to take the children with her, but Jason refused to let them go and she relented. He then agreed to let her take Lincoln before reneging: 'Jason changed his mind. I don't know why.'

Instead, the children would be looked after by the Lea family because they were well off financially, and the children would be loved and have a good education. 'I made the decision because I believed it would be the best for my children, and they have done very well financially. If I had taken them with me then, they might have been disowned, and I didn't want to take that chance.'

Hilke believed she kept in touch with her children while she was away, sending letters, cards and birthday presents. She assumed that her children had received her words and gifts, and it was only some years later that she found out Valerie had not passed on the correspondence. Hilke swats away the controversy: 'I guess she was being loyal to her son. She apologised later.'

Neither did she attempt to regain custody of her children, even when she returned to Melbourne. 'Valerie didn't want to give them up because she had taken care of the children for three years. I accepted that. I could have taken it to court but I tried very hard to keep things pleasant. I remained very close to the Lea family.'

We broach the subject of Lincoln's death, an event that understandably remains painful. 'It was an accident,' she says. 'If anything, I think Lincoln's death brought Valerie and I closer together. She kept asking me, "Do you forgive me yet, do you forgive me?" The answer was yes.'

And the decision not to tell her about Lincoln's accident until after the funeral? She has forgiven that as well: 'Valerie eventually rang my mother. I think they were nervous about telling me.'

'Looking back made me realise how strong a person I had become. To fall and pick myself up and start another day not blaming anyone but myself.'

∞

In the days and weeks after her grandson's death Valerie kept herself busy. She managed her latest property acquisitions—two houses in the city's eastern suburbs—and attended the funeral and the brief inquest, which came to the obvious conclusion of death by misadventure. She celebrated her 36th wedding anniversary and even organised a dinner at Gaela's flat to see off a friend heading back to South Africa. But none of these distractions could shake her guilt about Lincoln and her sense that destiny had taken him from her.

She went over and over the details of the accident in her diary, questioning how it could have happened, who might have been at fault and whether it could have been avoided. She acknowledged but then dismissed her son's anguish, that she had ignored his warnings about the dangers of living above a factory. Instead, she latched onto Mungah's observation: 'His time had come. Move on.'

'I knew we could never keep him,' Valerie wailed, insisting he was too adventurous. He was a dear sweet little boy who created havoc when he accompanied her to property auctions, clambering over stacks of furniture to the dismay of salesmen, or slipping from her grasp during shopping trips and disappearing; he would watch her from behind a door, emerging only after she yelled out in embarrassed frustration.

She was the most important person in his life, the one he turned to when he was hurt, whose cheek he would kiss at night, whose hand he would hold before stepping off a footpath to cross a road. And she was the caring parent who taught him his childhood prayers—'Gentle Jesus, meek and mild'—which he would recite each morning when he climbed into her bed.

She overlooked Lincoln's bad behaviour at kindergarten where he had a habit of pushing other children; she protected him against 'Jacie', who she would 'whack and whack again' if he touched his younger brother. She related to Lincoln 'more than any of my children', somehow drawn to the boy and yet wondering why he didn't resemble anyone in the family, as if he had been switched at birth.

> The trouble was we loved him too much, and fate has to step in and teach us what?? It was all because I tempted fate by being so happy at having the three of them, and thought that maybe God had given them to us to make up for the loss of the three adopted ones. But nothing will ever make up for his loss.

Then Valerie's grief spilled over into regret, the closest she had ever come to acknowledging her mistake in trying to create the family she couldn't produce naturally. She even acknowledged her callous treatment of the adopted children: she couldn't relate to them and, in turn, they had rejected her as their mother. This was God's revenge on her and her alone. Not on the dead boy, nor on his siblings and his distraught parents. This was His revenge on her:

> Oh dear God where have I failed that you've punished me like this. Is it because I couldn't find the money to help Bretton in prison? What have I been punished for? I felt that if I had been bringing up the adopted three now that I may have now turned a blind eye to the things that they did that were wrong but if I had, I cannot imagine that they'd have been any different. Should I have persevered more,

238

showing an outward love for Honey although she rejected it so openly, did I give up too easily? It was an impossible thing to do, to try and bring up natural and adopted children together because no matter what we did, the psychological situation always cropped up . . . We should never have adopted them, we should have just been foster parents and had the Government pay for their upkeep and medical expenses and the three of them may have grown up with an entirely different mental attitude to us as parents and we could have taken more than just the three of them and if their parents came back and wanted them at 14 or 15 they maybe would still have considered us and kept in touch and we may even have kept some of them.

But after weeks of revision, Valerie came to a single conclusion:

I don't suppose I will ever get over losing him. Oh Lincoln, why did you do this to Mummy?

Somehow, as Valerie repeated the tragic event over and over again in her mind, it had become twisted, as if moulded to eventually comfort the grief of a narcissist. Perhaps, she considered at one point, she should get another orphan:

It would, to some degree, make losing little Lincoln more worthwhile if it could help some other little soul.

On the other hand, perhaps God intended her to give Jacie and Angeline more attention, but she found it so difficult. She felt soul-less. Empty. Was it love or was it guilt?

I could add a thousand IFS that conspired to kill that funny dear little boy. He was the only one I ever was a real mother to.

☙

A few weeks after Lincoln's death, Honey telephoned out of the blue.

Valerie had rarely spoken to Honey in the five years since she'd left home. She and Charlie had just returned from a trip around the world—London, New York, Hong Kong—buying film rights, including visiting Charlie's cinematic hero, D.A. Pennebaker, who had hosted a dinner for them in his spectacular Fifth Avenue apartment while they negotiated buying the rights to his latest documentary, *Monterey Pop*.

But Honey wasn't calling about her trip. She was 21 years old, pregnant and 'freaking out' about her identity, desperate to find out more about herself. Who was she really? Honey had remembered being picked up at the doctor's surgery at the age of four and wanted Valerie to contact her natural mother.

It was a confronting question, fraught with ethical and legal problems, and one that Valerie wasn't keen to answer. Honey, like Shelton, had been acquired in what was almost certainly an illicit baby trade run by Basil Rush, the child welfare officer.

Valerie knew not only the identity of Honey's real mother, Shirley Newman, but also that she had promised to give Valerie Lea her baby as soon as she was born, not four years later, as actually happened.

Rush had risen quietly through the ranks, ran an agency called the Infant Life Protection Scheme, a hangover from the nineteenth century, which gave him access to refuge centres such as The Haven, run by the Salvation Army in North Fitzroy, and the freedom to organise private adoptions. This was fine and above board except that it enabled Rush to source babies for the city's wealthy and powerful—children to order, at a price. It was little wonder then that Shelton's mother, Gwyneth Roberts, had concocted a story about her baby's father being from an aristocratic British family.

There was lawful provision for a payment to cover the cost of an adoption, but Rush was charging under-the-counter fees, sometimes hundreds of pounds, to pay off expectant mothers and to line his own pockets.

Shirley Newman had fallen pregnant to a man she didn't want to marry, despite his offer, and had no interest in keeping the illegitimate child. Instead, she had made a deal with Rush, agreeing to have the baby and hand it over to Valerie Lea, who had given birth to Charryce a few months earlier and wanted a girl the same age—a 'twin'.

Honey's birth certificate would reflect this 'deal', stating that she was the youngest of seven children born to Valerie and Monty. It made no mention of Shirley, even though it was issued four years *before* the adoption. Because Valerie had been unwell after Charryce's birth, she put off the adoption until she recovered. By then Shirley was wavering, and in the interim she had given the baby a name—Gayle—and handed her over to the care of Dot and Jack Quinlan. It would take four years, a new relationship and another pregnancy, plus pressure exerted by Basil Rush, before Shirley would sign the consent form, retrieve Gayle from the Quinlans and hand her over to the Leas.

Valerie justified the adoptions in her diary: 'I'd told Bretton that he'd been "grown" especially for us and I'd tried to explain the same to Honey so she'd feel she had really belonged,' she wrote, adding: 'None of it worked anyway, with her or Bretton.'

When Honey now asked about her mother, Valerie told her nothing about Shirley Newman.

27

A MISCARRIAGE OF JUSTICE

After Shelton fled Sydney, Brett soon headed north. He 'went bush', as far from the city and its sins as possible, he told his brother. He was unwilling to go back south, where the temptations were just as bad and there was no compensating family support.

Even though Brett kept in contact with Valerie via the occasional phone call and letter, she had let him go. But he was a vulnerable young man who needed support and guidance. He hardly had the life skills to find a pair of matching socks let alone set up a life of responsibility, open a bank account or rent a flat. Life for Brett was focused on finding enough money to fill his belly each day, whatever the means.

He took odd jobs, mainly as a storeman or labourer, but his casual attitude meant the work never lasted long. He worked for a couple of years in a sideshow, first as a spruiker selling entrance tickets to the Big Top and then as a performer of cheap deceptions inside the tent—a snake charmer, a character named Bullet Proof Boy and a half-man, half-woman act. It was all pantomime—dress-up games, where he could avoid being himself for a while—and it only came to an end after his boss got into a fight with another worker and killed him. Brett thought he was next, so he left.

Somewhere along the way he met and married a girl named Margaret Lynette. He appears to have told no one except Shelton about his marriage. If Valerie knew, she didn't think it important enough to note it in her diary, let alone want to attend the wedding or wish the couple well.

In May 1970 Brett and Margaret Lynette were living in the Gulf Country town of Karumba, when he received a letter from the Australian Army. Brett had been called up for national service.

In 1964 the Australian Government had introduced a national ballot to bolster its troop numbers and meet their commitment to the Vietnam War. Once a young man turned twenty, his name went into a ballot: if his birthdate, written on a wooden ball, dropped from a wire barrel in a bingo-like draw, he would be called up for two years' national service, followed by three years' part-time service in the regular army reserve.

Brett's birthdate—5 July—was not among those drawn in the lottery of September 1967, which meant he had dodged the national service bullet and should have been excused indefinitely from duty. But somehow he was drafted. It is difficult to understand why, unless he was included in a second draw held in March 1968, which was supposed to be for young men who were 'absent from Australia' when the first draw was made. This time, Brett's birthdate came out.

There is another explanation, strange but possible nonetheless. In the 1966 ballot the ball inscribed with Shelton's birthdate—25 August—rolled down the wire chute, which meant he should have reported for duty. He didn't. Was there a mix-up between the brothers' birth records? One document among Brett's prison files suggests that they had been given each other's birthdates, at least for a period of time, before the mistake was realised.

Whatever the cause of the error, Brett got the call-up in 1968, but because of his itinerant lifestyle he didn't find out about it for another two years. By the time authorities tracked him down, he was classified as a draft dodger.

The ultimatum left him torn: if he failed to turn up for duty, he might face a lengthy military prison sentence, but if he obeyed he would lose his job, potentially leaving his wife in financial trouble.

In the end, despite Margaret Lynette's protestations, Brett heeded the army's threats, packed a bag and headed back down to Brisbane. He could have applied for a deferment, as many did, for any number of reasons—that he had a criminal record, he was married or he was a conscientious objector. But he didn't make the application, almost certainly out of ignorance, and was signed up for two years' service just as Australia was beginning to wind down its involvement in Vietnam.

As he cooled his heels in Brisbane, waiting to be escorted to Sydney for basic training, Brett received a note from Margaret Lynette, pleading with him to return home. She was two months pregnant and was experiencing complications. It changed everything: 'I decided to skip,' he later told authorities.

CB

Private Bretton Lea, Service No. 1736827, lasted just six days in the military. When the train from Brisbane arrived at Sydney Central Station on the evening of 12 May 1968, he managed to evade his escort and vanish into the crowd. His responsibilities lay elsewhere.

Brett was on the run. He headed back north as far as Townsville, where his wife was clearly ill. She would miscarry a few weeks later, but that changed nothing. Regardless of his motives, he had gone AWOL and there would be serious consequences if he were found.

The couple drove to Sydney, where Brett got a job in the factory of a Sunday newspaper, but he didn't stay there long. Afraid he might be tracked down, he moved again, this time back to Melbourne where, in desperation, he cashed some cheques even though he knew they would bounce.

They again returned to Sydney where, in a brazen departure from his usually clandestine operations, Brett blagged his way into a job as a credit manager with the hire firm Radio Rentals. He lasted three weeks before he took off with $2700 in takings and wages, leaving Margaret Lynette in the process.

In the space of four months he had gone from a married man with a steady job and his first child on the way to a man with no job, no wife and no child who was being sought by the military police, and by civilian police in three states.

He was Clyde without Bonnie, and he was bound to come unstuck. Soon after he scarpered back to Melbourne with his takings from Radio Rentals, the Victorian police caught up with him. Brett was sentenced to a year's jail for passing dud cheques, then extradited back to Sydney to face charges of larceny for the Radio Rentals job.

When he appeared in court in Sydney on 16 June, he pleaded guilty to the larceny charges but, instead of being sentenced, Brett was handed over to the military.

Everyone had to stand in line to have their piece of Bretton Lea.

☙

On 22 June 1971, six days after his conviction for larceny, Brett's court martial was held behind the sandstone walls of Victoria Barracks in Oxford Street, Paddington.

As he waited to be called into court, Brett was locked in a bare room in the middle of the barracks, where a small window gave him a view across the clipped lawns towards the main gate. He sat quietly awaiting his fate when, unexpectedly, there was a tap at the window. He looked up.

Shelton stood there grinning, a fag hanging from his lips, holding up a plastic bag to show its contents. Supplies. Brett had asked Shelton to be his character witness, in the hope that he could use his facility with words to somehow persuade the tribunal to treat his case compassionately.

Shelton said nothing as he handed the bag through the window. Then he moved away before he was spotted.

Brett was flabbergasted. His older brother had somehow walked straight into the grounds of an army base carrying two bags of takeaway food. Inside the bags were a bucket of Kentucky Fried Chicken, a couple of bottles of Coca-Cola and a packet of cigarettes and matches. Brett tucked in, with the guards outside none the wiser.

When the door was unlocked half an hour later he was smoking and sipping the last of the Coke, the chicken bones and wrappers spread out on the table in greasy triumph. The guards who had been sent to retrieve the prisoner were stunned.

'Where did you get all this stuff?' one managed.

Brett grinned. 'It was here when I got here.'

He managed to wipe the smile off his face before he entered the courtroom. Once inside, he realised the seriousness of his situation. His would be the first of three hearings for the day, in front of a jury of nine senior officers headed by Brigadier E.J.H. Howard, Chief of Staff, Eastern Command.

The brigadier already had in front of him Brett's psychological report, which offered little explanation of why he had absconded, but it confidently concluded that he had a 'detached attitude' and was expecting to cop a minimum two-year sentence.

The proceedings were straightforward enough, his crime indefensible. Brett had gone AWOL, would plead guilty and would be punished. He would be given a chance to explain himself in mitigation, and to call his brother to give a character statement.

Brett began with an appraisal of his adult life, delivered not as a weeping plea for leniency but as a matter of fact. Rather than lay blame at the feet of Valerie and Monty, he cast himself, a child, as the person most responsible when he left home, as the court transcript read: 'I left home due to some disagreement in the family, most of which was my fault.'

In doing so, Brett had accepted Valerie's view that he was to blame. He knew what had happened to him as a child wasn't fair, and yet he copped it as his lot in life. He told the steely men on the bench about his wanderings—'odd jobs to sustain myself in food'—and his failed attempts to try his hand at the confectionery business before ending up in Queensland, where he was notified of the call-up: 'There was some statement to the effect that I had been called up previously, but I never received the notification,' he told the court. This had led to his decision to go AWOL, the miscarriage, his marriage problems and the subsequent crime spree.

When he was arrested in Melbourne he was only facing two charges of passing dud cheques. It was then that he said that he decided to come clean:

The police had not found out about anything else. I told them about being absent from the Army and that I was involved with Radio Rentals. To the best of my ability, I intend to settle down and try and make something of my life. That is the main reason I gave myself up in Victoria; to try and clear everything up and start afresh. I would like to try and get back together with my wife.

Up stepped Shelton to plead mitigation. He was dressed in a crumpled suit jacket over an old striped T-shirt, a pair of mismatched trousers and shoes with no socks. The chain tattoos around his ankles were clearly visible as he sat on the stand with his legs crossed. It said a great deal about Brett's relaxed mindset that he was able to take in the finer details of his brother's attire. In life, he met every setback with the same infectious, squinty-eyed grin and set jaw that characterised his appearance in Valerie's home movies.

Shelton's appearance may have been dishevelled, but his speech to the court was impressive. It was from the heart. His brother had been treated badly and should be dealt with leniency. It underlined the intellectual chasm between the brothers: one of them was inspired by the writings of Ezra Pound and John Donne; the other was an unformed adolescent, forced to become an adult, who took every day as it came and tried to turn it into fun.

Shelton was in performance mode, but this wasn't like delivering a poem in a smoky pub—he was talking so fast that the court stenographer couldn't keep up. She begged him to stop for a moment. When he started to ramble once more, she asked him again. Shelton became annoyed: 'Look, if I continue to stop, I'll lose the thread of exactly how I want you to listen to this and how it's coming out,' he protested. 'It's all the truth.'

The impasse would have been funny if it wasn't so serious. Eventually, Brigadier Howard put up his hands in defeat: 'It's okay, just let him talk.'

Brett watched with bated breath, full of admiration for his brother as Shelton continued with his story, confirming that letters he had received from Margaret Lynette indicated the situation had put the marriage under enormous strain. He concluded:

Brett should not have gone into Army service. His wife was sick in Karumba, and he needed to be with her. As a result of going into the Army, his wife miscarried and family problems resulted. It seems very much that he was, in fact, forced to take the action that he did from hard realisation.

I am very upset myself for Brett because he tried to make a go of it. The Army was unfair to call him up and this turned on the incidents at the time which caused his marriage to break up. I believe there has been a lot of unnecessary trouble with the police as a result of this. He is still having trouble in not being able to get back with his wife and he still has a further court charge to face.

The defending officer concurred: 'Private Lea has had a very troubled life since the age of sixteen when he left home. Since then he has had no guidance from his parents, which probably helped him on his way into trouble with the police.' But it was a military matter and, as such, Brett had pleaded guilty to being AWOL and had to be punished: 'I would ask the court to consider when coming to a sentence that he said he would like to make a new life for himself and his family. When it comes to the penalty to be imposed, I would ask the court to be as lenient as possible.'

It is difficult to know what impact Shelton's speech might have had, but he certainly didn't seem to harm Brett's case. Maybe he helped. The stony-faced officers seemed to listen. Whatever his faults, Shelton was truly his brother and someone Brett could count on. Perhaps the only one.

Shelton looked pleased with himself as they waited for the jury to return their verdict. It didn't take long, and it was unusual for a military court to show any sympathy towards the accused. Brett would serve only twenty-eight days' detention. It was a bloody good result, considering he had expected two years, and easy time compared to the other jail stints he'd survived as a teenager.

28

FOREVER YOUNG

Well this could be the beginning of the end for us.

Valerie was livid and frightened. Petrified, in fact. As if dealing with Lincoln's death wasn't difficult enough, it looked as if their life's work might collapse in a pile of debt, with Mungah's savings, so diligently acquired, squandered.

There were times in her life that, as resilient as she seemed, the weight of responsibility would become too much for Valerie. And this was one of those times. A series of visits to specialists to ease her recurring back pain had reopened old wounds and grievances dating back to the 1951 car crash. After her legal costs, she had only received £1100 compensation for the accident, still a painful and vivid memory for her. Valerie had felt she was owed £50,000 for all the suffering and the whole episode only served to highlight the cost of the mistakes made by Monty over the years.

In the early 1960s, when Monty's secret losses were revealed, they had been forced to cash in their life insurance policies, sell off Valerie's jewellery and raid the children's bank accounts to repay the company debt.

Then there was the Brighton Savoy fiasco. She totted up the losses in her diary, almost two pages of names, money and blame—from the non-payment of wages to outrageous legal fees, neon signs, surplus furniture and even unused bridal catalogues. She reckoned it had resulted in a loss of $85,000 to Mungah's Bulwark Against Disaster, supposed to be shared by her natural children. Its value now hovered below $200,000. As Valerie's diary entries on this subject mounted, so did her fears that they and the children would be left penniless.

She was also distraught that the Sydney management team had overtaken the empire she and Monty had created in Melbourne. It had not only stripped them of their manufacturing base and slashed the number of their outlets from nine to five but had also taken her husband and children away from her, to Sydney. Jason and Lael may have occupied management roles at the Kogarah factory but Darrell paid them peanuts. And Monty was forever travelling between the two cities: 'I resent the Sydney influence on our children and that they have them and we don't.'

To make matters even worse, another of Monty's business ventures was in trouble. This time it was a company called Direct Foods Limited, which he had set up with some business associates to deal in freezers and frozen food. It was a complicated arrangement, in which the company was not only selling and leasing appliances but also providing frozen produce to store in the freezers.

According to Valerie's assessment, Monty had invested over

$500,000 and been led up the garden path. She estimated they were $160,000 down on the deal, and it could get worse:

Monty just laughs and proceeds to hand over money to perfect strangers for them to squander,' she railed. 'I do feel very bitter over what Monty has done to his family although I couldn't ever love anybody as much as I do him. Of course, when I come to think of it, Monty is so nice to live with simply because of these soft qualities that make people fleece him.

There was clearly a developing rift in the relationship between Monty and his younger brother, Darrell, who was now suggesting that Monty sell his quarter share in the family company and go his separate way. Valerie wrote:

I wanted to do that ten years ago, but he wouldn't. I have felt so frustrated for years now, because everything that Monty has done that I've not wanted him to do, he's lost on.

He is a complete enigma to me. He wants his children to have nothing. He forgets how little work he has done in his life. He forgets that anything he ever wanted, he got. Jason is twenty-eight and doesn't have a penny of his own, neither does Lael or the two girls.

She hadn't bought herself a new dress since 1965; instead she spent between $1 and $4 on second-hand outfits from charity shops. Not that she was complaining too much. Valerie had never been flashy. She liked cotton sheets, sturdy boots and balanced meals with vegetables, but she also watched the pennies and rarely socialised outside the home.

They were an odd, daggy family in a suburb where most households drove expensive cars and holidayed overseas or in their own beach house; the Leas went on camping holidays. Now, as Valerie struggled with the weekly grocery order, it seemed that all that prudence was for nought: 'I really don't know HOW the average family manages.'

There was no mention of Shelton, Brett or Honey and their financial welfare. Valerie had washed her hands of the adopted children. They could fend for themselves.

Jason Jnr would observe the disagreements and disappointments as they unfolded. As he described it many years later:

Monty was a man who could never answer his own front door. He always had someone chasing him for money from deals that had gone bad. Sometimes it was because he had gone guarantor for someone like a business mate who was buying a Rolls Royce and then took off and left Monty with the debt.

Did Monty just have bad luck?

No, he tried to do too many things. The family's skill was making chocolates and lollies, but Monty wanted to get involved in everything else and it was bound to fail. Harris did the same thing to an extent, getting involved in a Queensland tin mine at some stage and a hotel [on] Sydney's North Shore. Both turned to crap. We all came back to the lolly business. We knew what to do. Maurice was the retailer, Harris and Monty were the manufacturers.

⁂

Jason Snr and his girlfriend Biddy Tapper were getting married. They had begun planning their wedding before Lincoln's death and saw no reason to change the date, although the Catholic Church was refusing to marry them in Sydney because Jason was divorced. Instead, they would wed in New Zealand, Biddy's native country. The ceremony was set for September 1971 and, despite her money worries, Valerie had booked the tickets, although Monty was not keen to go.

Valerie liked Biddy, and was pleased that Jason was planning to buy a house in Woollahra—the Sydney equivalent of South Yarra in terms of social status—so perhaps there was hope for the future. The house was tiny but a bargain, she thought, and, when Jason struggled to raise the funds, she convinced Monty to offset the loan against his company shares. Jason and Biddy needed a marital home, particularly as Valerie was hoping the couple would have children quickly; triplets preferably, so they would be too busy to 'pinch' Jason Jnr and Angeline from her.

Meanwhile Lael was sweet on a girl named Janice, but Valerie wasn't sure: 'A gorgeous girl,' she wrote, 'but I'm sure she is not of a healthy strain, and an ailing wife would be murder for any marriage.'

Gaela had settled into life in South Africa with her new husband. Compared to Jason and Biddy's house, theirs alone was worth a diary entry. Not only did it have three bedrooms and separate dining and lounge rooms but also a bar, rumpus room, double garage 'and five more rooms for servants—blackies of course'. Gaela bought furniture for the house at auctions while Charl settled into his job as manager of an engineering firm which paid $400 a week.

Valerie wondered how her daughter had managed to land such a catch, particularly as Charl did all the chasing of 'her ladyship'. Gaela's shyness had been a frequent source of frustration, sharply contrasting with her own pursuit of Monty all those years before.

And they were trying for a family. Gaela had been off the pill for a year but, sadly, there was still no sign of a baby. 'Infertile Myrtle,' Charl called her. Valerie was desperate for a new grandchild.

By contrast, Charryce and David were 'meandering along', living in one of the family flats in Lambert Road while David looked for a job. They were trying to find a house to buy with his war service loan, but their dithering was annoying for a woman who was always impatient to find solutions.

At the other end of the family spectrum, Mungah had turned eighty-five. And after years of denying her age—even insisting that Valerie not refer to it when she 'pegged out'—she was now proud of having lived so long. Boasting about it in fact, kept alive by a mountain of pills that she wouldn't have dreamed of taking had they not been free on prescription.

On her last trip to Melbourne Mungah had even returned a favourite ring that had once belonged to her eldest daughter, a knuckle-duster of a thing—a central diamond surrounded by three smaller ones inside matching gold spheres. Her return of the ring was Mungah's way of acknowledging that she was coming to the end of her life, but it only served to heighten Valerie's sense of mortality: 'Oh MY GOD!! I've turned 58. No, I can't believe it. I think I'll stay 29.'

And Valerie would find a way to stay young, even if it was superficial. She packed Jacie and Angeline off to Sydney to spend the summer holidays with their father and new stepmother, then checked into Malvern Hospital for a lengthy operation: 'Going into hospital for a week. Tell you later what's being done,' she teased in her diary.

It would be another year before Valerie revealed the details of the operation. Despite claims of desperate financial straits and sacrifices, she'd had a facelift, her eyes and skin tightened, wrinkles stretched and plumped. Even with her bandages on, she pouted for the cameras, recording what must have been one of the first such operations the city had seen.

'I looked a fright for a couple of months but wore my wig to pieces,' she wrote. 'Monty seems pleased and Bubbie thinks it is a big improvement. I don't have to think about my wrinkles showing so much so it has helped me psychologically. I'm not so conscious of looking old.'

◌ঽ

Soon after Lincoln's death, Valerie and Monty moved out of Chapel Street, so they were now back at Lambert Road. Jason had insisted on it, although it seemed too little too late. Nothing would bring the little boy back, and Valerie could not shake the image of him lying dead from her head.

Her diary would continue to reflect her rolling grief, alternating with guilt and smothered by excuses. Jason should blame himself for not allowing Hilke to take her children and Monty could shoulder some of the responsibility for moving the gate. God was punishing her for not being a good mother to Shelton, Brett and Honey. After all, it was her loss rather than Hilke or Jason's because she loved Lincoln more than anyone else. And so it went on.

Jacie and Angeline were now settled in local schools, but Valerie remained convinced that her eldest son would try to reclaim his children against her wishes. And Hilke could even return from Britain. What then? Did she have any rights as their mother? She couldn't bear to lose them.

Then there was Mungah, whose health had deteriorated over the past year. A bout of food poisoning had reduced her to skin and bones, and when Val's sister Lola put her in a nursing home, Mungah protested by going on a hunger strike and almost died. Doctors were amazed by her tenacity, that she was still alive. In desperation, Valerie agreed to take care of her mother permanently. After all, the house was big enough, and most of its rooms were now empty.

Monty was also worried about his own mother. Esther, two years older than Mungah, was now living in a Sydney nursing home, where she recognised no one and was tied to a chair to stop her wandering—a devastating end to a feisty life. She too was brought to Melbourne, and Valerie put the two old women in what used to be the children's playroom.

This was the room—then full of toys, dolls and a rocking

horse—that had held Honey spellbound the night she arrived in 1953. It was where Charryce had practised her ballet, with a barre and mirror that ran the length of the room. But the sparkle had all gone now: the carpets had been replaced with linoleum and the toys had long been discarded. It was empty, save for two single beds facing one another so that Valerie and a nurse who came once a week could attend to the needs of two incontinent old women.

Jacie and Angeline had been moved from a dangerous industrial property to what was virtually an aged-care home, where there was an overwhelming odour of urine amid constant moans, shrieks and calls for help.

Esther refused to eat and sat upright in bed calling out, 'Come on, Dad! Come on, Dad!', as if her late husband Harry was in the room. And Mungah didn't seem to recognise anyone other than her daughter, whom she treated as if she was still twelve years old.

Jacie, aged nine, watched his grandmother rush into the room one day after one of his great-grandmothers called out.

'Val, Val! Who's that lady there?' Mungah said, pointing her finger at Esther.

'Mum, that's Esther. You've known her for 40 years.'

'I don't know her. What's she doing here?'

Esther didn't show any sign that she'd even heard this exchange. A few months later, the matriarch of the Darrell Lea Chocolate Company was returned to the nursing home, where she would soon die.

ଔ

Esther wasn't the only one leaving Lambert Road. Jason wanted his two surviving children back. Valerie had begged him to let her keep them, but Jason's mind was made up. Lincoln was gone and he should make an effort with his two older children. Biddy wavered, but ultimately supported her husband. The children would move to Sydney. 'I've lost them. It will be very lonely without them.'

But Valerie could already see there was trouble ahead. In her opinion, Biddy was not happy. Jacie and Angeline were not her children yet Jason, who was working long days at the factory, was expecting her to bring them up. The marriage itself was going to come under pressure, she predicted. 'The children will not do any worse with us than with them and we are their BLOOD.'

There was another issue. Jason had received legal advice that Hilke, who was back in Melbourne with her new husband, Ted, could be granted custody of the children by a court. Valerie could not bear the thought that a mother might want her own children back.

29

KITTENS FROM CATS

> A Sydney baby whose birth was attended by two paddy
> wagon loads of policemen, two ambulances, most of her
> neighbours, and nearly all the kids and dogs in her suburb,
> is the newest recruit to her mother's campaign for 'babies
> liberation'. Angel Bell, born to Honey Bell at home—with
> the assistance of Honey's husband Charles and two of her
> girlfriends—is progressing nicely at home in Balmain.
>
> *Sydney Morning Herald*

In June 1974 Honey gave birth to her second child with Charlie
Vodicka. Her first, a son named Kaja (the Czech version of
Charles), had been born three years earlier in the isolation of a
rented shack on the beachfront at Coolum in Queensland, but
Angel would be delivered in the middle of Australia's biggest city
amid a blaze of accidental publicity.

They were now in Sydney, renting part of a beautiful sandstone house on the Balmain foreshore, but behind the artistic
and entrepreneurial success there was instability. Honey's life

with Charlie was a torturous tug-of-war between free love and a longing for commitment and security. He could give her plenty of the former and none of the latter, but he was still an intoxicating character she was prepared to follow.

Charlie may have left his wife, Desi, to be with Honey but he remained in contact with his previous family, as well as making a play for almost any woman who walked through the door. Honey tried to ignore the obvious.

Kaja's Coolum birth had been surreal, and not just because Honey had wanted a home birth in an ideal setting. When the labour pains began one evening, Charlie disappeared from the house to telephone Desi, who turned up the next morning with their two children, arriving just after Honey had given birth and was about to be taken to hospital because she couldn't expel the placenta.

While all this was going on, Chuck had meanwhile moved Desi and her children into a rented house across the road, so that Honey, nursing her newborn, found herself watching her lover walk hand-in-hand down the street with his estranged wife.

When they all returned to Melbourne, it grew even weirder when Chuck moved both his families into a house he owned in Ferny Creek, at the foothills of the Dandenong Ranges. It felt like a freewheeling commune: both Charlie and Desi courted numerous partners. In the end Honey fled the scene with Kaja, ending up in Sydney, and Charlie finally chose to leave his wife and be with her. They changed their surnames and became Charlie and Honey Bell, 'because it rang true', but they did not marry. The monogamy would not last.

And now they had Angel. But her birth, which was supposed to be a serene and beautiful event, had turned into a farce. Honey had spent months negotiating with nearby hospitals to allow her to give birth naturally, rather than rely on drugs. Most importantly, she didn't want the baby taken away at birth and placed in a nursery. But no hospital would cooperate, so she had chosen another home birth.

Honey had spent the morning of the birth lying in the sun, but moved back inside during the afternoon when the temperature dropped and clouds scudded across the sky. Inside, the stone walls of their basement apartment made her feel even colder and Honey began to shake. Panic set in and, when the first contractions hit, she let out a wild scream.

Upstairs, Charlie suddenly felt scared and called a gynaecologist, who refused to attend 'because it's Sunday', so he called an ambulance, which turned up just as Angel's head was crowning. The noise attracted neighbours and their dogs, who were soon crowding out the front of the house, wondering what all the fuss was about.

The ambulance crew, one of whom later admitted he'd never delivered a baby and was 'more scared than the mother', wanted Honey to agree to go to hospital, but she refused. The ambos called the police and two cars arrived soon afterwards.

'It felt like being in some Fellini movie,' Honey laughed, later recalling the circus that had developed. 'I saw this huge police officer walk into the room as if he owned the place, just as I was trying to push Angel out. I decided to let out this primal scream and he scuttled back out of the room. About fifteen minutes later, the baby was born and everybody cheered and left.'

Then the media arrived, a flock of seagulls alerted by police radio, looking for a feed on a slow Sunday. Honey wanted them to leave, but Charlie insisted that she give interviews, barely two hours after giving birth. She had a view about birth and hospitals and, ever the entrepreneur, he insisted she speak publicly about them while she had the chance. Honey spoke to the reporters who crowded into the room, her criticism enmeshed with misgivings about her own life.

In hospital, my baby would have been ripped away from me, and that's the greatest trauma anyone can suffer.

Hospitals aren't geared for humanity—for the baby's sake or the mother's. There's a general sense of sadness in every maternity hospital I've ever visited. The baby is taken away from the mother and put in a room with twenty or thirty other babies, all screaming their heads off. They put drops in its eyes and weigh and measure it and dress it. It's exposed to glaring lights and different temperatures.

The mother is left lying there, empty-handed, wondering where her baby is. The whole thing is absurd, absolutely ridiculous. People don't take kittens from a cat. Even the most sensitive person wouldn't rip a kitten from its mother—they wait for five weeks. I don't see why they can't apply logical standards to human beings.

ೞ

Overnight, Honey had become a flag-bearer for a new liberation movement—natural childbirth and babies. For a woman born in a Salvation Army home and abandoned by her adoptive mother as well as her natural mother, it had special meaning.

Sensing an opportunity, Charlie organised a media tour from Sydney to Brisbane and then back down to Melbourne. There was no shortage of interest from local newspapers, nor from women, who came along to town hall meetings with their own stories of frustration and fear. Ever the entrepreneur, Charlie realised there was potential for a book and a film.

Honey mentioned nothing about her own troubled background to reporters, who continued to ask for her opinions, not just on treatment at birth but on the broader issue—women were being ignored, their instincts dismissed by a system that put the decision-making into the hands of male doctors.

'You are told to go to the doctor each week and you ask him something and he just pats you on the back and says everything will be all right,' she railed to her old employer, the *Women's Weekly*. 'You're given only the vaguest of details; treated as if you're not even involved. The doctor is supposed to know everything, but he considers you too uninteresting or stupid to be told anything.'

Likewise in hospitals:

One of the problems of nurses and sisters in hospitals is that they get you in their clutches. You've been conditioned all your life to accept the laws of mothers and schoolteachers and they're just an extension of them and you let them bluff you. You're not allowed to ask why you should do something, or why you allow someone to stick a needle in you or give you a drug. You're just told 'do it'.

If you ask why they treat you as if you've asked them for a ticket to the moon.

Worst of all, she said, maternal instincts were being ignored:

Women in western countries are not encouraged to have faith in our natural resources as women. We're not reared to be women. We're not even encouraged to breastfeed our babies, and yet that nourishment is perfect for them, and irreplaceable. If women followed and trusted their instincts and felt more secure in their womanhood and their ability to have babies and bring up children, life would be better for them and their children.

There was one surprise supporter. Valerie Lea, herself a victim of lazy hospital treatment and traumatic experiences, embraced her estranged, adopted daughter's campaign. As Honey reflected in an interview: 'Valerie had always said that she didn't want drugs and wanted to have children her way. Somehow she was proud of me because I'd stood up to the hospitals and had my babies at home the way I wanted.'

It wasn't the first time Valerie had considered her estranged daughter kindly and with a sense of regret. After the birth of Kaja in September 1971, she wrote a diary entry revealing that she would have liked to play a new role in Honey's life. In particular, she was worried about Honey's living arrangements with Charlie, which were tenuous at best, but she stopped short of offering help: 'I wouldn't mind having her and the baby but I'd be frightened of how Bubbie would react,' she wrote.

Three years later, as Honey continued her post-birth media tour, Valerie asked her to pay a visit to her old home. There Honey found a subdued woman. Valerie had words of encouragement for her and also a gift—a collection of photographs she'd kept in an envelope marked 'Honey's'.

She handed them over without explanation—a 'propaganda collection', as Honey would describe them. They included several photocopied collages of photographs that tracked Valerie's own life, from a shopgirl in the 1930s, modelling her famed Darrell Lea uniform creation and courting a moustached Monty, through to Val as a young mother nursing her own babies, whose care would be traded for her aspirations and the business—'All head, no heart' as her eldest son would describe it. 'Business first . . . always business first.'

Among the photographs in the envelope there were several group family shots of Honey and her brothers and sisters, their names carefully printed in Valerie's square handwriting, as if Honey wouldn't recognise her own siblings. There were also numerous pictures of her and Charryce—on a billy cart, nursing the pets, modelling dresses and dancing—as if to show that the sisterly relationship had once been happy. It was true in part, Honey thought: the sisters *had* once been close, up to a point, and it was only their mother's decision to separate them at school and create artificial differences between them that had destroyed the bond.

There were also tiny proof sheets of photos taken during Honey's first days at Lambert Road in 1953, showing her learning the routines of the new household—dinnertime, washing her hands and playing in the wonderland toy room. Three had been developed into full-sized prints; one was of Honey hugging the rocking horse that had so attracted her attention—a gift of Mungah's some years before, according to the caption on the back.

The biggest print, however, was of a smiling Honey embracing Valerie. The young girl's apparent joy hides the reality of the moment, when her new mother insisted she take off the dress in which she'd arrived and put on a new one. Far from joyful, the other two prints showed a confused and worried child being stripped of her dress. It was the moment that Gayle Lesley Johns became Kestin Ferne Melani Lea.

Tucked into the back of the envelope was a pocketbook-sized photo of Honey. The caption, written in a different hand to the others, read: *My darling daughter 3 and three quarters. March 1953.*

The photo had been taken not by Valerie or Shirley Newman but by Dot Quinlan, the childless woman who, with her husband, Jack, had loved and taken care of the little girl for almost four years before Shirley took her away and handed her over to Valerie.

Dot would send photographs to Shirley, who turned up occasionally for a visit, but the couple never took steps to formalise the adoption because Honey's mother never showed any interest in reclaiming her daughter. Nor were they aware of the arrangement that already existed with Valerie. The Quinlans had thought their golden ray of sunshine was theirs to keep.

Then Jack died of a heart attack, and soon afterwards Shirley arrived and took her daughter back. Dot, already distraught at losing her husband, was devastated. She and Leslie Rough tried to find out where Gayle was taken but gave up when they learned that Shirley had given her to another family—the Leas.

30

UNTOUCHED GOODS

The death of Harriet Everitt came slowly; a life that had been hallmarked by effort and determination simply ebbed away. Some may have regarded Mungah as a slumlord, but she did not live in luxury while her tenants wallowed in hovels; rather she lived as they did—a modest lifestyle in a relatively humble abode.

She was regarded as formidable and grim, and perhaps she was in her business life, but Valerie's videos also show a softer countenance—a smile even—as she relaxed, surrounded by the fruits of her labour—family.

Putting her in hospital was never considered, even though Valerie could no longer deal with Mungah's physical needs: her bad back was making it impossible to move, wash or dress her mother. Instead, she brought in paid nurses on rotation, just as she had done with her children when they were young.

Mungah eventually died on 29 December 1973. Valerie had

been sitting with her that morning; when she left her, she thought the old lady was sleeping. But when a nurse named Anna went in to check her soon afterwards, she found Mungah 'stone cold'. 'She must have gone while I was with her and I didn't realise,' Valerie later wrote.

As she often did after momentous events, Valerie did not write immediately about her mother's death; in fact she didn't reflect on its aftermath until mid-1975. Ever pragmatic, Mungah had discussed her imminent death openly with her daughters, who had shared the care of their mother in the last months of her life.

Lola and I had talked to her about what she wanted and that's exactly what she got. I hope my end is as satisfactory as Harriet's was, even though I was an angel when she was with Lola and Lola was evil, and vice versa when she was with me. She had a lovely coffin (not black as instructed very definitely) and I sent her off with all the things she liked. The undertaker PROMISED he'd see she had them all on—her woolly singlet, her prettiest deep pink nightie, the bed socks sent down to her . . ., her lovely blue blocked dressing gown Lola bought in Asia. The fur cape she loved and photos of herself and me and Lola. If I could have found her fur hat that would have gone too but it was in Sydney. Oh and the gold watch Monty and I gave her in 1936. Then they put her on a plane (at least she'd be on a plane ONCE even if it wasn't in her life) to Sydney.

The funeral was at All Saints Anglican Church in Petersham, just a few hundred metres from the John Street house she had bought more than 40 years before to establish her Bulwark

Against Disaster. It was a happy event, Valerie thought, although the minister, who did not know Mungah personally, couldn't really capture her spirit: 'I felt like getting up and making a speech of my own to tell them all what an extraordinarily wonderful person she was but I knew I'd break down if I did.'

Harriet was cremated in her bed socks, and the urn was buried at the foot of the family plot at Rookwood Cemetery, where her parents, Maria and Joshua Evans, lay: 'We did everything just as she wished and I'm sure she is satisfied.'

03

24 March 1974

I do so thank the Lord that we have the children back for good, I trust.

Jacie and Angeline were finally back under Valerie's care and control. Her prediction that they would not stay with their father had proved correct: that interregnum lasted a little over fifteen months in Sydney before the pressure on the marriage—the combination of Jason's business demands and Biddy's desire for children of their own—became too much.

Within a few months of Jacie and Angeline returning to Melbourne, Biddy would be pregnant with her first child—a double bonus for Valerie, because it meant she would not only get the children back but also have a new grandchild, a girl named Carissa who would be born in April 1975.

And any fear that Hilke might pursue a claim on her children through the courts seemed to evaporate when they received news that she had given birth to a daughter named Samantha with her husband, Ted, a senior manager with the Ford company in the United Kingdom.

Things were falling neatly into place family-wise, although Valerie had concerns that, despite being married for some time, neither Charryce nor Gaela had any children yet: 'I'm sure Charl has never seen Gaela naked. I do hope David's doing a little better,' she quipped.

Valerie was also worried about the next generation. She hoped her granddaughters could eschew what she regarded as low modern-day morality and peer pressure, and marry as virgins—'a package of untouched goods'.

She and Monty had been pure: 'I think Monty and I are extremely lucky. He doesn't know what other girls are like (I hope not, otherwise there will be pinking shears for him in the middle of the night) and I'd be frightened to find out about other men. It's better to just keep on wondering.'

For all Monty's business mistakes, she could not imagine life without him. In fact she had been waking in a cold sweat some nights, fearing she had lost him: 'I'm sure I would lose my onions,' she wrote. Valerie was sure that her husband of 40 years was unique, because he didn't drink or smoke, and he even smelled nice: 'I do wish I could thin him down a little, though,' she wrote. 'I'm so scared of him having a heart attack. He's too fat. So am I.'

To this end, she had devised a regimen of eating health

food—'no fats or greasy food and plenty of good meat, fish, vegetables and fruit'—that began with a daily drink of orange juice, cod liver oil and warm water, strained into a jar and shaken vigorously seventy times.

Valerie was also intent on writing a 'resume on arthritis and common sense', which included drinking lukewarm milk fifteen minutes before meals and avoiding water for three hours afterwards, to give the natural oils in food time to settle in the joints between the bones and stop them grating together.

Despite her reservations about pre-marital sex—'I don't want MY daughters and granddaughters doing it that way!!!!!'—Valerie was glad that son Lael had been 'experimenting' with girls to find the right one, someone who would treat him 'like a god'.

It's a peculiar situation today—in the past the men wanted sweet, pure, untouched girls . . . and the girls who were promiscuous were very much looked down upon. Now the sweet pure ones are considered not good wife material, as being 'frigid'. What they want is a pure wife who turns wanton after marriage.

A month later, Valerie's concerns were lifted, at least partially, when Charryce announced that she was pregnant.

ɞ

Five years after his death, Valerie could not shake her grief over the loss of Lincoln, still asking 'what-ifs', wondering if it was better that he died rather than be crippled. Her trauma was causing disquiet among the others: 'No one will let me talk about it,' she complained. 'This sort of happening does make one think hard about the Afterlife and if we will ever see him again.'

And Lincoln's brother and sister weren't making it any easier. Jacie was now fourteen and attending Caulfield Grammar, following in his father's footsteps, but his reports were 'disgusting'. To make matters worse, his attitude was drawing comparisons with Jason Snr. One of his teachers, a Mr Wright, made reference to the fact that he'd taught both father and son, and that Jason Jnr was not shaping up. It was the situation Valerie had sought to avoid by sending her children to different schools, and she was now considering sending Jacie to a trade school.

Angeline too was being disruptive in class and Valerie could think of only one reason: 'I think they still have a chip on their shoulder as regards "Why aren't we living with our own parents?"'

She objected to the question and implied criticism. They were lucky to have her and Monty, rather than live with their step-mother—it would cause unhappiness for their father, and 'we are both their own blood once removed'.

She was 'obliged' to Hilke. At first Valerie had not wanted Jason to marry her; later she watched him refuse to let Hilke leave the country with her children, one of whom later died. Without Hilke, 'we would have been far behind with our grandchildren production program'. Even so, she was not looking forward to the next ten years of bringing up Jacie and Angeline: 'They're harder than the first lot.'

As much as Jason's children disappointed her, Valerie's attention was diverted by the birth of Charryce's baby, a boy named

Guy, in January 1976. It had been a difficult birth, not unlike her own experiences, but he was a healthy child, the image of his mother and 'going like a bomb'. The little family was about to move into the old Lea home in Lambert Road.

Gaela's marriage was struggling, however. Charl had admitted to several affairs, but he was begging to be allowed back. Gaela was not convinced.

31

AN INEVITABLE CRIM

Brett Lea would spend many of his young adult birthdays behind bars. He was in an army base holding cell on 5 July 1971 when he turned twenty-four; on a Queensland prison farm at twenty-six; behind the oppressive colonial walls of the old Maitland Gaol at twenty-nine; and inside the minimum-security Cessnock Correctional Centre when he was granted day leave to celebrate his thirtieth birthday with a girlfriend.

It may not have mattered to him. After all, the annual milestone was just a reminder of the day he was discarded by his mother and handed over to another woman, for whom he was just a number—the fifth child—to fill an obsession.

Even his Christian names—Bretton Carrick Grantham—were monikers cobbled together from a baby book. They collectively referred to a native of Brittany, a rocky Irish headland and the name for an old English homestead; their false grandiosity merely emphasised their hollow intent.

His real persona was the unpretentious Brett, and the sorry tale of his adult life to this point lay in a thick paper file held by the NSW Department of Corrective Services. It contained mostly formulaic and numbered reports, compiled for committees of prison bureaucrats and psychologists who were tasked with classifying prisoners and creating meaningful lives for them inside prison; the aim was to help them reform and find a new path in normal society.

Somewhere in that file was hope for the future. Hope, but not expectation, as the documents made clear. Experience and statistics told these committees that an overwhelming percentage of criminals would reoffend and be back inside within five years. Brett Lea would be no exception, although there seemed no shortage of optimism expressed about him in the reports.

Brett Lea wasn't a bad man, they seemed to conclude. Rather, he was a petty thief who had wandered into a life of crime as a result of circumstances and a lack of self-worth, as noted by a probation officer named Paul Winch in a 1975 report to a classification committee which read in part:

He is the fifth eldest in a family of seven children, three adopted, and was raised in an affluent environment, attending Caulfield Grammar School to intermediate standard. He now has no contact with his family and no desire to change that, believing he was never fully accepted by them or given the emotional support and affection as an adolescent that was enjoyed by the children who were not adopted.

Reference to his education would be made repeatedly over the years, as if it was surprising that a boy who attended the prestigious Caulfield Grammar in Melbourne could end up a burglar, drug dealer and occasional fraudster. Brett was bright compared to most of the prison inmates but he would have judged himself harshly in comparison to his older brother, whom he admired.

Brett was a sociable man, unassuming and wiry, with a pleasantly gravelly voice from years of smoking. He seemed to inspire a level of confidence in his abilities, even in his trustworthiness, as noted by a senior officer soon after Brett entered prison for an eighteen-month stretch for receiving stolen goods in September 1972.

> The prisoner is usefully employed as a second clerk in the Assistant Superintendent of Industries office. I respectfully request that consideration be given for his being classified for the position. He has only been here a few days but shows the ability and trust needed for employment in this office.

A poor employment history reflected Brett's struggles, beginning with the first years after he dropped out of school—*Father (1 year), self (2 years) confectionery shop plus factory*—he wrote on one assessment form to indicate he had worked for the family business for one year before striking out on his own.

Shelton had an intellect and literary passion that gave his life purpose and direction; similarly, Honey had the will, passion and moral compass that made the most of opportunities. But Brett was alone; without guidance and familial support, it was inevitable that the young man born to a 'Spanish' factory worker and with a fractured education would get into trouble.

C3

Brett was ping-ponging between courts. After serving his time at Holdsworthy Army base he was sent back to the Central Magistrates Court to be sentenced for the Radio Rentals scam, but he got lucky for a second time, avoiding jail and being put on a $200 good behaviour bond for over for a year.

He appeared before the newly appointed Chief Stipendiary Magistrate Murray Farquhar, whose links to organised crime would later destroy his reputation and lead to his own stint in jail. But Farquhar also had his good points, including a notion that criminals often had undiagnosed problems that should be taken into account. He often referred alcoholics and drug users to welfare agencies for help, and clearly felt that Brett Lea fell into the category of someone who needed leniency and assistance.

But Brett was not yet ready for change. The life of a small-time crim was still more appealing; the pockets of his favourite pale blue suit were usually full of cash, because his ill-gotten gains were so easy to fence.

It was still a game in many ways. Like Shelton, Brett received an adrenalin rush from his exploits, and from thumbing his nose at society and its judgment. The two brothers had occasionally done jobs together: they didn't always turn out all right, but in later years he would look back on these adventures with delight, as if they were still teenagers riding all night on the St Kilda dodgem cars.

One of his favourites was the night that he and Shelton tried to rob an office in the inner-Sydney suburb of Newtown during a Christmas party. Brett waited outside in an old car (unregistered, of course, so it couldn't be traced) while Shelton clambered up the side of the building and climbed through an open window. He'd reckoned he would only be an hour but he got careless. Instead of searching for the safe, he stumbled on a table full of food, intended for the party, which was under full swing in a nearby room.

Shelton couldn't resist and began making himself a turkey sandwich. But he was 'snookered' when the party guests decided it was time for dinner. He dived under the table and hid behind the tablecloth, munching his sandwich while the party went on around him. It would have been farcical if it hadn't been so serious.

Meanwhile, Brett sat outside in the car, increasingly convinced that his brother had fallen out of a window or been caught. It was several hours before Shelton finally reappeared; he became so bored under the table that he eventually just stood up and boldly walked out of the room in front of the increasingly drunken revellers.

Brett's freedom after the Radio Rentals let-off didn't last long. Seeking a fresh start, he strayed across the northern border into Queensland. Perhaps inevitably, he fell into old habits and began robbing houses on the Gold Coast, where he was caught and sentenced to another eighteen months. He did catch a break, however: he was allowed to serve the sentence on a fenceless prison farm.

The Numinbah Correctional Centre was paradise for prisoners—an 1800-acre reserve not far from the Queensland–New South Wales border, with no fences and few demands, other than to behave and serve your time. Nonetheless, after getting into some sort of dispute with other inmates over a gambling debt, Brett wandered off, escaping back over the border and high-tailing it to Sydney.

The lax, almost non-existent interstate cooperation between police at the time made it relatively easy for escapees like Brett to remain at large. He was low priority, non-violent and not worth the time and expense of a manhunt. The only one way someone like Brett could risk recapture was if he was arrested for a new crime, and inevitably he obliged in June 1975, on the eve of his twenty-eighth birthday. With an accomplice, he embarked on a series of robberies on homes in the streets of Sydney's inner west.

They weren't caught, but the robberies set up a series of unlikely events, if Brett's version is to be believed. He would later tell a parole officer that his personal life was in turmoil. One relationship had ended badly and he'd begun another with a woman who'd clearly had enough and told him that he had to make a choice between her and his brazen lifestyle of easy money and cheap suits. Brett chose the former. The June 'busts', as he called them, would be his last, he promised. It seemed that his life had turned a corner.

But his plans were upended when his former partner-in-crime decided to continue the spree on his own, 'got ambitious' and was caught. Under questioning, the man not only admitted to his solo crimes but also coughed to the robberies in June and, worse, named Brett as his accomplice.

The charge stuck and in late August Brett was sentenced to another five and a half years, the courts clearly tired of his recidivism. And when he got out, he was extradited back to Queensland to serve the rest of his sentence and any penalty for his escape:

'Seems to accept his fate (possible 1–3 years) with amazing ease and equanimity,' a prison psychologist reported to prison officials. 'Has big plans! Wants to start his own importing/ exporting business . . . This will be his last time in! Has his life sorted out now!! Left home at fifteen, and is unsure if he will seek assistance from his parents on release.'

Brett would make his own plea to the parole board for compassion:

I have tried to outline that I've changed my attitude towards the way of life I've been leading. I now see that I've been getting precisely nowhere all these years. When this is all over I want to marry the girl I love and who loves me, and settle down for good, raise a family and start a profitable business, so that we and our children can be happy and content for the rest of our lives. God has never changed me; it's only me that's doing the changing. I think it's about time I knew what life was all about and that this crime etc. gets me nowhere at all. I sincerely hope that my request to go to a gaol where I can receive visits from my future wife will be considered as we will be apart for some years, both here and in Queensland. It's extremely hard to keep a relationship strong with letters only.

Respectfully yours,

Bretton Lea

It would be Brett's last stint in jail. He would go straight when he got out.

32

THE FLYING BABY SHOW

Charlie and Honey called it *The Flying Baby Show*, a proposed talk show about birth and child-rearing attitudes in the counter-culture of the 1970s. After the blaze of publicity around Angel's birth, it seemed like a great idea as they assessed their future in the discomfort of a Fijian village.

They were supposed to be doing some early research for the show, seeking out examples of communal living and non-nuclear families, but Honey was also searching for the perfect maternal experience, even washing her clothes in the Sigatoka River along-side the local women while they pestered her about the joys of a washing machine. The irony—that the women she thought lived in paradise hankered after Western luxuries—was lost on her until many years later: 'Yes, it was idyllic but the realities of living in an environment where everyone had lice and there were cock-roaches in the refrigerator, meant that it wasn't going to last.'

If they wanted to pursue the idea of the baby show then they would have to go back to the city, and Australia was the wrong place, Charlie insisted. It was too small and too conservative; its newspapers would rather listen to stubborn old doctors than to new ideas. They needed to think bigger. California was the place to be—people there weren't afraid of new ideas and he could use his contacts to get some development money.

In early 1975, with four-year-old Kaja and her breastfed nine-month-old daughter, Angel, Honey followed Charlie to his land of promise. As in Australia, their arrival attracted plenty of media interest in what was dubbed 'baby's liberation'. It was also an opportunity for Charlie to break into the world of film and television as a creator, like D.A. Pennebaker.

The couple had little money. But somehow, in the hippy culture of Los Angeles, they were able to make ends meet, renting part of a palatial house in the Hollywood Hills, a faux castle dubbed Pickfair because it was built by screen legend Douglas Fairbanks Snr in the 1920s as a weekend retreat for him and his wife, Mary Pickford.

It was a bizarre existence in a wealthy neighbourhood surrounded by some of the most successful musicians of the era. Joni Mitchell lived opposite in a house once owned by escapologist Harry Houdini; here Crosby, Stills and Nash first sang together as a trio. Carole King had a house in Wonderland Avenue at the top of the hill; Jim Morrison lived nearby, as did Frank Zappa, Neil Young and members of the Eagles.

But money was tight and Honey wrote to Valerie and Monty asking for help. Valerie recorded her response in her diary, revealing Charlie's mother had also approached her about giving the couple some financial help. Her response was bitter: 'I've been sending money to Honey in Los Angeles, $200 so far because she and Charlie and the two children are in dire straits again. She could have married ANYBODY instead of committing herself to Charlie!!'

But there was hope on the horizon, according to a letter from Honey, who had written to thank her for the money: 'Her last letter says she thinks they are on their way to a bright future, at last, with the Flying Baby Show re natural home birthing so I do hope that comes to pass. She now has Kaja and Angel (same name as our Angeline)—four and one year. They are bringing the children up "permissive" which unfortunately precludes them from ever being invited back anywhere although she told me they were all fine.'

Valerie was wishing them well, but only offering minimal support—a few hundred dollars—while drawing a line in the sand between Honey's daughter Angel and *our Angeline*. Honey was in a different family now.

Charlie now called himself Chuck, the American version of his name, but, like his efforts, the change was to no avail. His contacts were either uninterested or unable to find the development money needed to progress *The Flying Baby Show* past discussions and meetings.

In the end it was a contact of Honey's who provided financial support. Michael 'Chalky' White was a famous London producer, whose theatre credits included *The Rocky Horror Show* and *Joseph and the Amazing Technicolor Dreamcoat* and whose film successes included *Monty Python's Holy Grail*. He had recently produced the film version of *Rocky Horror*, which would become a cult classic.

White partied hard and loved taking a gamble on ideas, losing as much as winning. He was also the boyfriend of Lyndall Hobbs, Geoffrey Hales's half-sister and a close friend of Honey's, and was happy to invest $10,000 in *The Flying Baby Show* project.

Charles and Honey had already moved on from the Laurel Canyon mansion. They decided to rent a beach house at Del Mar, just north of San Diego, where they could write and finalise their project while providing a base for their family.

But rather than inspire energy and success, their stay there eventually highlighted their problems. As Honey recalls:

> I realised at this point that the man I looked up to and thought was a genius wasn't really up to it. As with many Hollywood projects, *The Flying Baby Show* came to nothing. I would write up treatments for other films and then he would take them off to try and sell the ideas to get development money. But nothing ever happened.

ः

For once Valerie was right. Chuck Vodicka/Bell was a disappointment. Honey was studiously ignoring his womanising and had her head stuck in the sand over money, never questioning where it came from or how it was spent. And he took full advantage of the situation: 'We had two children, no home and no money. I was totally dependent on him. He used to call me the ostrich because I didn't want to see the reality of our position, but at some point I told him that I'd had enough and I wanted to be involved in the money.'

As White's development money slipped away and their work on the show stalled and was finally abandoned, Honey found a new way to prop up the family. She became a baker.

They had occasionally dined at a beachfront restaurant that did not serve dessert. One night she offered to bake a carrot cake. It was such a resounding success that the restaurant asked for more. She opened a home-based bakery business, trading as the Cadillac Carrot Cake Company and supplying restaurants in the area. Business boomed and her baking profits enabled them to rent a less salubrious house further north at Solana Beach, another small coastal city on the coastline between LA and San Diego.

When she looks back at this period, Honey regards it as one of the happiest times of her life. The bakery was in full swing; she rode the kids to school on her bike; there was a vegetable garden, a dog and cats. There was also a constant stream of visitors, who came from LA and Australia to stay and surf.

However, Chuck still believed in open marriage and indulged in other women, often disappearing for long periods without offering an explanation. There was little Honey could do about it. It was clear that their dreams of a television show were gone, as was Chuck. With no support—and sick and tired of baking carrot cakes—she had to close the bakery.

Despite a lack of money and a meandering partner, life was engaging. Honey was poor—cleaning nearby homes for a few dollars and relying on the vegetable patch for much of their food—but she embraced poverty as part of the experience. The house was rundown, but it was on the beachfront, with a huge fireplace and a seemingly never-ending trail of visiting friends. Then Charryce showed up.

In she came, wearing Valerie's best jewellery. I recognised it—a big round diamond ring that we used to talk about when we were kids. I was told that the family jewellery had been divided, and it was all going to Gaela and Charryce. It was as if I didn't exist. Wasn't I part of this family? Here I am struggling, and she's flaunting Valerie's diamonds.

I remember that she went out and bought shoes for the kids, and when she left I found $500 on the table, so I went out and bought a car so I could drive the kids to school. I was thrilled. It was the first time I had owned a car. It wasn't about money. It was about family.

I was later told that the Leas were worried about me and any claim I might have. There had been $10,000 put away for me. Five hundred must have seemed pretty cheap.

33

A CONCEPT OF BELONGING

Of all her worries, complaints and misgivings, Valerie's greatest fear was accidental death. Over the years she had delivered endless lectures around the dinner table about traffic accidents, and cut out dozens of newspaper articles about the consequences of children playing near dangerous things like boiling water and fire. And she insisted on them wearing clean underwear, just in case they ended up in an accident as she had done in 1951, in the gutter with her dress over her head.

There had been other near misses. Jason had walked away unscathed in 1958 when a car driven by an older friend rolled over near Anglesea, and she and Monty had been involved in a second accident in 1964 when their Citroen was hit by a stolen car. Then there was poor little Lincoln crushed by the gate at Chapel Street, a tragedy she kept reliving as if there was something that she had missed.

Then, on 30 November 1978, Valerie's world almost fell apart again. Monty had left home just after 1 pm, later than usual, and was driving along the four-lane Dandenong Road, heading to one of his warehouses. The afternoon traffic was heavy. He was in the second lane, as he would remember, wary of two big trucks coming towards him in the third and fourth lanes to his right.

Suddenly, he sensed he was being pushed towards them. It felt as if the car was on a skid but, glancing back, he realised that the car immediately behind him had moved into the empty left-hand first lane but, in doing so, had made contact with Monty's little Holden Gemini and pushed it across in front of a huge Kenworth truck in the third lane.

With no time to react, the truck driver smashed into the right-hand side of Monty's car. The momentum flipped it, tossing it onto the truck's hood and off again before pushing the car across into the fourth lane where another huge truck smashed into the front of it.

Monty, his seatbelt unbuckled, was hurled backwards by the impact, somehow slipping through the narrow gap between the two bucket seats before the roof itself was crushed. He finished up in the back of the car.

Everything came to a standstill; the trucks were now stopped in front of the crumpled Gemini. A crowd quickly gathered. Monty could hear a voice calling to him: 'Are you all right in there?'

Monty felt okay, but he could smell the fumes of leaking petrol and was worried about a fire: 'Get the door open. Get me out quick!' he called. Somebody managed to wrench open one of the back doors and Monty eased himself out backwards.

The Gemini was a complete write-off. The front windscreen had shattered and there was glass throughout the car and in his scalp; Monty sat watching as dozens of people scurried around collecting a pile of paperwork strewn across Dandenong Road.

Someone called an ambulance and a tow truck. They arrived five minutes later and the police not long afterwards. But it was too late; the driver responsible for the crash had vanished. Anyway, all that mattered was that he was alive; a couple of scratches on his hands and head were the only visible signs of the accident that could easily have killed him.

The truck drivers had both stayed to help, anxious to ensure Monty was okay. The Kenworth driver said he had seen enough to at least slow down before he hit Monty's car, otherwise the impact would have been much worse.

A nearby resident had heard the crash and rushed out to see if she could help. She now bundled Monty into her home and plied him with cups of tea, the shock of the accident evident as his hand shook uncontrollably while signing the form for the tow-truck driver to take away his ruined car.

'It was a miracle that anyone could walk away from that crash,' the woman told Valerie when she telephoned the next day to thank her. 'His time had not come.'

Valerie was exhausted, but deliriously happy: 'It's 7 pm and he is still sorting out all his tumbled papers, calm as can be and it's ME who had to take a relaxation tablet as my hands were trembling so. The Lord is certainly looking after him for me. The first two accidents, in 1951 and 1964, were caused by fellows in stolen cars, thirteen years apart, now this one is fourteen years later. Thankfully, this time he was on his own.'

It would not be her last scare.

Loma Carey walked out on Shelton in 1975 after they'd been together almost four years. It was alcohol, she would later say; she could no longer tolerate his binges and wanderings. Sometimes he would be gone for weeks, interstate on occasion, and then reappear as if nothing had happened, unable to understand her anger.

The couple had lived in Sydney in the early seventies, where Shelton and Brett had reunited, returning to their old, bad ways of doing the occasional burglary. But the excitement was finally starting to wear thin for Shelton, as he told Michael Sharkey many years later, describing the moment he decided to retire.

I was eighteen storeys up, on the outside of a building in Edgecliff, and I'd just done this bloke for his lot. They were asleep, he was snoring and she was mumbling and moaning. I was tickling their tank right in front of them; I wasn't disturbing the molecules of the air, and as I left, on the eighteenth floor on the outside, about to make a rapid descent, I saw the sun rise, and I was stuck there, like a butterfly, watching the absolute beauty. And the jewels in my pocket faded. You know how you recognise beauty? It has integrity. You get rocked to your heels. Poetry allows you to capture the light, density. You get *all* that.

There was another contributing factor. Loma was pregnant, and in December 1971 Shelton's third child, Destiny, was born. Her birth brought home to him the fact that he was missing Chaos and Zero, so he and Loma moved back to Melbourne where he opened a bookshop in Gertrude Street, Fitzroy.

It was an unashamedly disorganised place. Shelton held court there, brewing tea in an urn under a lean-to out the back for anyone who dropped in for a chat—from book lovers and friends to the homeless and the drunks, even the local street prostitutes who, between clients, came in and sat on an old couch. This prompted a raid by the vice squad who thought, wrongly, that Shelton was running girls.

Of course there were women—groupies who found him magnetic and drove Loma mad as she fended off phone calls and put up with all-night parties. By the end of 1975 she'd had enough and headed back to Sydney with Destiny, now aged four. It would be eight years before Shelton saw his daughter again.

During their years together, Shelton had not said a single word to her about his childhood and background. It was only when Loma finally let him back into her life, so he could see their twelve-year-old daughter, that Shelton told her about the Leas. Suddenly she understood, as she later told Diana Georgeff: 'I loved him. He was a special person and, without that damage, he was the most extraordinary human. He tried and wanted the family; but we got in the way of the creative drive and he'd go and get blind.'

Shelton had his pick of the adoring women who hung around him, and he exploited their attention. Among them was a

24-year-old named Barbara Robertson, who had been two years behind Honey at St Catherine's. History would repeat itself as Shelton swept Barbara off her feet with a heady mix of romantic words, jazz and booze.

Barbara soon resigned from her job as a high school teacher to become his muse. They travelled first to Sydney and then to Queensland before returning to Melbourne, where Shelton was hospitalised with a ruptured oesophagus caused by vomiting from alcoholism.

On Barrett Reid's orders, Barbara dragged Shelton out of Melbourne so he could dry out. They walked most of the Ninety Mile Beach, from Port Albert to Lakes Entrance, then hitchhiked their way up the east coast to Sydney. Along the way, Shelton worked on a book called *Palatine Madonna*, based on a Sydney hooker he once knew. And Barbara fell pregnant.

Shelton's response—he couldn't support the child financially but he could offer it his love and emotional support—seemed brutal, but Barbara accepted it. In fact, she wanted to avoid a traditional marriage, as she wrote in a personal diary entry she later showed to Diana Georgeff. It read, in part:

> The concept of 'belonging' was brought into our relationship by Shelton. He expressed a need to belong to someone. Although he is ideologically opposed to the concept of possessing someone, he is not emotionally opposed to it. For him to belong wholly to me, I have to belong wholly to him. I find these emotions frightening.

ᘒ

When Barbara gave birth to a boy, Danay, on 2 January 1979, she and Shelton were living upstairs in a house in Elgin Street, Carlton. The Gertrude Street bookshop had gone and they were using their ground floor as a store, selling second-hand books and clothes.

It was a meagre existence, but that didn't stop Shelton's roaming; he often found a way to travel to festivals interstate. He once wrote to Barbara from the Adelaide Writers' Festival, triumphant that he'd performed twenty readings and been hailed as a genius, although he'd made no money—'I'm penniless but have arranged a fare back'.

In another letter, addressed 'Dearest Barbara', he declared his love but defended his lifestyle.

> Reality, my girl, is what you make of it. The source of every dream has its basis in reality. It is a thing I learned in jail. Time is malleable. How do you determine the difference between objective and subjective time? By using a clock? Bullshit. Time is what you make of it. So too is your sense of reality what you make of it. Look, the process by which I continue to live is one of magic. I am a story teller and as such have a deep-rooted need to embellish 'reality'. To live within a dream is the most exciting thing we can do, because not only do we live within the confines of a given landscape, but we can help ourselves to create our own landscape. The internal one.

It was inevitable, Barbara knew, that the relationship would not last and by the beginning of 1980, around Danay's first birthday, she had moved out. She would eventually move to Papunya, near

Alice Springs, to teach Aboriginal children, returning only when Danay was old enough to attend secondary school.

In a little over a decade Shelton had fathered four children with three women, a trait that annoyed Brett: 'Shelton just persists in having babies with women and then leaving them,' he told Diana Georgeff. 'Sometimes he stays a while, but he leaves in the end. Never marries one. He's just looking for the next woman. There's never a right woman.'

Diana disagrees. Shelton did not easily fall into new relationships and was conflicted about his inability to settle down, she said. When she pressed him about his behaviour, Shelton had first tried to deflect the question before becoming serious: 'You know the answer,' he told her. 'I don't trust women. Women have never given me any reason to trust them.'

34

DEAR OLD SAUSAGE

At 7.20 pm on 30 October 1980, a fire broke out in the packing materials store of the Darrell Lea factory complex in Kogarah. The first fire engine responded within thirty minutes but it was too late.

More than sixty firemen from twelve brigades would fight the firestorm that spread through the factory, fed by acres of cardboard packaging. The flames leapt twenty metres into the air, lighting up the Botany Bay foreshore in a hail of sparks and acrid smoke.

The fire would burn for three days and destroy 80 per cent of the complex and manufacturing plant. In its aftermath, the buckled giant vats and twisted steel girders were evidence of the intense heat generated by the fire. The melted light switch that had started the fire later hung on a plaque in the new boardroom, alongside the clock that stopped when hell broke out.

For the family members who watched the catastrophe

unfold, it was devastating. Harris Lea stood to one side with tears streaming down his face. At that moment it seemed that everything his family had created over more than 50 years had been destroyed, the business wiped out in a moment: 'My life, my whole life. Gone!' the newspaper reporters heard him cry.

The operation was in ruins. Plans for opening eight new stores were now abandoned. One-third of the staff was retrenched and most of the others ordered to take leave while temporary production plans were formulated.

Comprehensive insurance would ultimately build a new factory, but in the meantime Darrell Lea shares plummeted and the dividends due to be announced at the annual general meeting a few days later were slashed. If it hadn't been for some of their competitors—like Nestlé and Life Savers, who provided factory space, and Red Tulip, who agreed to manufacture extra product until the factory could be repaired—the company might have collapsed.

But by Christmas they had opened two kitchens at the back of the burnt-out shell. Although reduced to a production rump, they were making limited lines such as barley sugar, butterscotch, caramel and Bulgarian rock. It was as if the company had regressed to the home-spun cooking of the 1920s, when Harry Levy began selling confectionery from his fruit and vegetable shop on Manly's Corso one winter.

൭

Valerie watched from Melbourne, but wrote nothing in her diary about the fire and its impact. Not a word.

It was as if it had never happened.

Her first entry after the event detailed how she had sold one of the Atlantic Steel Corporation's houses in St Kilda at a tidy profit while buying three adjoining maisonettes in Caulfield, which she had plans to renovate and rent for a combined income of $300 per week.

The entry almost reads as if she was trying to convince herself of the wisdom of these strategic decisions, as if she, and she alone, was keeping the family afloat and Mungah's dreams alive. Her silence on the Kogarah blaze was deafening.

Behind the scenes, family relations were disintegrating. The brothers and their wives, once so close, were now at odds over business strategy and, worse, sniping over personal mistakes. Even the next generation was involved. When regret about the decision to float the company surfaced, Jason, who was soon to be chief executive, reminded his uncle Maurice: 'You, the controlling shareholder, Godfather, must have given your approval or we would not have gone public.'

And Valerie was angry that her husband had been crushed and belittled by the Sydney management. Harris, in particular, constantly reminded his brother of his business mistakes— his personal losses, using company funds as well as misusing Mungah's money, now totalled an astonishing $1.7 million. As a consequence, Valerie and Monty had been stripped of any income from their shares in the parent company since 1976.

It was a bitter pill to swallow, particularly as their younger brother Darrell, who had resigned in 1972 after suffering a brain disease, had been allowed to continue spending money, including buying a luxury townhouse, which he rented out while he lived in Honolulu.

In her diary Valerie wrote:

Nobody could ever imagine the amount of money he must have spent. Quite colossal and also quite stupid and unnecessary. Nobody knows what he is living on or where he gets his money. I still feel so bitter that we are the only ones to produce any heirs, real blood heirs, to the business, and yet no help now for over four years, and none forthcoming. It's always 'Look how much money we've put into Monty's losses'. Monty and I are bleeding ASC [Atlantic Steel Corporation] with every single facet of our living costs. Absolutely everything; rents, gas, electricity, food, fees, doctors' bills.

The last point was particularly concerning. Monty had been in and out of hospital all year, struggling with heart palpitations and mini-strokes, and recovering from several operations. Two had been in late 1979—the first to remove a papilloma on his bladder, and the second his prostate—and yet again in mid-1980, when another growth was detected. At various times he had caught pneumonia, suffered pleurisy, and had to have his blood thinned to remove a dangerous clot in his leg. He now wore stockings for his varicose veins.

'My poor dear old sausage. He's had a rough trot,' Valerie wrote in deliberate understatement. But watching him struggle made her cry.

Whatever the mistakes he had made, Monty was the man she had chosen 50 years before to share her life, and she loved him as if he were still the confident twenty-year-old she met in 1930. Probably more: 'It's hard to believe that all those years have gone by. We've been married almost forty-five years and it doesn't seem like three weeks. I am frightened to the very marrow in case I lose him. I honestly couldn't face the vicissitudes of life without him.'

Valerie had her own health problems. Her back was a constant issue; her bones were thinning; she had a heart scare; and she had two hernias under her ribs caused by straining after a haemorrhoid operation. The frustrations were still there, but she was becoming more sanguine about life: 'I give up. I'm stuck and I'll have to put up with myself as I am.'

Most seriously, Valerie was going blind. She'd first noticed a problem in 1972, before they moved from the old factory back to Lambert Road, when she watched a man walk towards her one day and then suddenly saw two of them.

It was now much worse. Her retinal cells were dying, slowly but inevitably. A series of specialists could do little but hope the decline would be slow: 'It's just as though I'm looking through a glass with grey splotches all over it', she wrote, adding that, now limited to a narrowing band of vision, she could only read and write slowly.

☙

Did I mention that Jason and Biddy went on a three-month world tour?

As if needing to balance her concerns about Monty's health, her complaints about the company and her money worries, Valerie turned to her children, whose success she measured in terms of property assets, travel, marriage and children. It was hardly surprising that she judged success in these terms, and that she was unable to appreciate Shelton's creativity, Honey's entrepreneurial zest and Brett's earthy survival skills.

Jason and Biddy had been in the United States, checking out a deal to take on a chain of shops. They had turned the business trip into a holiday across Europe and Asia, and left their two children—Carissa, aged five, and Nathan, three—with relatives in New Zealand. In a few days they were due home, to settle back into their house in Vaucluse with its dramatic harbour views across Shark and Clark islands to the Opera House and the Harbour Bridge. The recently knighted businessman Sir Peter Abeles was a neighbour, Valerie added.

Charryce and David were also on a buying spree. Valerie's once maligned son-in-law had found his feet in the property business, his latest success being the construction of a house on a block of land in St Kilda. The project had cost him $33,000, including paying himself a wage, and he'd sold it for $83,000. They had furnished another in Toorak, bought a renovation job in Richmond and were considering four flats in Abbotsford: 'He has certainly made a SUCCESS of his life,' his mother-in-law noted.

Charryce's son, Guy, was now four years old. It was time for another grandchild, Valerie hoped. Charryce had been in the Darrell Lea shop in Elizabeth Street, where a long-time employee, a Mrs McGrath, had recognised her: 'Your mother was the most wonderful woman,' Mrs McGrath told her. 'A lot of the girls were frightened of her, but I liked her and we got on well.'

'That was nice to hear', Valerie noted, not making it clear whether she was happy that one person remembered her fondly or that she scared the hell out of a dozen others.

And Lael, aged 32, was finally married, to a woman named Joy Barkley. Valerie couldn't have picked a better match herself, she exclaimed. Joy came from a religious family that still said grace at the dinner table; she would not tolerate swearing and had even managed to trim his pot belly—just the type who would make a career out of being a good mother'.

Valerie hoped they would have four children, adding to the five grandchildren she already had: 'Monty and I had four,' she added, wiping Shelton, Brett and Honey and their children from the ledger.

Lael and Joy's wedding on 7 July 1979, was beautiful. It was at St John's in Toorak, where Lael had been christened and attended Sunday school, but Valerie forgot to check the address of the reception, an old house owned by the National Trust. She and Monty arrived late and missed the reception line. She was afraid that Joy's family, who had to greet the 120 guests by themselves, might have thought it was deliberate.

The newlyweds honeymooned in Queensland and moved into 26 Lambert Road, with a generous wedding gift of cash. But Lael was becoming frustrated with his role at Darrell Lea—he was still a window dresser while his older brother Jason, who had a harbourfront home and four children, was a senior manager and would be chairman of the company within four years.

Valerie could see that her two sons were very different: Jason had the confidence to override opposition, but gentle Lael was keenly aware of criticism. She believed her youngest son wanted out of the family business: 'Lael would like to go into business on his own . . . maybe a newsagent or a toy store in a country town. I am worried about it yet I don't know how to handle the situation.'

The brothers' differences would continue to fester, only to explode in unimaginable circumstances a decade later.

Valerie's joy was also dampened by Gaela's continuing marriage problems with Charl which, after a reconciliation, looked like it was on the rocks again. They had been living in Perth, having returned from South Africa, but now Gaela sought refuge back in Melbourne, at least temporarily while she decided if her marriage was worth another try. Valerie didn't think so.

A man whom Val had once declared the perfect son-in-law had turned out, in her eyes, to be a philandering gold digger who wanted his wife to be a servant to his needs. The fact that Gaela was his third wife only confirmed Valerie's opinion although, perhaps remembering her own pursuit of Monty, she lauded his gall: 'I cannot blame him for making such a quick effort to marry Gaela after being told her father was a millionaire and her mother has a stack of houses. Any man would have done the same and would have been stupid not to.'

Charl wanted Gaela back, calling her twice a day, and Valerie was convinced that her oldest daughter would eventually weaken: 'I think she will give in and go back for the fifth time. Well, it's her life, and she'll muck it up again.'

But Gaela would prove her wrong. She wanted to be by herself with an easy job and a little flat. A husband was not required.

By this time Gaela was 36 years old and Valerie had all but given up hope that her oldest daughter might deliver her more grandchildren.

If she was frustrated by Gaela's situation, at least Valerie was delighted that Hilke had 'not caused trouble' since returning from London with her new husband. Despite Val's fears, Jacie and Angeline had remained living with her and Monty. Hilke visited them occasionally, and the two families had even socialised together on special occasions such as birthdays and Christmas; the wounds of her divorce and Jason's dismissal a decade before were now apparently forgiven.

Angeline, now sixteen, had a twenty-year-old boyfriend, a trainee fireman inspector named James, a 'nice boy' whom Valerie was determined to keep from ravishing her grand-daughter. But any concerns about Angeline's moral wellbeing were put into perspective in March 1980, when she and James were involved in a car accident. They were on their way home after a disco when a car suddenly appeared out of a side road. James could not avoid the collision—his car spun out of control and crossed to the other side of the road, where he hit an oncoming car.

James escaped serious injury, suffering a stiff neck, but Angeline, who had refused to wear a seatbelt, was thrown from the spinning car and rushed to hospital with concussion and badly lacerated legs. The scars would take a year to fade.

For Valerie the accident was more evidence of the family's misfortune, particularly after Monty had escaped serious injury two years before. And there were the general health problems. Charryce had a recurring sciatic nerve problem, Gaela had bald patches, Lael a bad back and Jason's neck was constantly sore. To add to Valerie's misery, the world seemed a dangerous place and she felt sorry for future generations, 'especially our own descendants', with the risk of 'the bomb, ecology, communism and the attitude of the young to work'.

These were strange sentiments from a woman who had lived through two world wars and an economic depression.

35

THE DRIFTER AND THE
CAREER WOMAN

The night she met Brett Lea, Moana Wilson was not interested in finding a husband. It was 1985 and she was enjoying a drink with her best friend, Wendy, at a pub near her home in the inner Sydney suburb of Paddington.

The two women worked together as computer operators at nearby St Vincent's Hospital and enjoyed the routine of Friday nights at the Rose & Crown, where they could sit and chat without being pestered. They felt safe among friendly faces. Old Jack at the bar had bought them a beer, as usual, and they had just settled into their seats when a bloke Moana hadn't seen before waltzed up and announced himself.

'Hi, I'm Brett and I drink Fosters.'

It was clearly a line he'd used before, but she was still amused, particularly by his larrikin grin. However, her mood changed quickly when he asked if she'd been on holidays recently.

'No, why?' she asked.

'Well, I haven't seen you in the mornings lately.'

Moana's smile dropped. She had always walked to work along the same road until recently, when she realised that someone was watching her through a curtained window as she walked past. It had happened a few days in a row, so she had changed her route. She now discovered that the man standing in front of her had been her mystery observer.

'I was taken aback at how forward he was. I wasn't used to it,' she later recalled. 'Wendy and I finished our drinks and left the pub.'

Raised in a conservative Mormon family, Moana had spent her early years on a New Zealand sheep station. Although no longer religious, she was quite shy. The pub wasn't really the place where she expected—or wanted—to meet someone with whom she would form a relationship, hence her routine with Wendy.

She had grown up with a map of Australia on her wall and had moved to Sydney after finishing high school. She then spent two years working as a machinist, sewing belts in a factory. It had been monotonous work, but necessary financially, she decided, so she could study commerce and then computer science, a passion ignited by her father.

It was 1976 and Dad had been reading a newspaper article about computers going into the workplace. It was the future, he told me, thinking I might be interested in a career. It was very empowering. I became very goal-oriented and keen to learn and move through the ranks, from data entry to network systems and computer engineering. I was not looking for a husband.

It would be two years before she saw Brett again, this time at a wedding where his easy-going nature shone through his, on this occasion, more constrained behaviour. The age difference of fourteen years didn't seem to matter. He was a charmer, a knockabout bloke who loved a beer and Chinese food. Most importantly, he made her laugh.

In 1990 the drifter and the career woman were married at the registry office in Chinatown in front of fourteen people—mostly Moana's relatives but none of Brett's.

Likewise, the party of 80 or so people back at 'The Nash' Hotel in Paddington, where Brett knew the manager and cadged the back room for nix, was full of friends, but no one from the Lea family until Jason popped his head in for ten minutes and then left. If Brett invited or even told Valerie and Monty, they chose not to attend. Honey was still living in Los Angeles and Shelton had been disinvited because his son Zero, now nineteen, who been staying with the bridal couple a few weeks before, had stolen the wedding ring.

Brett was a boisterous rogue, a rowdy rascal with a beloved dog named Manzil (after the iconic rock venue, Manzil Room, in Kings Cross). He could be temperamental but he was warm, ever friendly and had a heart to match. He was Moana's opposite in so many ways—a boy from a broken home with a broken education and no plan in life, other than to live it as best he could.

Brett ran a handyman service around Paddington; he called

it Brett Lea Services, or BLS when he was feeling cocky. Actually, he was more of a fixer than a tradesman, a young Arthur Daley who could be found in one of three pubs in the area—the Grand National, the London or the Imperial. His 'office hours' fell between four and six o'clock most evenings, often to meet friends, who might know someone who needed something procured as much as something done.

Brett carried the latest copy of the *Trading Post* newspaper in his toolbox in case someone wanted to buy something he might be able to source, taking a modest success fee for his trouble. Brett never had designs on a big payoff—just enough to pay the rent, buy groceries and/or his next beer.

He was also quick to lend a hand with odd jobs or give advice to those with addiction problems, using his own experiences to discourage others from using hard drugs. He occasionally blurred the line between friendship and business, always to his own detriment.

One incident stuck in Moana's mind as an example of Brett's easy-going attitude. They were at the London Hotel one afternoon when a young bloke they'd never seen before walked up and asked if Brett knew anyone who could give him a hand carrying a cabinet. He was new to the area and was moving into a nearby house. The two men shook hands, then Brett patted the man on the back and followed him out the door.

He was gone for more than an hour, moving not only the cabinet but the rest of the furniture into the house: 'I wasn't surprised, because this was how Brett behaved,' Moana recalls. 'He said he didn't accept payment for that job but instead told the guy if he was looking for a car, boat, furniture or a handyman to give him a call.'

Moana was the second eldest of eight children in a close-knit family, a mother figure among her younger siblings in a family of working parents. While Brett struggled to find consistent work, she was diligently working her way up through computer systems and upgrades in male-dominated company structures to become a computer analyst.

Her feelings about having children were mixed:

I adored children, but had no intention of having my own. I felt I had raised children most of my childhood into teen years and didn't want to continue to do the same in my young adult years. I did keep my options open, that if I met the right person and the time was right I'd consider having children. One day Brett would want children; the next day he would change his mind. We agreed that if he gained meaningful employment and spent more time at home, we could discuss having children.

They moved around, renting in Paddington and Rose Bay, minding a friend's house in Coogee and once spending three months travelling around Australia in a four-wheel drive. Eventually they settled in the southern suburb of Pagewood, out near the airport, although Paddington remained Brett's haunt.

Moana sensed an untapped intelligence behind Brett's tough exterior, a front to hide his disappointments and fears. She hoped she could provide him with the security he had clearly missed, but she knew deep down that Brett would never be fully grounded.

Moana tried to reach past the facade to understand the real Brett, but his feelings remained largely hidden and he acknowledged only that he, Shelton and Honey were treated differently by the Leas, and that he wondered occasionally if he and his natural mother, whoever she was, had ever unknowingly crossed paths. Despite his reluctance to discuss his feelings, Brett revealed that he felt responsible for Honey, that she needed 'protecting' from the Lea family.

There were snatches of conversation about the Leas over the years, but the only time he sat down and discussed his childhood was when Jason gave him a copy of the family video, as sanitised by Valerie. He and Moana watched it together, replaying it several times. At one point she asked him why he always wore dull-coloured clothing. Brett didn't move, saying: 'It was to distinguish the adopted children from the real Leas.'

Moana couldn't help but like Shelton. He'd come to visit occasionally, when in Sydney for readings: 'A captivating man. I enjoyed listening to him,' she said of her then brother-in-law. 'He and Brett were different—they looked different and acted different, but they were brothers.'

The only 'real Lea' sibling that Brett seemed to like was Lael. When she and Brett stopped in Melbourne during their round-Australia trip, he had insisted on Moana meeting Lael and his wife, Joy. They had a pleasant lunch, during which Brett and Lael reminisced about childhood mischief, but Lael also seemed to concede that the orphans had been regarded as second class. Joy, in particular, was unhappy about the way Brett, Shelton and Honey had been treated as children.

During this stay in Melbourne, Brett went back to 22 Lambert

Road. He hadn't seen Valerie and Monty for several years, and the last time he'd visited them—a crippled man and a virtually blind woman, living in a small section of what was once a grand house—had been quite distressing. Whatever misgivings he had about his childhood, Brett felt sorry for the people he still regarded as his parents.

They were staying in the room where they used to punish me and Shelton. Downstairs, even though all the bedrooms were upstairs. It was a long, skinny room at the back part of the kitchen, with windows on one side. There were bunks at each end. There was rubbish piled up in the room, odds and ends. They had no TV or radio. No one was looking after them.

But this time it was Charryce who answered the Lambert Road door. She stopped when she recognised her brother, blocking him from entering: 'Charryce wouldn't let me in the door. She said, "Wait there and I'll get your phone number, and you can ring another time."'

Charryce remembers the meeting as well. Her brother had caught her off-guard, his arrival unannounced and just as she was about to leave: 'He probably thought I was shutting the door in his face. That was the last time I saw him.'

Brett left without waiting.

⅓

A year into their marriage Moana found out about Brett's criminal past. It was a Saturday morning and they were on their routine walk around Paddington Markets where Brett was always on the lookout for a bargain. At some point he turned to her and mentioned that he'd arranged to meet two men at the London Hotel. It wouldn't take long, he said, so she went along.

The men were sitting between a second entrance door and a window when Brett and Moana walked in. It was only 10.30 in the morning, so there was no one else around. Brett introduced her and they chatted for a few minutes before Brett wandered off with one of the men, leaving her with the other. They were only gone five minutes, but Moana sensed there was something amiss.

'How do you know each other?' she asked the man who had remained behind.

'We went to school with one another,' the man said with a half-smile.

He didn't look like he'd been to a posh Melbourne school, so she pressed him: 'Which school?'

The man grinned: 'The school of hard knocks.'

Moana was shocked and confused. Why hadn't Brett told her before they were married? It wouldn't have changed anything, but didn't she have the right to know? When she questioned him later, he brushed off her questions about what he'd done and where he had served time, admitting that there had been 'quite a few' and that he'd originally been convicted of vagrancy. He said he didn't like small spaces and being enclosed in tiny rooms; this was clearly a result of spending so much time in prison cells, but he would not be drawn further. It was in the past, and that's where it would remain.

Despite her compassion, Moana realised that after two years the marriage, or at least the love, was over. It wasn't the prison time or the lack of transparency, nor was it Brett's inability to settle down to a steady job. The problem for Moana was his inability to commit.

Despite being abandoned at the moment he most needed his parents, Brett remained nostalgic about the Lea family. Valerie was his mother because he had known no other. He was sad rather than angry, unable to see that his poor decisions in life had been in response to his treatment and not, as he had been told by Valerie, the other way around.

Brett was like his older brother—a free spirit with little sense of responsibility, often spending several nights a week socialising and then falling asleep on someone's couch. He was faithful, at least as far as Moana knew, but any joy she experienced in their relationship was quickly fraying.

His behaviour wasn't what I expected of a husband. There were too many nights away from home. But I continued in the marriage because I had a strong desire to care for him and provide a sense of stability. His troubled childhood played on my mind constantly and I wanted to give him a place to belong. So we stayed together for another eight years.

36

HE COULD MAKE A WEEKEND FEEL LIKE A YEAR

The loss of Barbara Robertson had unhinged Shelton. But rather than force a reassessment of his life, it only exacerbated his bouts of binge drinking, which were now worse than ever. His writing had suffered as a consequence, according to Barrett Reid, who had become the anchor point in his life. One night Barrett thought his friend was dead because he was so comatose, he wrote in his diary. 'When sober, Shelton was the most honest and loving of men, but drink made him maudlin and he hid behind the veil of booze, pretending it was necessary for the life of a poet—ugh'.

Barrett was now living permanently at Heide. He was also battling cancer and Shelly, as he called him, would become one of his closest carers. In a 1985 diary entry, Barrett pondered their friendship after Shelton had nursed him through a hellish night of chemotherapy-induced pain:

How I love Shelton. What a joy to have him here [at Heide]. Our love for each other is so familiar and unforced. What an odd, unexpected history, our friendship—could any two people be so dissimilar. What curious histories: crying against the cold stone, naked under the groundsheet in a storm, prisons, hospitals, drying out tasks, all leading to this—family I suppose. Family things, and joy.

Barrett and Heide had become Shelton's sanctuary, the friendship now close enough for Shelton to reveal his childhood with the Leas: 'Shelly would not complain about Valerie,' Barrett told Diana Georgeff. 'He would say there must have been something *wrong* with her. I inexorably said she was a prize bitch and of course he ran away! He stayed true to his essential self. He has a healthy soul.'

It was inevitable, though, that another woman would take Barbara's place, just as Barbara had replaced Loma Carey, who had replaced Mary Craig, who had replaced Wendy Liddle, not to mention the women in between.

Christine Webb met and fell in love with Shelton one night at the Albion Hotel, in North Melbourne. That was normal enough, then the next step wasn't. Shelton wanted to take her to Sydney, but she convinced him to escape the city life for a while and move into an abandoned hay shed on her parents' property outside Warragul in country Victoria.

The area was called Mountain View and, at first, it provided the respite Shelton needed to emerge from the alcoholic haze, to win government arts funding and to begin a new phase of writing that would produce two more books—*Poems from a Peach Melba Hat*, published in 1985, and *The Love Poems*, published in 1993.

Christine planted a herb garden and sketched, content to provide the peaceful foundation she thought Shelton needed. They built their country house with their own hands. It was a home, a garden, a place where Danay could visit. They held legendary parties, at which Christine played the piano, and they worked together on books of poetry. She illustrated the work.

Barrett watched the change, which he described as 'lurching toward maturity', and thought it was time that Shelton addressed the question of his identity. He knew Valerie had the answer and he thought that if Shelton went to her she would unlock the mystery. Instead she brutally dismissed him. It was a massive setback and Shelton reverted immediately to binge drinking and taking enough drugs to kill himself.

It was the trigger for his relationship with Christine to unravel; by 1988 it would peter out. Despite the hurt, Christine retains memories of a man she describes as 'an affirmation of life', as she told Diana Georgeff: 'He opened me up to whatever I wanted and taught me to tap the beautiful, worthwhile things. He gave me joy and confidence and he brought out every ounce of creativity in me. He showed me that life held something more, that life was worth singing about.'

CB

Leith Woodgate had heard about Shelton Lea before she met him.

His reputation as a hard-drinking and hard-loving rebel did not seem to be a natural fit with the well-established North Fitzroy

GP, who shared custody of her three children—aged eleven, thirteen and fifteen—with her ex-husband, another doctor. But it was danger that provided the intrigue.

The first time she sighted Shelton was at a pub, Lord Jim's, where she went one night in 1990 to listen to Frank Hardy read from his short story collection. Among the audience was a prowling Shelton Lea, although they did not speak to each other.

A few weeks later Leith was at the Lord Newry in Brunswick Street for a poetry reading with Shelton on the bill. She was talking to another friend after the performance when Shelton walked up and started a conversation, then handed her a copy of his latest book of poetry, *Poems from a Peach Melba Hat*, in which he had inscribed an invitation to go dancing.

She accepted, despite his reputation, as she recalls:

> I had heard about him as a troublesome poet. People cared about him, but he was a shambolic personality. I didn't know what I thought, but I agreed to meet him.
>
> As a doctor you have to live a constrained sort of life. I'd been married to a doctor and didn't want to go down that safe track again. I was attracted to people who were creative, who thought differently, which is exactly how Shelton presented. A male friend told me not to worry, that he'd probably get drunk and forget about it, but he didn't.

A week later they met in a local restaurant for a meal and, as promised, went dancing in a nearby Spanish club. 'The relationship just grew from there. I kept telling him it wouldn't work, but he was very persistent. He introduced me to a whole new world, a magical world where he could make a weekend feel like a year.'

It would be the most enduring, if largely conventional, relationship of Shelton's life. He was living with a woman who had not only a busy professional life but also three children and, more importantly, no desire to have any more. If the house ever felt crowded, he would remove himself and stay with Barrett Reid for a few days so Leith could have time with her children.

His role in the household was a constructive and thoughtful one, Leith says, looking back—not an overpowering, drop-in parent but an adult with enough authority to insist, for example, that the family eat together each night, in conversation around the dinner table, rather than in front of the television.

This was in stark contrast to the often difficult relationship with his own children, probably summed up by the second oldest, Zero, who would stay with them on occasion and told Leith: 'He said to me once, "I love Dad, I just don't like him." I think it showed the difficulty of their upbringing. He didn't see them growing up. He always loved them, but he wasn't there for long periods.'

There was another change in Shelton: he was no longer the angry and confused youth who used poetry to explain his world, but a maturing middle-aged man whose art now expressed his wonder and raw observations. There were still painful memories about his childhood, of course, but Leith listened to them as one might listen to a storyteller, rather than someone still seeking answers and justice: 'Shelton wasn't my patient. I didn't treat him or examine him; I lived with him and loved him. Obviously his past disturbed him. He got angry at times. The memories were ever-present, but it wasn't the dominant thing in his life. Once perhaps, but not in his forties.'

Together, Honey and Brett were the nearest thing Shelton had to family. They were related by survival, something more powerful than mere blood, and typified by the bond between Shelton and Brett, who were brothers not in looks, likes or personalities but in their shared life experience.

೮೩

Valerie and Monty were now living in a house beside the Kogarah factory and still going to work each day: 'I'd hate to be doing nothing,' Valerie retorted when Diana Georgeff expressed surprise and admiration.

Valerie had agreed to talk to Diana in 1994 at the urging of her son Jason, but she soon regretted the decision. Some memories were distant and difficult, or too painful to recall, her answers to questions about why she and Monty had wanted to adopt Shelton, Brett and Honey were brusque and defensive: 'We were looking for a big family. That's what we were looking for. I know we enjoyed them very much. We gave up all our friends and spent Saturdays taking them out.'

Diana asked her if it was it difficult to raise adopted children alongside her own.

'Well you get horses from horses and draught horse from draught horses,' she offered. 'We were placid people and our children are placid people. They [the adopted children] were just normal kids, and we just did the best we could for them.'

She didn't like thinking or talking about Shelton and his childhood: 'I'm old now. When I look back I see that you need to be very clever, a psychologist, to be able to bring up adopted children with your own. We just did the best we could for them.'

It would be a recurring answer during the twenty-minute conversation, as if she and Monty had taken in children as a good deed, at the request of authorities, rather than made a deliberate decision to use adopted children to artificially enlarge their own family—living, breathing playthings for the children of rich people.

Shelton's incarceration at Turana still haunted Valerie, and she remembered standing out in the middle of Lambert Road at night calling out his name when he ran away.

'He never came back,' she said sadly.

It upset her to be reminded of Shelton's troubles. The whole house had reverberated at night when he banged his head on the bed as a young child, and they had spent more money and time on him than any of the other children. Her best memories of him were of a child she regarded as brave, willing to take on improbable physical challenges, clever enough to second-guess the questions of doctors and, with his curly hair, the most beautiful of the children.

When strangers met all the children (whom she'd line up in a row), Valerie knew what the response would be: 'They'd turn around afterwards and say, "We like the one with curly hair; he's lovely, isn't he." That was before they got to know him, of course.'

But Shelton's poetry left her stumped. At one point she had been given some examples, which she still kept in a folder somewhere,

326

although the fact that he had published eight volumes of work seemed to make no impression on her. She gave up trying to read it: 'I just could not understand them.'

As she spoke, Valerie remembered more. Her voice grew in confidence as she recalled her decision to send the children to different schools—'teachers are human' and tend to compare family members. What was left unsaid was the comparison she feared: that her own children would be seen as less capable than those she adopted.

37

A DIARY ENDS

Valerie had a name for her approaching blindness. It was called scotoma, she declared in her diary, as if this eased the anxiety. At the age of almost 70, she had found a way to live with a bad back, but she knew that the loss of her eyesight would be a far more profound disability and that her diary was coming to an end after 40 years.

'The retinas are degenerating and it is progressing so fast that I will be lucky not to be quite blind this time next year,' she wrote in November 1981. 'Hope I'm wrong!'

A few months later Valerie handed over the pages of her diary to Jacie's girlfriend, whom she paid to type it so she could distribute it among family members. This was not a document to be locked away but to be read by others, so that even her most private and unfiltered thoughts, fears and regrets could be understood. And her children saw no reason why it should not be read more widely. Jason Snr gave Diana Georgeff a copy to use in her book. So did Lael's wife, Joy. Honey also has a copy of the document that, in her mind, confirms that she was judged and treated differently and abandoned when she was a vulnerable teenager.

Charryce and Gaela acknowledge that the diary shows the unfiltered nature of their mother's thoughts. But that's how she was: 'She didn't write very nice things about me,' says Gaela in reference to Valerie's comments about her oldest daughter's teenage weight problems.

Charryce is content to let her mother's words speak for themselves: 'She was a bit direct in certain instances. Is that terrible?'

The first few diary entries, in 1946, are mostly a collection of motherly anecdotes about her children, their measurements and their first attempts to communicate. But she had made no attempt to cull her political rants, threats of violence or what might be regarded as racism, nor toned down her frequent criticism of others, including her beloved Monty. She did not hide her personal misgivings, a vanity that often tipped into narcissism, her clear favouritism of Charryce and Jason, and her antipathy towards Shelton and Honey, in particular.

The diary entries emphasise the complexity of a woman driven by family and blood, who considered herself to be godly but chose to measure life and success with money. She was clever and inventive, open to creative ideas and business practices, and she embraced the evolution of medicine, yet she was also utterly rigid in her regurgitation of the beliefs of her less educated forebears. Most of all, she laid bare her story of motherhood—the admirable and the awful.

Familiar themes return as the diary approaches an end she may not have foreseen. She had sellotaped into the diary copies of some of the articles she'd used to warn her children of hidden dangers, believing that her lectures around the dinner table when they were young had made a difference to their lives. There were snippets lamenting the lot of mothers forever slaving to feed their families (even though she always employed a cook) and newspaper cartoons of the fifties and sixties making light of the troubles faced by large families, from their behaviour in public to keeping breakables out of their reach at home.

She worried about money and how they might never be able to afford to repay the company what they owed, and she tried to justify snatching Jason's children, insisting that Jacie and Angeline were happy to go along with the plan and had even asked, 'Can we call you Mummy?' By contrast, she made no mention of her adopted children or their progress as adults.

Most of all, she was distraught about Monty's deteriorating condition. The cancer had returned and his prostate had been removed, leaving him weak and lethargic: 'He is seventy-two now, and I'm still twenty-nine.'

But there was other news—Charryce was carrying twins. Valerie had known that her daughter was pregnant before she and her husband left on a European holiday, but she was sworn to secrecy until their return in time for Charryce to have the baby. Then she received a telephone call from David, who was in Germany: 'There are two of them,' he'd gushed.

'I am so THRILLED. I have been madly laughing uproariously to myself when I have been alone in the house,' she wrote on 24 May 1982, the day of her 47th anniversary. 'It has been most difficult talking to them on the phone and trying to answer sensibly because Monty has always been around.' It would be another month before Charryce gave her mother the all-clear to announce the news to the rest of the family, and begin making preparations for their return to Melbourne, and to Lambert Road.

Delighted as she was, Valerie couldn't help feeling envious of her daughter: 'I would have given my eye teeth for twins,' she wrote and wondered if her oldest, Jason, might have been the only surviving baby of triplets, given that she lost two huge blood clots early in her pregnancy back in 1941.

Valerie wrote her last entry on 22 September 1982.

That morning she and Monty had been overseeing the Darrell Lea stand at the Royal Melbourne Show where, ever the businesswoman, she had admonished the staff for handing out show bags that had already been prepared rather than encouraging customers to wait while the bags were made up in front of them. This marketing strategy kept a crowd in front of the stand for longer and attracted more people: 'It looks busier now,' Lael told her.

But her mind was firmly on the hospital where Charryce had given birth to twin boys, her sixth and seventh grandchildren: 'Monty and I are extremely lucky... and if [Lael's wife] Joy comes up to scratch we may glean a couple more,' she wrote, ignoring the existence of the six children of Shelton and Honey.

38

BROTHERS AND SONS

In 1987, Jason Durard Lea fulfilled his mother's wishes and became managing director of Darrell Lea Chocolates. For Valerie, it was vindication of her belief that family came first and that nothing was stronger than blood ties. It made sense that a Lea should run the firm and that Jason, the oldest of Harry's blood descendants, should lead the new generation.

Jason had always expected he would one day run the firm. It was obvious from the moment he joined, according to Brian Cook, the employee given the task of training him: 'He wanted to be the boss,' he told the ABC's *Dynasties* program in 2005. 'When we done ten batches he wanted twenty, because deep in his heart he knew that he was going to own that place. Jason is like his father—they've only ever wanted more and more for the factory. They're like alcoholics.'

Jason would head the company's operations and direction for

the next fifteen years before stepping down to join the speakers circuit and deliver speeches such as 'How Not To Stuff Up a Family Business', a title other members of the family would regard as ironic, given his turbulent ride and the later trajectory of the company.

More than anyone, Jason knew how the company worked. He had lived and breathed it since leaving home at the age of seventeen—often to the detriment of his five children and two wives. His marriage to Hilke had fallen apart; Jacie and Angeline had been mostly raised by their grandparents; and by the early 1990s he was divorced from Biddy, who was selling their harbourside mansion in Vaucluse.

These were the sacrifices that a driven man was prepared to make. Nonetheless, the company he cherished—apparently more than his wives and children—was at a crossroads and now faced challenges in trying to keep up with new technology, changes in the buying habits of consumers and increased pressure from multinationals. It also had to weather the worst economic environment since the 1930s.

An overwhelming number of Australians knew the name Darrell Lea but, according to the company's own research, less than five per cent regularly bought the company's products: 'People know we exist, they just don't know why we exist,' Jason told *The Age* newspaper in August 1992. 'Darrell Lea is a household name, but people don't know what we stand for.'

It seemed a remarkable statement about a company that had established its place in Australian corporate history. In its desire to become bigger, had Darrell Lea lost a generation of consumers?

Its share of the confectionery market was sinking under the pressure of multinationals such as Cadbury, which had sued Darrell Lea over the use of purple in their packaging. After a five-year stoush, the courts ruled in favour of Darrell Lea's argument that Cadbury did not own the colour, nor were customers being misled.

But the legal victory did not hide the act that the company was struggling and, just as the introduction of shopping malls had forced the company to make changes in the 1970s, so the pressure of multinationals meant it would have to evolve or it would perish, reduced to a happy childhood memory.

Jason conceded his strategy was ambitious, but he envisaged new product lines copying European-style confectionery, revamped stores and extensive advertising that revolved around its freshness and reliability: 'They can't do what we can do. They can't manufacture this afternoon, deliver to the shops tomorrow morning and sell the product that afternoon. It's a matter of sticking to a particular niche and excelling at that.'

It was a return to the 1930s marketing philosophy of Value and Freshness—to produce and sell quicker and cheaper than their opposition—but it was going to cost money and that meant overturning one of the family's rules about keeping debt levels to an absolute minimum. In the past they had usually only borrowed when short-term loans were needed to finance production peaks at Easter and Christmas.

The public float of the company in 1966 had been designed to open up the value of the company, but even then they had avoided the temptation to borrow big and diversify. The public shares had been bought back in the wake of the 1980 fire because they could not guarantee attractive returns for investors, so now the company was back in family hands.

'We always just stuck to the knitting,' Jason quipped in *The Age* interview. 'We are a manufacturing, warehousing, distributing and retailing company on very low margins. It's really a two-bob business.'

But all that was about to change.

ɔ

Like his older brother, Lael had been around the traps in the family firm, starting at the age of eighteen when he worked in the bowels of the Kogarah factory and helped with deliveries: 'I wasn't great scholastically, and I knew, deep down, that there was nothing else I wanted to do, or could do.'

In 1966 he had headed to Europe for a three-year stint, broadening his experience by working in other confectionery companies—a rite of passage, like Jason's during the failed Twisties venture. When he returned to Australia in 1969, Lael turned to the retailing arm of the operation, firstly in Sydney and then in Adelaide, before embarking on a ten-year slog as understudy to the Victorian state manager.

In 1983, at the age of 37, he took over the Victorian operation and, with Jason at the helm, began opening new stores across the state. According to the official family history, this expansion was successful, but behind the scenes there was growing disharmony as Jason's decision-making and management style became increasingly authoritarian. As Lael would recall: 'It would not be unusual to get a ten- or twelve-page letter from him after a visit that he had made, telling me everything from how you tie your shoelaces up to how you bank the money.'

There was an added complication when their Uncle Darrell died in 1990 and his quarter share in the company was divided among Harris and Maurice, who each received half of the shares. Monty got nothing, because of the company bailouts he had received over the years. He and Valerie were furious, but there was little they could do.

It meant that Harris and Maurice each had 37.5 per cent and Monty only 25 per cent. Lael was frank about the impact: 'It was his [Monty's] own bloody fault and it disadvantaged Jason and I, because we had less of the pie than anyone else.'

Around the same time Valerie decided to carve up Mungah's Bulwark Against Disaster. According to Lael, his mother had insisted that the property assets be distributed to Charryce and Gaela only, because Jason and Lael would get the lion's share of Monty's share of Darrell Lea when he died. Charryce was given four-fifths of the pot, because she had three children, while Gaela, childless and divorced, received only one-fifth.

Jason and Lael regarded this as evidence of their mother's favouritism towards Charryce. After all, their father was still very much alive and his share of the company had been diluted. The bond that drew them together—blood—was being tested by money: 'It caused a lot of angst within the family,' Lael remarked.

The relationship between the two brothers was becoming fraught for other reasons too. Jason was still behaving like the big brother of their childhood and did not like Lael questioning his decisions, particularly the increase in the number of shopfronts that now stretched across the continent to Perth: 'The only business model in Jason's time was to build the business by opening more shops, and that just increased the costs,' Lael recalled. 'I told him what I thought and he didn't like it.'

Lael believed it should be more strategic because, although more shops had given the company more exposure, the expansion had coincided with a huge increase in rents, and many of the shops were not even paying their way, let alone turning the required profit. Much of the machinery was also expensive and makeshift, bought second-hand from overseas and shipped to Sydney where it had to be re-engineered to fit the factory.

By the early 1990s the company was producing 80 tonnes of confectionery each week and servicing 411 stores, many of them agencies in regional towns. A new store was being opened every month and the transport bill had grown exponentially.

Also the new, re-engineered machinery was producing more chocolate than the company could sell in its shops, so they began making generic Easter eggs for other confectioners, but that required new and bigger warehousing facilities.

To make it all work, the company needed to double its market share. It was the biggest gamble the Leas had ever taken. As Lael recalls: 'Our problem was that we never had the volume and the turnover to be able to pay for some of those machines and the shops. The intention was there, but it was a vicious circle.'

છ

There is a photograph that Jason Lea Jnr treasures more than most. In it he holds centre stage—a man in his thirties, stocky and bearded, with a boater hat and a broad grin. He is shaking hands with a dignitary. Behind him are rows of young male and female employees and mountains of show bags filled with Darrell Lea goodies.

The photograph was taken at the Sydney Royal Easter Show in 1983, and Jason had just accepted the trophy for the best display in the Royal Hall of Industries from the then Sydney lord mayor, Doug Sutherland. The group was celebrating with gusto. More than three decades later, the moment still makes Jason smile. Not because the trophy was particularly important but because it was a personal triumph—it was the moment he proved he was an important and valued part of the family business. At least in his own mind.

The previous year he had been given the job of running the Easter Show operation, a huge task given its importance to the company's public image. It was a difficult time of year for a chocolate company. The number of staff was doubled, if not tripled; they worked in three shifts over 24 hours as the factory struggled to pump out thousands of Easter eggs in addition to its normal fare.

The show-bag stand was just another layer of the operation, but one that couldn't be ignored. Since the mid-1950s it had been an important part of the business, a showcase for the company's wares and marketing power. Its typically bright and flamboyant window displays were transferred to huge stalls that were often several storeys high.

Their very first stall had been called the Candy Castle, erected for the 1954 Royal Melbourne Show. From that stall they had sold a bag containing twelve products, each in mini form, from nut bars and nougat to coconut ice, mints and chocolate, all packed in front of the customers. In her Darrell Lea smock and giant bow, Valerie had been front and centre while other family members manned the stall over the seven-day period. As the Lea children grew older, they would all play a part in this annual event, as did Jason Jnr and his sister Angeline when their turn came. Honey, in particular, loved the atmosphere and even co-opted school friends to help out on the stand by filling bags.

Like his father and uncle, Jason Jnr had left school to join the family business, helping to run factory maintenance until the day his father told him he was to take over the show-bag operation. He was thrown into the deep end, with no real experience other than those childhood holidays when he had sat out the back, filling bags with chocolates.

Jason recalls the brief conversation with his father; Jason Snr offered no help, not even a modicum of guidance.

'Righto, young fella, you can look after the show bags down at the Easter Show.'

'Okay, but what's involved in doing that?'

'Don't worry, you'll be fine. Just go in and do it.'

That was it. No advice on how to set up the stand or manage staff, even what product would go in the bags. He'd been left to sink or swim.

But the award was vindication of the fact that he hadn't sunk. Jason had not only survived the induction but thrived. Here he was, the boss, at least for a few days, with the freedom to experiment and express his own flair for marketing. All that mattered was the financial result, and it was spectacular: 'I revelled in the independence. I let my natural instincts take over, and I loved it.'

Jason took that confidence to the Brisbane Show the next year, taking a prominent place near the entrance to the industrial hall, in front of his main competition, Cadbury, Nestlé and Mars. 'It was an absolute rocket of a show,' he recalls with a roar of laughter. 'Far better than any other show we did. In ten days we delivered 250,000 show bags at two and three dollars a pop. It was chaos—forty staff madly packing bags out the back and in front of the customers. The crowds were fifteen-deep, all holding out their money. You weren't allowed to use a microphone to spruik so I did it the old way, with a rolled-up cone of paper: "Just wait, we'll pack one for you fresh. Don't go away. We'll bag one right away."'

The stall was decorated with clowns and liquorice men. Then came the jingle. Jason could still remember the words he wrote, their childish simplicity capturing the pure joy of the show bag experience:

Golly gosh golly gee,
here it is from Darrell Lea;
Hurry hurry, snappy snappy,
here's the bag to make you happy;
Goodness gracious goodness me,
buy a bag from Darrell Lea.

'It sounded good when one person sang it but when you had the whole staff in unison then the sound reverberated around the hall and people came running.'

Back at the Sydney Royal Easter Show the following year he came up with a unique way to get rid of unwanted Easter eggs, the excess stock that had been trucked over from the factory the night before and loaded onto palettes at the back of the stall. No one wanted to buy Easter eggs in that volume, he figured, so he tore off the silver paper wrapping, placed a dozen or so in each big clear plastic bag and smashed them into broken chunks of chocolate.

Back at the front of the stand he held out a bag of broken chocolate: 'The boys have just had an accident out the back and dropped a load of eggs. The first one with twenty bucks in their hand can have them.'

The bags sold out in a few, frenzied minutes of excitement. Jason waited until the crowd moved on before going out the back to repeat the 'accident'. By the time he'd returned, there was a new and eager crowd, so the story was retold: 'Bingo bango, we sold the lot and everyone was happy.'

The glee with which he tells such stories contrasts with his sadness about the business; Jason Lea Jnr is a man in whom the family instincts were clearly ingrained—a candy man, like his father, grandfather and great-grandfather. If only someone had listened.

39

REUNION

Chuck Bell was long gone. He didn't leave as such, but was always going somewhere, and occasionally coming back. Honey never questioned their strange relationship. They were still attached, at least by their two children, but she'd learned to be self-reliant, mother to Kaja and Angel. Nothing else mattered really.

She had no contact with the Lea family. Some years later, she wrote to Valerie and Monty in desperation, asking for help for dental work. When there was no reply, she wrote to Jason who, she felt, had been kind to her when they were children. Perhaps he would be prepared to talk to his parents. The response was hard—a blank refusal that was confronting. She recalls sadly:

He wrote that I was always blaming someone else for my mistakes. The letter had been dictated to a secretary and was not even signed. It wasn't true. I had only asked for help twice in the years since I left home, as any young person might if they were in my position. I had always worked and made my own way in the world. I thought the people who were family would help if I was in trouble. Instead they shut the door.

Her breakthrough came in 1983 when Lyndall Hobbs moved to Los Angeles, thanks to a successful short film called *Dead on Time* she had made with the British comedian Rowan Atkinson, who was still developing his Mr Bean character. Lyndall, who had secured a feature film deal at Twentieth Century Fox, hired Honey as her assistant. It was the steady job she needed, given she had an absent partner and two children now aged twelve and nine.

Then came another break. Her old boyfriend Geoffrey Hales had also moved to Hollywood and was dating the actress Darryl Hannah, who had just appeared in the classic science fiction movie *Blade Runner* with Harrison Ford. He was supposed to be housesitting for the recently married Australian actor Bryan Brown and his English wife, Rachel Ward, who owned a beach-front property in Malibu. The star couple were building a bigger home on the block and needed someone to watch over its construction while they travelled and worked in films. In return, she would have a guest cottage at the bottom of the block. Honey, who had already met the Browns through Lyndall, leapt in and offered to take care of the project.

She had a home and a job that paid a decent wage. The only drawback was the distance she had to drive each day—a ninety-minute round journey into the heart of LA after dropping the kids at school. It lasted a couple of years until, tired of the daily travel, she opened a new business, this time as a personal assistant to people who were prepared to pay for someone to manage their lives.

Among her clients were a farmer, a producer, a builder, a naturopath and a psychotherapist, all either too busy or too lazy to manage their own affairs, from paying bills and balancing account books to hiring staff and making dinner reservations. 'I'd just come in and tidy, up their lives. I swear, some of them wouldn't even sign their own cheques. It has always given me the greatest satisfaction realising that I could walk into a mess and leave it tidy, that I could manage other peoples' lives even though I struggled with my own. It was like a balm to my soul.'

Chuck had been back in Australia for more than a year. He'd left LA promising to organise passports and visas for Honey and the children, whose documents had long expired. Although nobody had bothered checking, they were living illegally in a country that Kaja and Angel identified as their home.

When he eventually returned to LA, Chuck took Honey for a walk. She remembers it vividly because they walked up a steep hill on the coast while he reported his news—that he had organised paperwork not for the family but for a new girlfriend, a former St Catherine's girl he had stashed at a nearby hotel.

'She was me minus twenty years,' says Honey.

As if sensing the absurdity of his behaviour, Chuck had something to offer. He had found Honey's mother—not Valerie Lea, but the woman who gave her away when she was four years old.

⊗

Honey waited anxiously in the arrivals hall at Los Angeles Airport, ignoring the bustling mass of bags, bodies and shrieks of delighted reunions around her. It was January 1993 and she was there to welcome a woman she hadn't seen in 40 years—her natural mother.

It had been a strange few weeks. First, she had been woken in the middle of the Californian night by a phone call from Australia; a man from an 'agency' claimed he could tell her the names of her birth parents.

She had been half-expecting a call ever since Chuck had told her he'd tracked down her mother, but not like this. She felt numb, unable to process the idea that she was finally about to solve the biggest puzzle of her life. She acknowledged that she wanted the information. It was given without fanfare and she had gone back to bed with two names—Shirley Newman and Brian Andrews.

The second call came a few days later. Shirley was calling from Warrnambool, a port city south-west of Melbourne, where she worked at a women's shelter. Shirley's first words made the woman she gave away cry in relief: 'Honey, I always loved you. You were always loved.'

The conversation was brief but surprisingly comfortable, although there was no attempt to unravel the mystery of why Shirley had handed the girl she named Gayle to Valerie Lea. That moment could come later, when they met. Shirley wanted to visit.

And now Honey was at the airport, checking again the arrivals board above her head, which confirmed that Shirley's flight from

Melbourne had landed almost an hour ago. She should have cleared customs and retrieved her luggage by now; she should be walking through the doors soon.

Honey had tried to imagine what Shirley might look like but failed. She knew her when she was four years old, of course, but Valerie had cut Shirley's history out of her life—no discussion and no photographs, as far as she knew—so the image of her mother's face had slowly faded with time.

But Honey knew Shirley as soon as she spotted her. There was nothing she recognised as such, more the sense of the tallish woman with short, fair hair who appeared in a gap in the crowd of people walking down the ramp. Shirley looked up and recognised her too.

Honey's mother would stay for several weeks. The conversation barely touched the elephant in the room—the adoption—because Honey was more interested in the present than the past. Could there be a future? They could never be mother and daughter in any real sense, but perhaps they could be friends.

Honey hoped so, and then one night she came home from work to find the wood fire laid and ready to be lit. She couldn't remember doing it that morning, but there it was, exactly as she would have done it herself in her own meticulous fashion. Just so. A funny habit of hers.

But it was Shirley who had laid the fire. The next day Honey watched, fascinated, as her mother collected twigs outside; she recognised some of her own characteristic habits. It was such a tiny, inconsequential thing, and yet it said so much.

A trip was planned. Honey wanted to show Shirley her

world—the delights of the West Coast and its Spanish roots, including the eighteenth-century missions, built to bring Christianity to California, that still dotted the landscape, and Hearst Castle, the fairytale home of the publishing magnate William Randolph Hearst. They seemed to represent the wonder and excitement of the world in which she had landed unexpectedly two decades before.

Honey revelled in the experience, still fantasising about having a mother but also aware that she had a relative stranger in the car next to her. There were moments of delight when they visited the castle and joined a guided tour: 'Oh, you are so like me,' Shirley commented. 'You are up-front in the group and ask questions.'

But then cracks began to appear. They were nothing Honey could pinpoint. Shirley's manner more than anything. It was 1 pm and she had to have lunch now, as if Honey, the working mother, had let her down. Punctuality. The small things were magnified—the good and the bad.

When she finally waved goodbye, Honey was relieved and downhearted. Shirley seemed unaware of her fragility. Far from being contrite, she was defensive; her manner implied that she had retained her maternal rights and would exercise them.

As she left, Shirley pressed a handful of photographs into Honey's hand, insisting that she take them. They were of Honey's life before Valerie and Monty: a photo of her mother and father, a confident, handsome couple astride his motorbike, their relationship clearly more than a one-night stand.

There were several of Honey as a toddler. In one Shirley,

beautiful in a pale checked dress and shoulder-length hair, posed in front of a rose bush, her wedding finger bare. In another, Honey was being nursed by Shirley's mother in a neatly fenced yard with clipped lawns. None of the photos suggested poverty or the desperation that might have forced Shirley to give her up for adoption.

The last photo was of Honey as a baby, perhaps a year old, in the arms of her foster mother, Audrey 'Dot' Quinlan, who beamed in delight at the prospect of raising the child she knew as Gayle. Instead, that child would be ripped suddenly from her and handed over to Valerie Lea as a playmate for her daughter.

Honey put the photos away. Shirley thought they would show that she was loved, but they only confirmed she had been abandoned for no good reason.

♋

A few weeks after Shirley left, Honey received another phone call, this time from the man Shirley Newman refused to marry in 1949. He now called himself Brian Andrews, although his name had been Leslie Rough when she was born. He gave no explanation for the change, which just seemed to further confuse the events of her early life. Everyone—especially the Lea family—seemed to hide behind new names and identities.

Brian told her that he was living in Tasmania, where he and his current wife had a large house in the northern city of Devonport, and offered her a place to stay if she and the children ever wanted to come back home. The proposal seemed ridiculous—why would she uproot her settled life in LA and move back to Australia?—but he persisted with the idea, a seduction of sorts.

But then she suddenly received a letter from the US immigration authorities demanding that she and the children present themselves for assessment as illegal immigrants. Her world had turned again. Suddenly Chuck's waywardness had taken a serious turn. He had never provided any financial security, let alone emotional stability, but now she, Kaja and Angel had been totally abandoned—left without identity documents and now faced with the threat of deportation.

Somehow she had managed to survive for twenty years without help. She'd raised two children, lived well in Malibu in a movie star's house, and gained work at the Paramount and Fox studios. But now, at the very moment when she was handed the possibility of discovering her past, the life she had established for herself and her children was all being taken away. The final straw was a call from Bryan Brown, telling her that he and Rachel were selling the house and she would have to move out of what had been her home for the last decade.

It was time to go back to Australia and head for Devonport. She left LA in July 1993, but would soon regret the move. By the time they'd arrived in Tasmania, Brian Andrews had lost his big house and was living in a flat above a shop in Devonport. It could not have been worse timing for a dream reunion. Brian and his wife were under immense financial strain and there was a clash of culture between Honey's Californian children and their archetypal Australian grandfather.

The experiment would last only a couple of months, ending

in September 1993 on Kaja's 22nd birthday, when the man who had wanted to be Honey's father stood in the street and screamed at her and his grandchildren. They packed their gear and left for Melbourne later that day.

40

MOTHERS

Diana Georgeff first learned of Shelton Lea when she was four-teen. She and Honey had been sitting with their friends in the rose garden at St Catherine's during a lunchtime break and Honey asked if anyone had heard of Ezra Pound.

Honey's sixteen-year-old brother was locked up in Turana, where he had discovered the work of the controversial American modernist poet. Diana wondered—a 'slip of a thought', as she would later describe it—what sort of a person could find literary beauty in such an awful place.

Her friendship with Honey endured after school and when, as a young woman working in the city, she met Shelton, his appearance and manner answered her question: 'Shelton was a heartbreaker, a danger zone and he drove his own reputation as a hard, wild boy,' she would later write. 'There was caution stamped all over him and it was surprising to see the kinds of girls who fell under his thrall. The sixties and seventies were the days when artists and poets were the anarchists, protesters and pop stars. It was an era made for Shelton. He used the times as a vehicle, a schooner he could ride.'

Fast forward more than two decades. Honey had arrived back from California and her friends, including Diana and others from school days, had gathered to welcome her home. Shelton, worn and craggy, hobbled in using a cane, dragging on rollies down to his stained fingertips: 'He was nearly fifty,' Diana would write. 'He looked jaded and sallow. His dark hair was beginning to grey. His nose was broken, he relied on a stick . . . He seemed that day as though life's long toil was imprinted on his body. At first, I thought he'd become an old feral cat; he had the face that prison gives.'

Shelton sat quietly most of the day but suddenly came alive, his voice turning 'from husky to honey' as he recited a poem, still a vital man despite his broken appearance. Diana repeated from memory one of his poems, about a raindrop, back to him. He was chuffed but responded by trying to conceal it, by being cool: 'That unconvincing bluff betrayed a kind of vulnerability that did not tally with his knockabout image, or the wicked boasts about his past. That fleeting look was the trigger for telling his story.'

It was a few months later that Diana approached Shelton about writing his biography. She was captivated by his story and his literary gift, and the vitality of a damaged man who could open his heart so freely. He agreed to cooperate.

One of the first steps was to try to find Gwyneth Roberts.

Shelton, crushed by Valerie's refusal to help more than a decade before, was now excited by the prospect as he gave Diana the authority to search on his behalf.

It took her just a few hours of searching government adoption records to establish that Gwyneth had married Noel Lennard less than a year after giving birth to Philip Anthony Roberts (Shelton). Then she quickly traced Shelton's half-brother and within a few days had established, sadly, that Shelton's mother had died a decade earlier from cancer, going to the grave without revealing her secret.

She was known as Gwynne in the family and in her later years had become a charismatic matriarch, holding court with a 'cigarette in one hand and a gin in the other'. It wasn't the only similarity—Gwyneth Roberts loved poetry, and wrote it herself. And she had raised four children with Noel Lennard. Shelton had a half-brother named Kim and three half-sisters—Kerry, Kate and Katharine. It appeared that Gwyneth, like Valerie, had her own quirky approach to naming her children, but she named hers after poets.

When Diana broke the news to him, Shelton had two questions: was his mother alive and did his siblings want to meet him? The distress that registered on his face after hearing of Gwyneth's death was quickly replaced with joy: 'I've got a brother who wants to meet me!' he hooted, dancing around the room.

Shelton met his brother, Kim Lennard, two days later in the Lord Newry Hotel in Fitzroy. Having calmed his nerves with a double gin beforehand, Shelton kissed and stroked his brother's face—a younger man with a neat haircut and a steady job, who revealed that his mother had suggested the name Philip if he and his wife had a son.

The connection with poetry ran deep. Gwyneth's mother, Elsie, used to hold poetry readings at her house in Perth and counted Florence, the mother of poet Dylan Thomas, among her childhood friends in Wales. Another friend was Daisy O'Dwyer, better known as the writer and Aboriginal welfare champion Daisy Bates.

'An unstoppable gene,' Shelton laughed when told of the poetry connection. He had found the answers to questions he had been seeking most of his life.

By chance, Shelton's partner, Leith Woodgate, had met Gwyneth Roberts. Leith's children had gone to school with the children of Kerry, Shelton's oldest half-sister, with whom she had also attended meetings of People for Nuclear Disarmament in the early 1980s. On one occasion Leith had been invited to a party where she met Kerry's mother, sitting out the back in loud conversation, 'a wreath of Craven A smoke around her as she talked and gesticulated with her hands'.

Leith only realised the connection with Shelton years later, when his newfound half-siblings visited him at a bookshop he had opened in Brunswick. They came armed with family albums, including several photographs of Gwyneth. Leith immediately recognised her. When she mentioned it later to Shelton, he was taken by the serendipity.

The reunion was a revelation for Shelton and his siblings. The children of his half-sister Kerry came to work at the bookshop and attended poetry readings. His brother Kim also turned up at poetry readings; he would say that watching Shelton perform raised the hair on his arms. Now that Gwyneth was gone, the family loved having poetry in their life again; Shelton was their mother's song.

And Shelton loved having his blood relations around. It gave him a measure of closure even though it raised new questions. He was fascinated by the past, particularly his mother's literary connections. He wanted to know as much as possible about his maternal grandmother and her poetry soirées, and was also tickled to learn of his grandfather, Rhys Roberts, who sounded like a 'likely lad'; he carried a cane and had a liking for drink and women. As Shelton said in one of his letters to a cousin:

I wondered in my youth, why the metaphor, why the poetry and why me? I often mused that poetry in fact was genetic and that it, like a magic gene, was passed on, skipping generations here and there, but always emerging. Because poetry is a drive, an urge, an inbuilt thing. It only makes sense that it be a legacy of previous generations.

Shelton wanted to find his father, most likely a US serviceman rather than Anthony de Havilland, the apparently fictitious British officer. But the identity of his mother's lover would remain elusive. More importantly though, he had found peace about his mother. In a letter signed 'Shelton Lea (nee Philip Anthony Roberts)', he wrote:

My mother made an extraordinary journey to Melbourne in 1946, made courageous by distance and decision. She made an attempt not to relinquish me for a period of time, for which I am ever grateful. There are hidden parts of our history that we can neither condemn nor atone for. I thank my mother for my life.

I am one of the many thousands for whom the bonds of family are like ghosts occasionally seen in the corner of your eye or scattered about your life. You know you are missing something, and you don't know what. In the process of finding out the 'what' I have found my mother and her family.

Soon afterwards Shelton opened his new Brunswick bookshop. He called it De Havilland's.

☙

Brett had never expressed a desire to find his mother but when Diana Georgeff told him in 1994 that she was keen to trace Louise O'Brien, his response was visceral: 'I'm going to tell her what a bitch she was giving me away,' she recalled.

At first he swatted away the idea, but Shelton finally convinced him that the emotional journey was worth it. Shelton had fought his own demons when Diana had searched for and then found his natural family. Now he was rejoicing in the discovery of his brothers and sisters, and the fact that he could make sense of his own story.

Shelton and Diana tried to talk Brett down, telling him he should not be hard on his mother when he didn't understand the circumstances of his birth, and that life had been different for young single women back in the 1940s. But this held little sway with a man who was still crying out for acknowledgement by the woman who had given him away.

Despite his reluctance, Brett finally agreed and set Diana on a scant paper trail that would lead her to the town of Hamilton in Victoria, where she found three of Louise's siblings, including a brother who revealed the news that Louise, like Gwyneth Roberts, had died from cancer several years before, her secret intact.

Louise's brother insisted that his sister was not capable of having a secret child—'No, not our Louie'—and it was only when Diana sent him a copy of the consent to adopt form signed by Louise that he conceded it was, indeed, his sister.

Louise O'Brien had fallen in love with, and pregnant to, a US serviceman named George Weiss in 1946 and, like so many other women, including Gwyneth Roberts, she hid her shame from family and friends.

The similarity with Gwyneth's situation was striking: both fell pregnant to soldiers who had returned home before 'doing the right thing', leaving their women with the invidious choice of either keeping the child and risking shame, or giving it up for adoption and suffering the grief that entailed or, in some cases, taking the physical and legal risk of aborting the pregnancy. Louise had actually chosen the last option before Valerie intervened. Soon after she gave birth, Louise left on a so-called bride ship and found Weiss in Philadelphia, where she married him and took US citizenship.

Louise and her husband would have two more children, a

boy and a girl—Brett's full siblings—but her marriage ended in tragedy when George was shot and killed while working as a security guard. She returned to Australia in 1965, but tragedy struck again in 1974 when Louise died of ovarian cancer after a ten-month battle. She was only 51 years old.

There would be another twist. On her deathbed Louise, who had been working as a salesgirl and living in a flat in Hawthorn, made arrangements to see a mystery woman whom nobody in the family knew. When the woman arrived, she didn't give her name, just went into Louise's bedroom and locked the door. She left an hour later without explanation. A few weeks later, Louise was admitted to hospital and passed away soon afterwards.

When Diana asked Louise's brother about the mystery woman, he described her as high-end and high-handed; she had swept into the house with an air of assumed authority, just as Valerie Lea might have done. Perhaps Louise wanted to put her mind to rest about the son she'd left behind. She had cared enough about the boy to give him a name—David George.

If the woman was Valerie, what she told Louise in that room would remain a secret. Did she pretend that Brett had enjoyed a wonderful childhood, and was now a 26-year-old man with the world at his feet? Or did she tell his mother the truth—that he was a displaced wanderer somewhere in Sydney, on the run from Queensland authorities after walking out of a prison farm?

It is unlikely that the mystery woman offered to reunite them or that Louise wanted to see the child she gave away, but Brett was never given the option of knowing his real mother. He would know nothing about his birth family for another two decades.

In 1994, when Diana told Brett of her discoveries, his anger had drained away, to be replaced by sadness and curiosity.

His mother—a Spanish factory worker, Valerie had told him—had been living close enough for him to have been reunited with her, but that opportunity was now long gone. Brett telephoned his uncle who, far from being shamed by his sister's secret, wanted to meet and embrace his nephew: 'You are home now,' he said.

Brett, a man who had laughed his way through a total of nine years of prison, wept uncontrollably.

☙

Melbourne had welcomed Honey back with open arms, the city's laneways and cafes and clubs offering her the comfort of home, like the security blanket she always kept, even as a middle-aged woman.

The trauma of the short stint in Tasmania with Brian Andrews/ Leslie Rough had subsided. Although the relationship with her birth father would always be at arm's length, they would stay in touch. After all, her adoption was not his decision.

Honey, always pragmatic and capable, had fallen on her feet. She quickly found a place to live and a job running a digital imaging company. One of the first of its kind, it produced advertising material, using early Photoshop technology, for want of a better term, to produce niche images.

She saw Shelton occasionally, attending some of his performances and visiting him in his bookshop, where he would introduce her as his 'blood blister'. But, like most siblings, they had established their own adult lives and social circles, although both centred on the bohemian culture of Fitzroy where they had been born to mothers who didn't want them.

Honey found herself mixing with a group of expressionist painters, led by her friend David Larwill, who had opened an artist-run gallery called Roar. The mood there was laid-back—as one art critic observed: 'Dogs and beer were always welcome.'

This group had also started Artists for Kids' Culture, a charity for underprivileged children that was funded by an annual auction of paintings donated by members. Jo Darvall, who also helped establish the charity, remembers Honey's passion for the cause:

> She came in after we founded the charity and helped push us in the right direction. It was like herding a bunch of cats—a bunch of artists who thought they could change the world—but for Honey the idea of helping children was real, because she had lived it.
>
> I only found out later about Honey's childhood. It came out in little bits as I got to know her, hidden in some ways, because she didn't want it to define her. I knew Shelton as well, although I never saw them together. Shelton was grounded because he knew who he was, an artist with a love of words, but I always had the sense that Honey was a bit lost.

Honey also reconnected with old school friends such as Diana Georgeff, who had been instrumental in finding Gwyneth Roberts and Louise O'Brien, and was keen to meet and interview Shirley Newman.

CB

The pub Shirley chose was crowded and noisy, hardly the place for a conversation. But the three women who sipped their coffee and herbal tea seemed unaware of the clamour around them. Honey, Diana Georgeff and Shirley Newman were engrossed, nerves jangling a little as they tried to settle into a difficult conversation.

Surprisingly perhaps, Shirley did not shy away from direct questions about Honey's adoption. Now well into her seventies, her voice was clear and strong. Neither were her explanations at all defensive. The adoption had happened, and she could not take it back.

At the time of Honey's birth, Shirley's father, on whom she was depending to get a place to live, had died while she was in hospital with the baby. Her mother offered no support, so she'd had no choice but to put up 'Gayle' for adoption. She did not attempt to explain why she allowed the Quinlans to care for Gayle in the meantime.

Diana's questions were carefully inquisitive, not accusatory: what had led the then twenty-year-old to the Salvation Army home; what was life like in the weeks and months before she delivered the daughter she would name Gayle; and how had she felt when she left her behind in the crèche? The questions formed a slow and inevitable spiral towards the emotional core of the matter.

The Haven had not been what Shirley had expected, not that she really knew what to expect when she sought help for a predicament she regarded as bad luck. Honey, beside her, barely blinked at the notion of being a piece of bad luck or constantly being referred to as 'the baby'. Too much had happened to be offended by a throwaway line.

Shirley had entered The Haven through the back gate and in the seven months she stayed there, she never once ventured onto its wide front verandah. The 40 girls were not allowed outside its boundaries except to attend church as a group; the high walls even blocked the views of the world outside.

They slept in dormitories of ten and were treated like army recruits, with inspections at dawn, followed by prayers, roll call and a list of duties to be performed each day. Shirley avoided the laundry and kitchen, spending most of her time in the tiny on-site hospital. The food was decent, but she was peeved that they were charged board and she had to pay for a cardigan she needed as the weather turned cold.

Honey ventured a question: 'Was I hard to deliver?'

Shirley remembered with clarity: 'About four hours in labour; but it was the pain, nobody told me about the pain.'

Honey went quiet. She had gone through labour twice herself but the joy of birth overrode the discomfort. It seemed that even after 46 years, her mother still regarded her as a painful inconvenience whom she would give away again if given a second chance.

41

HE WANTED TO CLEAR THE AIR

Moana woke suddenly one morning in November 2002, startled by what she would describe as a short but vivid nightmare, in which she was sitting on a bar stool in the Grand National Hotel surrounded by all of Brett's friends. Although she couldn't hear their words, they all seemed to be sad—many were crying, hugging her and apologising.

Confused, she glanced down to see that she was dressed in black. She looked around the room, searching for her former husband so she could dispel her fears. He wasn't there. Was this his funeral?

That was when she woke up.

Two years earlier Moana had finally ended her marriage, more in sadness than in anger. She realised she couldn't change Brett, or ease his heartache, and that he would ultimately drag her life if she stayed with him. Still, they had remained in touch and on good terms.

The vision haunted her so she decided to call Brett. He answered immediately and listened as Moana recounted the dream. When she finished there was silence.

'Where are you, Brett?' she finally asked.

'I'm at the doctor's. I've just been told that I have cancer and I've only got three months to live.'

His voice was thick and slow, the reality that he was going to die sinking in. Moana stared at her mobile phone as if it wasn't real.

Things happened quickly then. The cancer was clearly aggressive and Brett's options were limited. Radiotherapy might delay the inevitable, but the quality of his last few months could be limited by such radical intervention. He chose to try treatment, but it wasn't effective and he stopped.

Knowing he only had a few weeks left, Brett flew to Melbourne to spend time with Shelton, the pain now so bad that he found it difficult to sleep. He didn't want to be alone in the frightening pre-dawn hours, so a television was set up in the spare bedroom to give him company in his wakeful hours. When Brett went back to Sydney, Shelton badgered Jason to buy a TV for his brother. It was the least he could do.

In the last days of his life, Brett moved into a spare room in Moana's house, his body wracked by a disease that was barely held at bay by the dozens of medications he carried in a small bag. He had few other possessions.

'I felt he wanted to spend time with me before he died, so I offered the room,' Moana recalls. 'He was delighted, and he apologised for his absences during our marriage. He wanted to clear the air.'

The doctor's initial assessment had been correct, and Brett died on 16 February 2003. The funeral was held at McKell Park at Darling Point, and afterwards a group of friends retired to the Mill Hotel in Bondi for a wake. The name of the venue was the only detail of Moana's dream that was not accurate.

Jason turned up. He told Lael about the experience later: 'Jason put $500 on the bar and then another $500,' Lael recalled. 'Then he left. He said that he'd never seen so many roughhouse people in all his life.'

Brett's ashes were scattered in two places—in the waters of Sydney Harbour, where he used to go fishing, and at the base of a tree outside the Lea family home in Lambert Road, Toorak.

42

BAD BLOOD

In 2003 Jason Lea did the unthinkable—he sacked his brother.

The man who grew up with his mother's edict—'blood' was everything—had decided that there was one thing more important—business—and that Lael could be sacrificed as the company went through difficult times.

The strategy to expand the Darrell Lea operation in the face of reducing markets and increased competition was backfiring; the company, once famous for its lack of debt, now faced a growing mountain of it as sales each Christmas and Easter fell short of expectation. A company that had once produced annual profits of 20 per cent was now struggling to break even.

Although there was an attempt to keep growing and adapt, by introducing lines into supermarkets for the first time, it would be too little too late; the company was being undercut by bigger brands as chocolate became as much a middle-class social statement as a working-class take-home box for the family. The Darrell Lea stores, once a blaze of colour and excitement, had become outdated and obsolete in the face of convenience shopping.

Behind the scenes, the factory was also struggling to maintain its output; shopfronts were being closed and agencies reduced. Darrell Lea was facing the biggest challenge in its 75-year history and the very heart of the operation—its family—was being torn apart.

Of the previous generation, only Valerie was still alive to watch the demise of Harry Levy's dream. Darrell had died in 1990, then Harris fell ill and died suddenly in 1991, followed by his wife, Sheila, in 1993. Maurice, the eldest brother, passed away in 1996 and his wife, Sharpe, in 2002, the same year that Monty was finally overwhelmed by his numerous medical problems at the age of 93.

They would all have been horrified by the spectacle that followed. In 2005 the row spilt into the public arena when some family members, surprisingly, agreed to discuss the rift on national television in an explosive episode of the ABC TV series *Dynasties*.

ᘓ

In the TV program, Lael was still trying to come to terms with his brother's treachery: 'At this point in time it's almost as though he doesn't exist because of what has happened to me. You put your whole life into the family business and you're out. You kid yourself you're still part of a concern when you really know you're not.'

His wife, Joy, was also angry about how he had been treated. She told the program: 'Lael went into a state of shock and grief; it was as if someone had died. If you love your brother you don't malign them, you don't betray them and you don't allow them to be betrayed. You stand up for them at all times. And that hasn't happened.'

Jason could not shake the notion that he was no longer the dominant older brother. They were two men either in or near their sixties, each with his own skill set—Jason in management and Lael in retailing. When Jason tried to press Lael into opening more shopfronts, Lael resisted on the basis that they would be loss-making, reckoning that unless there was a minimum of 13,000 potential customers a week, there was no money to be made.

Lael was accused of being an obstructionist and pushed into opening a store in a giant shopping centre near Essendon Airport that was moved twice, costing tens of thousands of dollars, to no avail. 'It was a dog,' was Lael's assessment.

Jason was unrepentant: 'I might be classified as cold and callous. But these decisions were made for the good of the business, not for the good of any individual, and so I've never felt guilty about any of these decisions at all, no guilt whatsoever.'

There was a tragic complexity to the clash. As the ABC program was going to air, Jason was in a hospital bed, battling leukaemia. He knew he had weeks, perhaps only days, to live and yet he allowed himself to be filmed, walking slowly through the hospital ward with the help of a nurse, handing out chocolates as he had done all his life.

'The chocolate man's here,' he declares onscreen before being led back to bed, his temperature rising with the exertion. 'Okay, we live for another day, kid. Good on you, thanks a lot. It's unbelievable. This just doesn't happen to me.'

Most people in his position might have been making their peace, surrounded by loved ones and friends and hoping the end would come without pain of any kind—physical or spiritual. Instead, Jason Lea was angry and lashed out at the only thing he could. Family, the mainstay of the business for four generations, was now a weakness.

'You may say that blood is thicker than water and where's your loyalty? Look, I don't know, I am what I am, and I'd say that my loyalty is more towards the business.'

He had already made that plain several years earlier when he sacked another family member—his own son. Jason Snr would die only a week after the *Dynasties* program went to air in December 2005.

ↂ

Jason Carey Lea is a wistful man, even though he is entitled to be angry.

The former 'Jacie', now in his mid-fifties, has plenty of money and lives in one of the grand mansions along the man-made canals of Queensland's Sunshine Coast. On this day in 2017, the much-vaunted sun is scarce. It is mid-May and autumn has finally worked its way north, turning the sky into a scudding mess of dirty white with occasional glimpses of blue. Flags on private jetties sputter and the muddy waters, mostly free of boating traffic, slide past.

Inside the house is dark and square, the dimensions of its rooms emphasised by a minimum of furniture. Jason has settled himself at a dining table; there is a couch and a giant flat-screen television between him and the glass sliding doors at the back.

'Everyone's out at the moment,' he offers, as if explaining the silence. 'Tea?'

A powerboat passes by on the canal, the motor a low murmur through the glass doors. Jason has not seen it. He cannot: his eyesight is slowly being destroyed by scotoma, the same degenerative disease of the retina that his grandmother suffered from. The cells at the back of his eyes are dying, and there is nothing that can be done. He may go blind, or he may not: 'Some people end up having a sliver of sight, in clock parlance from midday to 1 pm. I won't go full black [blind] but I will go grey, to what degree I don't know.'

His sight has been regressing for eight years, the light slowly receding. Three years ago, Jason's ophthalmic surgeon told him he was close to losing his driver's licence: 'Yeah, I know,' he replied. 'I'm scared myself so I've only driven twenty kilometres in the past year.'

He recently handed in the licence although he kept his boat licence because, he chuckles, 'It goes slowly and I can use binoculars.'

But the mirth is strangled. Jason hasn't come to terms with the disease and admits to a short wick and occasional bouts of depression. His resentment is understandable; the elements of his life he holds dearest are being taken away from him. First it was his life as a candy man, when his own father stripped him of his place in the company, and now the loss through disease of his capacity to drive.

His much-loved fleet of racing cars is being sold off. This is not a rich man's trophy cabinet of buffed luxury that rarely leaves the garage; it's a petrolhead's collection of bumped and buffeted race cars—an old rally car that once belonged to national champion George Fury, a sports sedan used to win a Queensland championship and a Datsun Sports 2000 used as a racing car since 1968.

The love of cars runs in the family; it is the one luxury that the Lea brothers—Harris, Monty, Maurice and Darrell—afforded themselves in lives that were otherwise filled with long work days. Jason rattles off the names of a dozen or more cars the brothers drove as far back as the 1930s.

The boys were always into cars. Even in the 1930s during the Depression, they had to have the thing with the biggest engine and fastest this and the best that. There is old 16-millimetre film footage of Maurice in the 1960s turning up in a big Mark VII Jag with big headlights. He would have driven that from Sydney down to Melbourne. There were no speed limits in those days so he would have been nailing it the whole way.

Monty was into Citroëns; Darrell drove American left-hand drives such as Corvettes, Pontiacs, Trans Ams and Camaros. Jason Snr and Lael also caught the car bug, and Jason Jnr continued the love affair. His collection is a part of motoring history that should be cherished, he reckons, and, although he will never drive his cars again, he is prepared to wait for the right buyers. The Fury sedan might go to a collector in Norway. 'The others will sell,' he adds, his voice trailing off in regret.

When Jason talks about his own story, he displays the warmth of a man in love with his trade who, against his own will and the harsh judgment of others, has been chopped off like the rotten limb of a giant tree.

He talks endlessly about innovation and the careful nuancing of recipes and marketing, the importance of moisture in liquorice and how to correctly light a shopfront. He delights in a company with heart and loyalty that would pay its workers cash bonuses and arrange interest-free loans. It was little wonder than many staff members spent their entire working lives at Darrell Lea: 'We were an amazing company for 70-odd years and a slow-moving dinosaur for the last twenty.'

But that's all long gone, although he can't help but wander down supermarket aisles, testing the liquorice bags for moisture and peering at bags of Rocklea Road to see if the marshmallow has dried out and sunk.

Like his father and his uncle, Jason worked at the Kogarah factory after leaving school. His first job was to crawl inside the vats, stripped down to his underpants, and dig out chocolate that was unusable—four tonnes of hardened mud that had to be shovelled into buckets lowered from above. 'The only good thing about it was that a Lea was doing this menial job. It gave me a lot of credibility among the other staff.'

'You watch the *Willy Wonka* film with Gene Wilder,' he continues, 'and it's lovely and it's pretty and colourful with rivers of chocolate and never-ending gobstoppers and bubble gum in purples and pinks and greens and blues, but the reality of a real factory is different; the only rivers of chocolate are created when you accidentally kick something over.'

Jason worked in the factory from the age of 21 to 27, initially as a 'white coat', learning how to make chocolate, liquorice and lollies. Eventually he would move into engineering and become a 'green coat'. Managers were known as 'blue coats'.

For a time, Jason and his father were close. One of his fondest memories is of the two of them making early morning deliveries at Kings Cross, where the hookers and drunks tried to buy lollies from them; Jason Jnr was eight. There is admiration for Jason Snr's work ethic: 'My father may have had the moniker managing director on his business cards but the Leas did everything; we were truck drivers, forklift drivers, chocolate makers, storemen and packers.'

But as Jason grew older, it all changed. His father rarely had time to talk to him or, conversely, would find a way to criticise everything he did. At least, that's the way it seemed to a young man desperate for approval.

My father was really great at critiquing everybody, particularly me. If you picked up a box of matches he'd critique you on how to pick up a boxing of fucking matches and then write you a four-page bloody letter about how to and how not to pick up a box of matches.

When it came to the dismissal, Jason Snr could not face his son, instead relying on another manager to tell him that his services were no longer required. He was being made redundant. When queried about this on the *Dynasties* program, Jason Snr's answer was brutal: 'I suppose the rock bottom truth is it's ten seconds of orgasmic bliss and bang, there's a child created. Does that necessarily give you the right to have to continue to have very, very strong family ties? I don't think so.'

And yet, Jason Jnr argues, if his father had bothered to look further, he would have discovered that his son's management style was worth saving. He had streamlined the Brisbane operations to the point where, in his own words, Jason had made himself all but redundant. The office was virtually self-sufficient.

He knocked back his father's offer of an engineering job in the Kogarah factory, deciding to stay in Queensland and go into business for himself, operating a storage company. 'My father described me as ten seconds of orgasmic bliss on national television and left me nothing.'

The words will always hurt. How could they not?

Angel Lea has little sympathy for her brother. She adored her father, despite his absences during their childhood, and was content to simply spend time with him in his office: 'I was just sitting there with him; it made me happy,' she recalls, underlining the little time that Jason Snr had with his children away from the business.

Angel also observed Jacie's difficult relationship with their grandparents. While she revelled in a household where Valerie imposed strict rules, her brother had rebelled, frequently clashing with Valerie and even the gentle Monty.

I love Jacie because he is my brother but he upset me by treating Valerie and my father badly so we don't really have a talking relationship. I don't blame my father for sacking him. My brother expected to be given things, to be given a higher position in the family business when the truth is that he was lazy.

Angel, by contrast, resisted family members who urged her to take a job in the company.

I didn't want to go into the family business. I wanted to work with children, to become a preschool mothercraft nurse, which I did for ten years before opening my own retail clothing business. I'm very proud of myself because I have done my own thing without any support, without asking for money. The inheritance money from my father came much later.

ဢ

There was a further complication to the father–son relationship. In 1994 Jason Jnr had become a proxy shareholder on behalf of his Uncle Maurice and Aunt Sharpe, who were living in retirement in Brisbane. As such, he was at liberty to ask a series of tough financial questions and even demand to see audited reports, which showed the company was in increasing trouble.

It was a question of how much you take and how much you make. My father was very good at answering the first bit, but was evasive about the second. He hated that I was asking the questions, but I was doing it on behalf of Maurice and Sharpe, the senior family shareholders.

The answer was confronting. The chocolate company may have been taking $100 million a year but its costs were invariably higher and, year by year, it was falling into compounding debt with the banks. The floating overdraft had become a line of continuous and expanding debt.

The strategy of expansion was failing. The company was now a slow-moving dinosaur that was trying to be all things to all people. The downward trend would continue after Jason Snr's death in December 2005. By this stage, his son had become the company's biggest shareholder, as he had been bequeathed his uncle's shares when Maurice passed away.

The company was still afloat only because it was being subsidised by rents earned from a subsidiary company that held the real estate assets. The real value of Darrell Lea lay not in its recipes and marketing skills but in the bricks and mortar that had been bought over the years and were ultimately owned by a holding company.

By 2012 it would reach a crisis point when the family shareholders were asked to put up private assets to meet a multi-million-dollar debt shortfall. None would do so. There seemed no choice other than to sell off the chocolate company.

Jason arrived at the meeting first, a habit he had developed so he could find a seat with his back to any window and accommodate his poor eyesight. The mood in the room was grave; the company's lawyers and auditors were present as the situation was assessed. The banks were owed $25 million and were demanding a $9 million payment. The company could meet the payment, but only if some of the real estate assets were sold off.

Everyone was in agreement that the chocolate company had to be sold off to clear the $25 million debt, but at the last minute Jason, by now the biggest shareholder, baulked: 'I just couldn't sign it. I needed to be sure there wasn't another way.'

After a delay, during which Jason discussed options with the company's financial officer, his second cousin Michael Lea, he finally succumbed: 'I had to sign the paper that said bye-bye. I had no option,' he says, his voice dropping to a whisper. 'That was 90-odd years of family—gone.'

The cloud had a silver lining. The Darrell Lea Chocolate Company would be sold to the Quinn family, the Queensland owners of a pet food company for $25 million, enough to pay out the major debt.

Despite its losses, the Lea family was far from destitute. Most importantly, the land on which the Kogarah factory stood was retained and three years later, after a series of wrangles with the NSW Government and Rockdale Council, the factory was torn down to make way for a real estate development of 500 homes.

As the biggest shareholder, Jason played an integral role in the negotiations, which cost $3 million in approval costs and another $5 million in community contributions—a child-care centre, improvements to parks and amenities, roads, traffic lights, even payments to local football clubs: 'As a piece of land without a development approval we might have got $22 million for it, if we were lucky. With the development approval we sold it to a Chinese-backed Australian developer for $75 million.'

Just like Mungah, the Lea family's Bulwark Against Disaster proved to be property.

CB

Rocky Road

February 2018

Lael is sporting a moustache, grown as part of a 'Movember' challenge and now likely to remain. He is tanned and has recently lost weight, according to his wife, Joy, who quietly chides him as only a wife of 38 years can do.

Lael and Joy have agreed to a follow-up interview. The timing is fortuitous because the previous day he had sat with family members to formally sign off on the winding up of the parent company. After 91 years, the Lea family had closed up shop.

Unlike the 2012 sale of the chocolate company, there is little sadness on this occasion. Lael is not even bothered that the Quinns, who bought the business and factory for $25 million had recently onsold the operation for $200 million: 'Everyone is making money. Good luck to them.'

The venue for the meeting—the function room in the Victoria Hotel in Collins Street, Melbourne—is nostalgic for both of them. The Darrell Lea company frequently held its annual Christmas function for its city shop staff here and Joy's parents had spent their wedding night upstairs.

But there is little happiness in their family reminiscences, particularly when discussions turn to Lael's late older brother. His usual laid-back demeanour hardens: 'I tell everyone that I have not shed a tear for Jason's passing, and I haven't.'

Lael's considers for a moment when asked if he really wants to say this publicly: 'Yes, because it's true.'

Lael's bitterness is hard-set. Behind his dismissal in 2003 were years of argument and underhanded attempts to belittle him.

When Lael was belatedly diagnosed with attention deficit and hyperactivity disorder (ADHD), an affliction he blames for his difficulties at school, Jason attempted to have him sacked: 'Jason kept trying to get other managers to do his dirty business because he didn't have the guts to do it himself.'

Jason even pleaded with their father to change his will and bequeath his entire 25 per cent ownership of the company to himself, leaving Lael with nothing. Monty had refused and they each got 12.5 per cent each.

'When they sold the company, only ten of the 70 shops were profitable,' he said, leaning forward. 'I told him. I warned them. Instead, he took me out. He was a bastard.'

43

CIRCLES OF OUR DEATH AND LIFE

February 2005

Shelton Lea was dying.

Jack Dancer had caught him and latched on tightly, filling his nicotine-fouled lungs with disease, the same disease that had taken many of those he loved, including his mentor Barrett Reid, brother Brett, former lover Mary Craig and his mother, Gwyneth Roberts. Now, unlike their fleeting time together in life, Shelton and his mother would be reunited in death.

Shelton and Leith had been holidaying in Coffs Harbour, catching up with Honey who had moved to the northern NSW city a few years before. By the time they returned to Melbourne it was clear that Shelton was unwell. The diagnosis confirmed the worst.

'Shelton's attitude to death is evident in his poetry,' Leith recalls. 'I think he accepted death as part of life. Not to be courted, but also not to be resisted if inevitable and he wasn't interested in any heroics, but he did want to keep as involved in life as much as he could until the last minute.'

Shelton knew he didn't have long. A few months perhaps, just like Brett, over whom he had watched and fretted two years earlier. Brett had feared being alone, discarded and forgotten; he'd copped too much of it in his life. Shelton didn't want to be alone either, as he told Leith the day he revealed the diagnosis. 'Don't turn anyone away', he instructed.

'And they did come,' wrote Diana Georgeff. 'Every day brought a procession of people he'd touched in their lives—all the poets, publishers, Aborigines, sculptors, actors, writers, old paramours, shopkeepers [and] filmmakers.'

Diana only found out about Shelton's prognosis a few weeks before his death. She had spent seven years researching and was now in the midst of writing the biography that would be published nearly two years after Shelton's death. When she went to see him, Diana realised she had made a mistake by shutting herself away from her subject while writing about him: 'He believed that because he hadn't heard from me, I had abandoned him. I thought he would understand but he didn't because he had been abandoned so many times before.'

A few days later, Diana went back to see him, so weak and fragile that she thought he would die then and there.

I asked him if he wanted me to read some of the biography to him. He nodded. I read the first chapter and I looked across the pages at his face. He was doused in perspiration. His eyes closed.

He barely laughed as he said, 'You did it, kiddo.'

'Do you want me to go on?'

'Next time.'

Shelton would make one final public appearance—in May 2005, when his book *Nebuchadnezzar* was launched at the Rochester Hotel in Fitzroy. It was his ninth book and a compilation of thirteen years of writing. He'd missed several of his publisher's deadlines but, after the cancer diagnosis, the project became urgent.

To most of the crowd who overflowed into the public bar that night, this was not the launch of a single publication but the celebration of a life—a pre-wake: 'Not many people get to launch a book on their deathbed,' one attendee noted.

A video of proceedings would show Shelton, wasted and tired, sitting on a yellow chair, smiling sadly at the crowd around him—a far cry from the piratical figure who had once leapt onto tables and demanded attention from strangers.

There were rounds of readings from his friends—either contemporaries who praised his earthy fire, or younger poets in awe and full of thanks for his enthusiasm and personal encouragement.

Canadian poet Ian McBryde related the launch of his own book some years before. Afterwards Shelton, whom he hadn't met, came up to buy a copy. 'Sure. What should I write in it?' McBryde had asked.

'Write that Shelton Lea is the best fucking poet in the world,' had been the reply.

The writer Dorothy Porter launched *Nebuchadnezzar*, booming:

This is a book with balls—red hot ones, Shelly—with the rhythm and swagger of sweet anger. Shelly tilts at all the serious windmills: sex, love, art and death, but also the book thrums with a gallantly old-fashioned political heart.

The poems stroll the streets of Fitzroy and Clifton Hill in Melbourne, or Redfern in Sydney—Shelly's haunts—but the people and landscapes of the poems haven't been gentrified. After reading these passionately empathic poems, I felt a kind of shame; that I have been walking these same streets and neighbourhoods with my head up my safe, middle-class bum. Like all good poets, Shelton Lea has ripped off my eyelids.

Despite being in pain, Shelton decided to give a reading of his title poem, based on a painting by Arthur Boyd.

I am nebuchadnezzar
my balls are caught tight with white wire.
I am caught in extremis,
falling,
paying the price for the poor,
my body pays with fire.
For I am nebuchadnezzar, I am the king of Fitzroy.
The clouds scud
And the subtle landscape of trees emanate from me
For I am the king of what's loud.
I am nebuchadnezzar and I am king of Fitzroy,
my skin is black, my heart is strong,
You see my gardens there in Gertrude street

Beneath the high rise flats,
That's my babylon,
The land that long I've fought for,
On behalf of all of my tribe
For this is my country and I am its king.

Shelton's voice, once magnetic, began to give out as he struggled to follow his own words across the page. He paused, kept going and then stopped. He'd given enough, and the eruption of applause and hooting calls for an encore overcame the sense that this was the last time he would be heard.

Shelton died eight days later, at home with Leith. It was sunny and the autumn sky was clear and blue. He was cremated and all but a handful of the ashes spread under a big tree at the back of Heide, near his friend Barrett Reid's ashes.

The rest were scattered in the gardens outside The Haven, the old Salvation Army women's hospital where he'd been born and abandoned 58 years before.

❧

During the weeks after his death, the tributes would flow. Shelton's fractured life and bawdy adventures were celebrated as much as his rambunctious poetry was admired. 'No one loved poetry as much as Shelton. Not even God,' wrote long-time friend and writer Barry Dickins under the headline, 'The man who walked into a pub, smiled and served up a poem with the lot'.

But it was a review of *Nebuchadnezzar* by critic Philip Harvey that raised another point. 'We did not hear everything we could have from Shelton Lea,' Harvey wrote. 'Perhaps that's true of all poets, but in this collection we notice attempts at reconciliation and personal resolve that are a change in his personal trip.'

The answers had been in Shelton's poetry, as far back as his days in Turana, when he discovered Ezra Pound. His poems are filled with poignant lines about abandonment, motherhood and love. Although he was troubled by his early life, his response to it did not amount to hatred or rage; if anything, his poetry allowed him to explore his own vulnerabilities.

He was 23 in 1969 when his first book, *Corners in Cans*, was published, much of it written in a prison cell. There was no rage, just the sound of prisoners' voices and childhood memories.

In the 1970s, in the midst of 'Vietnam', a poem about the horrors of the Vietnam War and the clouds of Agent Orange, he dropped references to adoption. In 'We Sat' he reflected on what he'd missed out on in his youth by being locked away. Shelton often explored love in his poems and wondered about the world. The only words he offered on hate were questions in a poem called 'Our Hands Describe the Nature of Our Society'.

'Shelton's poetry was more about a search for love and beauty than rage,' says Diana Georgeff. 'That was his uniqueness. He used to say life was about learning. No time for regret. He was hurt and often unable to control himself socially, but he turned it in on himself. That was Valerie's stamp on his personality—the fight against worthlessness.'

44

THE PRINCESS DEPARTS

Valerie Lea would live to the age of 94, spending her final days in a nursing home in Fremantle, Western Australia, close to Gaela.

Her parting on 6 June 2008 was peaceful according to the death notice, which quipped: *Our princess has departed—94 years, all teeth intact!!*

Of greater significance though was the reinstatement of the children whom she had adopted, abandoned and then specifically written out of her will. 'Devoted mother to Jason, Gaela, Leighland, Shelton, Bretton, Charryce and Kestin', it read, adding that she was also a loving grandmother—including to Honey's children, Kaja and Angie—and great-grandmother to sixteen.

In death, she had finally been granted her greatest wish—a large family.

45

CHARRYCE AND GAELA

Charryce is reluctant to talk. *Very* reluctant.

Over the years, she has watched the dissection of her family's business and personal woes on television and in newspapers, magazines and books—confessions and revelations that have shocked, saddened, angered and puzzled her.

What was there to gain from speaking out when others, including her older brother Jason, had sullied the Darrell Lea name and, if she did, would her words be reported accurately?

In the end, she agrees to an interview on the basis that she can vet the manuscript to satisfy herself that her views are being presented fairly. Others are entitled to their opinions, she says, just as she is entitled to express her own.

'Let me tell you that I only have admiration and love for my mother,' she warns. 'I am not going to say anything different.'

True to her word, Charryce is well prepared for the interview, her dining table covered with documents, files, photographs, newspaper clippings and family memorabilia. There are boxes and boxes of cassette tapes and microcassettes, all filed in plastic and labelled neatly.

Her desire is to be positive, to present the sunshine of her childhood, as she saw it, and the genius and love of her mother, Valerie. The evidence is there in abundance, she says, presenting as an example a copy of a teeth-cleaning song her mother had written, complete with illustrations and instructions on how she expected her children to brush each tooth. Charryce sings a few bars:

One outside at the back below
Two outside at the back above
Three outside at the back below
Four outside at the back below
And so on to the eighteenth tooth
It's you I love

Teeth were important to Valerie, she insists. That's why the death notice included a reference to dying with her own teeth intact. Taking care—whether it be wearing the right shoes, sleeping on cotton sheets or eating a healthy diet—were major bullet points in the Valerie Lea manifesto of good parenting.

In fact, everything her mother said or did was of value. Valerie Lea was a trailblazer who read widely and made decisions for her brood, pre-empting 'problems' by issuing dire warnings around the dinner table. The message was to be careful and conservative in life: 'The first chance you take may be your last,' she would write in letters to her daughter that always began 'My darling Bub'.

Then there was the decision to send her children to different schools: 'It was very wise,' says Charryce. 'Mum made it very clear that she didn't want us to be compared to one another but to be our own person, make our own friends and have our own identity. [Otherwise] Honey and I may have ended up in the same class because there was only four months between us.'

She produces another document, the eulogy she delivered at her mother's funeral: 'Reality is kinder than the stories we tell about it,' it begins, a clear rebuttal of the book *Delinquent Angel*, Diana Georgeff's biography of her late brother Shelton that she believed had unfairly demonised her mother.

In contrast, Charryce paints a picture of domestic bliss: 'My beautiful mother was a maverick woman of the highest order. She was exceptional, unique, somewhat eccentric and incredibly productive and the most loving and devoted mother to her children, her grandchildren, her great-grandchildren and crazily in love with Dad.'

Charryce recounts how she watched her mother working for hours on a sewing machine making scalloped blinds, bedspreads, cushions and chair covers to decorate the children's bedrooms, and hand-sewn party dresses and fancy dress costumes, later teaching her and Honey songs and dance steps to match the costumes.

Valerie designed bespoke furniture with built-in storage and fold-out desks and, outside, sat on her shooting stick directing landscape gardeners to create an outdoor wonderland for the children and their menagerie of pets, including cats and dogs, a galah, budgies, guinea pigs and a tortoise named Willoughby.

Charryce marvels at her mother's business innovations and recalls watching her work both the crowds and her staff at the Royal Melbourne Show each year, a larger than life figure with energy to burn.

True, Valerie Lea did not play the role of a traditional mother but, she insists, why should she be condemned for not being traditional?

She was doing what she loved to do. We were brought up by a succession of housekeepers which I thought was perfectly natural. We didn't much like them [the staff] but when Mum came home she would say to me: 'There is nothing nicer than coming down Lambert Road, into the house and having dinner with all my wonderful children. That's the highlight of my day.'

If you can organise your life like that then it's all right by me. Maybe some of the other kids, like Lael, thought that she wasn't a 'proper mother', maybe Jason did, maybe it shows a difference between females and males, and males need a little more mother love. But Gaela and I thrived.

Gaela agrees with her younger sister. She only knew a life in which her mother went to work each day but made the most of her time with the children. She laughs at the memory of Valerie, ever the innovator, sewing bikinis for her daughters, a woman of great creative energy who ruled her home with an unbending authority.

But Valerie's enthusiasm could be misguided, such as her attempts to force an unsporty Gaela into tennis and gymnastics backfiring, as did her insistence that her oldest daughter enrol in an accountancy class: 'I only got two out of 100 for arithmetic at high school, so I can't understand why she did it, but Mum always believed that a woman should have a job to keep her husband interested.'

ⱌ

We sit down to watch a video interview Charryce shot in 1994 with her parents, who were then both in their early eighties, during a family summer holiday at Clareville in Sydney's north. 'I haven't watched this in years,' she laughs, clearly delighted by the memories of a woman with a brain that fizzes with information—names, dates, places, relationships, anecdotes—delivered like a machine gun.

Occasionally Valerie pauses, forgetting where she is in the story: 'Oh Bub,' she laments before embarking again on a lengthy explanation of her family, which stretches back to the mid-nineteenth century when both sides of the clan made their way to Australia.

Monty, tanned and mottled, wanders into shot. Valerie leaps up to embrace her husband of more than 50 years and proceeds to unbutton his shirt and fondle his oestrogen breasts, a side effect of the treatment Monty is receiving for prostate cancer. She chortles as she grabs at the plump mounds while her husband shrugs and laughs. He is used to her shenanigans, the product of a long marriage. They are clearly still very much in love despite their ups and downs.

Charryce winces ever so slightly at her mother's behaviour, as inoffensive as it is. Valerie Lea had no filter, she says, and people had to accept her as she was. Perhaps that was why she was misunderstood:

Monty was always quiet and enjoyed standing back and watching Valerie be who she was. She drove him nuts at times because she could be quite undiplomatic. She did not tread carefully with sensibilities, like the way she spoke to Maurice and Sharpe about her brood without thought that they didn't have children. She was just being true to form. People can be easily offended. That's their choice but you can't quash someone's truth-telling . . . and Mum wasn't an eggshell person.

Mum had very little time for friends or socialising. She had Dad, a large brood of kids, her work in the factory, her work in the shops, and her planning and organising the renovation of houses purchased with monies sent from Grandma Mungah in Sydney.

Was it a mistake to adopt children with the intention of blending them into the family as 'playmates'?

It is a word that frustrates Charryce:

When parents have children they often try to have them close together so they can be playmates for each other. There is no mistake in that. My parents, notably my mother, adopted children, because it was a natural thing for her to do and they could provide a supportive and loving home environment within their existing family. Honey and I played together from the age of four. All we children were extremely close in age and altogether different to one another.

Lael felt differently. His mother had adopted children around the same age to make life easier. He called it the two-dog trick:

If you have one dog you have to walk the dog and exercise the dog. But if you have two dogs you don't have to exercise and walk them because they play all day and they're jumping and running around with each other. So there was less of a necessity to entertain each of the individual children because they entertained themselves.

This had repercussions for not only the adopted children but also for the natural offspring, like Lael, who felt that the presence of Shelton and, to a lesser extent, Brett in the family made life more difficult for himself: 'I was vying for the attention that had to be given to two children of the same age.'

Jason's view was even harsher, calling his mother crazy for adopting children: 'I think it's just bloody impossible for the natural parents to give the same love and affection to the adopted child as they would to their own.'

Gaela sits on the fence, hesitant to criticise her mother who told her once that she felt bad about the extra attention she felt she had lavished on Shelton at the expense of her natural children. But, she adds, 'I know that I would never adopt. There is something in adopted children that makes them wonder why were they given up and what was wrong with them to be given up.'

Charryce struggles to view her mother as anything other than the loving woman in the video: 'Mum's motives were genuine. She had a lot of love to give, a large house and a successful business. I think she wanted to help other parents and children and to enmesh us as one big happy family but it didn't work out that way because people are different.'

Contrary to many of Honey's memories, Charryce's childhood was idyllic, filled with activities such as weekend ballet classes and spectacular birthday parties with pony rides. There were outings to the movies, and friends dancing to the American folk group Peter, Paul and Mary in the living room.

If there was darkness around them, neither was aware of it.

'Mum hid her troubles with Shelton from me,' Charryce says, citing the opinions of the Apollo Bay police who believed Shelton had been treated too leniently at home.

I had little idea of the terrible times she and Dad were going through. My life was always enjoyable at home. I was a very compliant child, just happy to bob along and fit [in] as part of a big family. I stayed out of trouble, content to be a follower because it didn't bring me any distress or harm.'

Mum's overriding desire for every one of her children was that they be 'HAPPY'. What really hurt her was that Shelton was ruining his chance of happiness for the future. Mum felt she could have done nothing more for Shelton, and that nobody else would have persevered as much as she and Dad did. From the little I observed, I agree my parents did everything they could, but Shelton's behaviour was uncontrollable.

Gaela, who largely kept to herself, was also blind to the troubles: 'We all admired Shelton. He was so good looking with curly hair and a devil may care attitude. He was the star of the family. Bretton had the bedroom next to mine. He was the sweetest boy. I did ask him once why he left. He told me he just followed Shelton.'

Charryce admits that her relationship with Honey was imperfect, and that she was jealous of her sister: 'It was a quiet jealousy,' she says. 'Honey was very, very beautiful, more popular with the boys and faster to develop. She was a different personality than me, outgoing and fun-loving. I felt that she was smarter than me and a better artist than me.'

Was there a friendship with Honey? Were they close?

'In my mind yes, we were close, but apparently she didn't feel that way. We had normal kiddie rivalries but I felt we were close. I still consider Honey my sister and always will even though we haven't communicated for twenty-odd years. I'd be very happy to get back in touch.'

Charryce pauses for a moment, considering her last comment about reconnecting with Honey:

I don't think she really liked me and thought I was favoured in the family. If I was [favoured], I was, and she might have suffered but it's something that I can't revisit. So I think that she probably doesn't like me much, which is sad. I think she has harboured those feelings for years and years and years.

Her life was so different to mine. I don't know what she got up to or who she associated with. I just didn't know.

☙

There is another matter that makes for an uncomfortable discussion. The natural children of Valerie and Monty Lea all inherited either shares in the Darrell Lea business or a portion of the property fortune, founded on their grandmother's hard work and mother's reinvestment. The adopted children received nothing, and Honey now lives off a pension in a country town.

It is clearly a difficult issue. Charryce answers first by insisting that the pressure to exclude the adopted children from the family business came, at least initially, from Maurice, the oldest of the Lea brothers who, despite having no children of his own, railed against adopted children being part of the operation.

Harris ignored his older brother's view and ensured that his stepson Michael and three adopted children—Robert, Charon and Brenda—were included in his will.

And Monty? 'I don't know my father's views and reasons for doing as he did because it was never discussed.'

What about Mungah? She was also strident about passing on the proceeds of her Bulwark Against Disaster to only her natural, 'blood' grandchildren. Yes, that was true also, Charryce concedes.

In hindsight, does she agree with the decision to leave her sister out of the will, or should Honey be acknowledged in some way?

Charryce pauses before answering. There is a codicil to Valerie's will that deals with the thorny question. Charryce has spent several weeks considering whether to allow its publication to explain her mother's thoughts, but instead summarises its contents:

Mum's sadness and regret that, despite her very best efforts to bring them up with love and affection, good schools and an enjoyable home life, her three adopted children left home in their early teens and she had not seen or heard from any of them.

It was a bitter disappointment to her that they totally abandoned her and the family, but it was their decision and she had no choice but to abide by their wishes to leave home when they did. She wished them well, but wants them to understand that she did all she could for them and felt betrayed when they decided to take off on their own, wanting nothing to do with the family whatsoever. Now that's not entirely true because I know that there was a contact made with Honey.

What I think was very unfair was that the three adopted kids all left home so early. They all decided to up-sticks and go at fifteen or sixteen. They may have had their reasons but they left Mum in such a state of, let's say, anguish that she wasn't strong enough and she couldn't resolve the situation so she felt to blame. I don't believe that she was. That, to me, was a betrayal in a lot of ways; that they decided to go and never look back. They had been brought up by her, they had been part of the family, we'd all gone to The Prom together, we'd had Mother's Day together, Christmas days together. Behaviours came to the fore and they all went.

But they were children and it wasn't their choice to come into the family in the first place.

'They abandoned the household,' Charryce countered. 'They abandoned Mum. They will always be members of the family but anyone who chooses deliberately to not want to live with that family makes their own choice.'

Gaela concurs: 'If I ran away from my mother then I wouldn't have expected to get anything.'

Of her brothers' wrangling, Charryce despairs:

I didn't know that Jason was a bully as a child and it affected Lael as it did. I simply didn't see it. The ABC program [*Dynasties*] was horrible.

I didn't know that Jason, my own brother, was harbouring all this anger. I had no idea that there was any discord between the two brothers. My life has been quite separate.

I feel sad about it. When I was growing up, apart from Shelton coming in, the rest of us were just a part of one big happy family. When I hear the bitterness with which Lael speaks about Jason, his ill-treatment of Lael through the business and how he turned on his son, Jason Carey, I feel sad because it wasn't the family I recognise. I didn't think it was the relationship they had. Maybe I was so starry-eyed that I didn't realise Lael was suffering under Jason's bombastic ways.

How did she feel about a company that was essentially destroyed from within?

It was devastating. It shouldn't have happened. It just shouldn't have happened. I wasn't involved in the business and I will never know the reasons for its demise. Our generation's responsibility was to expand this highly respected Australian family business. Instead it oversaw its collapse.

46

ALL THAT COUNTS IS LOVE

August 2017

The pebbled driveway was bare and the upstairs curtains drawn tight. The Lodge at 22 Lambert Road, Toorak, appeared empty.

Honey stood silently at first, taking in the house that held such mixed memories. She wasn't fearful, just watchful. Valerie Lea was long dead, but her presence lingered.

'Come on,' she said finally. 'Let's have a look around.'

The tension broken, curiosity winning over apprehension, she strode up the side of the house and peered through a back window into what was once the dining room where the family gathered once a day.

'So much went on in there,' she said, almost in a whisper. 'It all seemed so wholesome and wonderful. Life was busy. We had school and gymnastics and ballet. We had friends. There was music and there was freedom because the adults were never around. But it was also the place where I was beaten black and blue and told that I was worth less than the others.'

Honey stopped, realising that her description jarred. How could a home provide such comforts, encouragement and opportunity, and yet be a place of such unhappiness?

'It was the hypocrisy that got me,' she said finally. 'Valerie pretended she wanted me but she didn't. She wanted a number.'

The moment passed. 'I didn't spend a whole lot of time letting them make me feel bad. I've gone through life with this attitude of forcing myself to cope, to Pollyanna along and hold most of my feelings inside. Shelton was different; he had a release valve that helped bring things out until the drugs went in.'

She continued the tour. Plants were sprouting from brickwork, the window frames could have done with a paint job, garden beds with weeding. It was clear that Valerie's firm hand was no longer on the tiller.

If there was anyone home, they stayed out of sight as Honey returned to the front yard. 'When we came back one summer holiday from The Prom we all had new bedrooms,' she said, pointing up to the second storey. 'I had those two windows, Gaela's were over there and that's where Brett watched out for Shelton. Bubbie had the next three—the best room, of course.'

A van rattled past. Honey followed its path with her eyes up the street. 'We would take the tram from the top, at Orrong Road, and change at Commercial Road to get to the factory at Chapel Street. At the other end of the street there was a metal factory. Can you believe it? We used to collect the off-cuts like metal coins.'

She smiled.

We had a lot of freedom, especially the orphans, because they didn't care as much. We roamed after school, knowing that we only had to be back by dinnertime, just in case Val and Monty were on time.

I had no idea that boys and girls were different that there was such a thing as inequality. I was shocked when I found out later that men and women didn't earn the same money.

I guess that's partly because Valerie was such an incredibly strong woman. She was a complex and impressive woman in many ways but, as Jason said on television, she was ruled by her head. What she lacked was love, at least for us.

There was a lot that I admired, but I did not like her. I couldn't touch her, I hated her smell.

We're back in the car. Honey has had enough. It will probably be the last time she ever returns to Lambert Road.

A sense of identity remains elusive for the woman who was born Gayle Leslie Johns, raised as Kestin Ferne Melani Lea, and now goes by the name of Honey Bell. 'I still feel confused and unsettled about who I am. Even the name Honey doesn't feel right at times. I always wanted to be an Elizabeth or a Margaret; something normal, something ordinary.'

She hasn't spoken to Shirley Newman for ten years. Their sense of connection had faded and then disappeared since her return to Australia. They had met occasionally, sometimes for a meal, little more, but the divide between them was clear. Shirley was either concentrating on her other children or was simply not interested in the daughter she gave away. Perhaps it was just too late to make that mother–daughter bond.

On her last visit to Shirley, Honey had noticed that all the photos of her had been taken down, and Shirley spoke about her excitement about the imminent birth of her 'first' grandchild, as if Kaja and Angel had not been born.

Honey left quickly, torn between sadness and anger. On the way out of town she stopped and went for a walk in the main street, stopping in front of a shop that sold homewares. A sign in the window caught her attention:

It read 'A mother is a person too', or some sort of wisdom like that. It sharpened my sense that perhaps it was my fault, that I didn't give enough to earn a mother. I didn't even know her birthday.

I'm sitting there, feeling guilty that somehow it's my fault, that I gave my mother a reason to abandon me for the second time in my life. I would have liked my mother to have liked me, having found me again, but she didn't.

I never had a scrap of nurturing or help. I still have moments when I feel black. I mean, how could one not when your mother gives you away and you go to a place where there is no nurturing and people are cruel? How could I have a normal relationship? I could only choose something and someone that didn't work.

And how does she judge herself? Honey considered the question: 'I've worked hard all my life. I haven't been able to give my children a lot, but they have certainly been loved. And that's all that counts.'

Acknowledgements

I understand that this book is a difficult story for some members of the Lea family to read and would like to acknowledge the willingness of Lael, Joy, Charryce (who provided dozens of family photos) and Gaela to be interviewed, as well as Jason Jnr, Angel and Hilke. I have made every endeavour to ensure that their views have been expressed accurately and in context.

I also realise that this has not been an easy exercise for Honey, rekindling difficult memories as it does, and thank her for her patience and cooperation.

I would like to acknowledge Diana Georgeff, who not only gave me her time and thoughts and the use of her biography of Shelton, *Delinquent Angel*, but access to documents and interview tapes of her discussions with the late Shelton, Brett, Jason Snr and Valerie.

Thanks my wife, Paola, for her indulgence and my publisher, Allen & Unwin, particularly my evergreen mentor Richard

Walsh, whose unique brand of encouragement keeps me on my toes. Thanks also to Annette Barlow, Clare Drysdale, Genevieve Buzo, my copyeditor Sarah Baker and Samantha Kent, who saw the project through to the end.

Notes

2 The candy man

'The Lea family history', *How Sweet It Is: The Darrell Lea story*, p. 3 [2012 and Brenda Lea]; 'The ceremony was of a pleasing and impressive character', *Jewish Herald*, 25 April 1905, p. 14; 'The answer to our success was family', *How Sweet It Is: The Darrell Lea story*, p. 16. [2012 and Brenda Lea].

3 The ticket writer

'They had to be tall', *The Age*, 14 November 1997, p. 10; 'I can imagine it happening', author interview with Lael Lea; 'Whatever they were selling, the displays were a kaleidoscope of colour—a shopfront version of a flamboyant Busby Berkeley Hollywood movie, as one writer would describe it', *Australian Dictionary of Biography—Harry Lea*, volume 15 [2012]; '*Miss* Valerie Everitt', *Sydney Morning Herald*, 22 August 1935, p. 10.

4 A new identity

'But she'd said no, unwilling to "make the same mistake my mother did"', interview with Diana Georgeff.

5 The Bulwark Against Disaster

'She was tiny but she was a tough lady', author interview with Lael Lea.

7 Displeasing God

'They would be sitting up in bed eating toast and jam', author interview with Charryce Lea; 'Brett remembered the lectures as life lessons', Brett Lea interview with Diana Georgeff [1995]; 'Her voice would come over the airwaves', author interview with Charryce Lea; 'She made it suspenseful', author interview with Gaela Lea; 'Very attractive appearance', Travancore Clinic report [November, 1949]; 'solidly built, good-looking', Travancore Clinic report [November, 1949]; 'This is probably largely a rationalisation', Travancore Clinic report [November, 1949]; 'hyperactive, aggressive and non-constructive', Travancore Clinic report [March, 1950]; 'factors in his history', Travancore Clinic report [March, 1950]; 'Mother said she wanted', Travancore Clinic report [April, 1950]; 'The conversation confirmed our opinion', Travancore Clinic report [May, 1950]; 'It seems entirely practical', Travancore Clinic report [May, 1950]; 'self-harming behaviour', Travancore Clinic report [May, 1950]; 'Mrs Lea is very pleased', Travancore Clinic report [May, 1950]; 'Mrs Miller concluded', Travancore Clinic report [August, 1950]; 'lengthy and damning', Travancore Clinic report [August, 1950]; 'Mrs Lea is unable to look at Shelton', Travancore Clinic report [February, 1952]; 'She cheerfully described', Travancore Clinic report [February, 1952].

8 Line up, camera, action

'We would sit there and laugh', author interview with Charryce Lea; 'It may have looked like a very happy bunch', *Dynasties* program, ABC, 2005; 'I spent four nights a week', Shelton Lea interview with Diana

Georgeff [1995]; 'It broke my heart', author interview with Honey (Lea) Bell; 'I saw what happened', author interview with Lael Lea; 'Don't you dare talk', author interview with Honey Bell; 'I loved my ballet', author interview with Charryce Lea; 'From the outside at least', author interview with Honey Bell.

9 The chocolate factory

'We kids sat on boxes', author interview with Honey Bell; 'Our pocket money was threepence per week', Diana Georgeff interview with Shelton Lea [1995/1996]; 'What Mum did, Dad didn't do', author interview with Lael Lea [2017]; 'We were expected to do it', author interview with Lael Lea.

10 The pinafore matriarch

The Argus, 27 November 1953, p. 6; *The Truth*, 6 December 1953, p. 7.

11 Seven children, seven schools

'St Cath's girls walked to a different beat', Diana Georgeff interview with Shelton Lea [1995/1996]; 'Diana Georgeff joined St Catherine's a couple of years later', author interview with Diana Georgeff [2017]; 'Diana, who would later write *Delinquent Angel*', author interview with Diana Georgeff; 'Honey was out there', author interview with Jackie Bing [2017].

12 Twisties

'Jason introduced me to jazz', Diana Georgeff interview with Shelton Lea [1995/1996]; 'His son was behind with reading', Diana Georgeff interview with Shelton Lea [1995/1996].

13 Chicken meat

'Shelton would detail his sad and lonely trip', Diana Georgeff, *Delinquent Angel*, Sydney: Random House, 2007, pp. 65–7; 'Diana Georgeff believes so', author interview with Diana Georgeff; 'He exploded the joint', *Delinquent Angel*, p. 92; 'I always thought the orphans were luckier', Diana Georgeff interview with Shelton Lea [1995/1996].

14 A ward of the state

'It opened my eyes', *Delinquent Angel*, p. 94; 'I haven't drunk any of that beer', Shelton Lea police statement, 5 February 1962.

16 The revelation

'It felt so barren', Diana Georgeff interview with Shelton Lea [1995/1996]; 'You never know when you're getting out', 'An interview with Shelton Lea', Michael Sharkey, *Southerly Magazine*, July 1989; 'Some people escape', *Delinquent Angel*, [p. 110]; 'it's an art, it's not therapy' Diana Georgeff interview with Shelton Lea [1995/1996]; 'fucken equisite', *Delinquent Angel*, p. 123; 'It was such a hopeful line', *Delinquent Angel*, p. 124; 'Shelton uses his intelligence', summary of institutional record, 22 November 1962.

17 Dodgem

'Sandor and I', 'An interview with Shelton Lea', Michael Sharkey, *Southerly Magazine*, July 1989; 'The Leas never tried to help', Diana Georgeff interview with Shelton Lea [1995/1996]; 'Brett had been heavily influenced', *Delinquent Angel*, p. 137; 'We did heaps together', Diana Georgeff interview with Shelton Lea [1995/1996]; 'He was as happy as Larry,' Diana Georgeff interview with Shelton Lea; 'Prahran cop shop was terrible', *Delinquent Angel*, p. 139; 'Diana Georgeff was convinced', *Delinquent Angel*, p. 145.

18 The bargain
'I was just a plump, lazy little girl', author interview with Gaela Lea.

19 Brighton Savoy
'Would some kind couple', *Sydney Morning Herald*, 30 May 1965, p. 2; 'He then made the mistake', author interview with Lael Lea; 'In true Monty style', author interview with Charryce Lea.

20 Go-Set
'I can still see her in the quadrangle', author interview with Diana Georgeff; 'Valerie was furious', author interview with Honey Bell; 'A love child', *The Whole Fruggin Scene: Melbourne and the rock 'n' roll revolution*, Jeffrey Turnbull www.poparchives.com.au/gosetcharts/whatwas.html; 'A sixteen year old fashion expert', 'Sex, drugs and Molly Meldrum: Behind the scenes of counter-culture mag *Go-Set*', *Crikey*, 5 February 2016, www.crikey.com.au/2016/02/05/sex-drugs-and-molly-meldrum-behind-the-scenes-of-counter-culture-mag-go-set/; 'I remember how sweet she looked', author interview with Colin Beard.

21 The origin of everything
'Brett would proudly tell her', Diana Georgeff interview with Brett Lea [1995/1996]; 'I was time keeper', 'An interview with Shelton Lea', Michael Sharkey, *Southerly Magazine*, July 1989; 'Shelton could see no problem', Diana Georgeff interview with Shelton Lea [1995/1996];

'If I were dealing with you', *Sydney Morning Herald*, 27 September 1967, p. 5.

22 A special somebody

'The *Go-Set* office was a vibrant place', author interview with Honey Bell; 'love, tenderness and emotion', author interview with Honey Bell.

23 A gypsy mind

'You have to write what's in you', *The Age*, 13 October 1969, p. 13; 'the best reader of poetry in Australia', *Melbourne Times*, 25 May 2005; 'Beauty in a gypsy mind', *The Age*, 13 October 1969. p. 13; 'Charlie's ambitions didn't stop there', *The Age*, 9 February 1970, p. 15.

24 Eight, nine and ten

'Would not have been as nice in the UK', author interview with Jason Lea Jnr; 'She told me that she was going out to dinner', author interview with Angeline Lea.

25 The cobra

'You've got to know how to deliver a poem', Diana Georgeff interview with Shelton Lea [1995/1996]; 'Shelton Lea is a loner', *The Age*, 13 October 1969, p. 13; 'the most important relationship of my life', Diana Georgeff interview with Shelton Lea [1995/1996]; 'He carried on a treat and I let him', *Delinquent Angel*, p. 193.

26 Lincoln

'It was pretty late in the afternoon', author interview with Jason Lea Jnr; 'I knew he was dead', author interview with Angeline Lea;

'For the last thirty years I have felt Australian', author interview with Hilke Lea.

27 A miscarriage of justice

'The police had not found out about anything else', court transcript [22 June 1971]; 'Brett should not have gone into Army service', court transcript [22 June 1971].

28 Forever young

'Monty was a man', author interview with Jason Lea Jnr; 'Jacie, aged nine, watched his grandmother', author interview with Jason Lea Jnr.

29 Kittens from cats

'A Sydney baby whose birth', *Sydney Morning Herald*, 24 June 1974, p. 1; 'It felt like being in some Fellini movie', author interview with Honey Bell; 'In hospital, my baby would have been ripped away from me', *Sydney Morning Herald*, June 24, 1974, p. 1; 'You are told to go to the doctor each week', *Australian Women's Weekly*, 24 July 1974, p. 3; 'Valerie had always said that', author interview with Honey Bell.

31 An inevitable crim

'He is the fifth eldest', NSW Department of Corrections report, 1975; 'Seems to accept his fate', NSW Department of Corrections files.

32 *The Flying Baby Show*

'Yes, it was idyllic', author interview with Honey Bell; 'I realised at this point', author interview with Honey Bell; 'We had two children', author interview with Honey Bell; 'In she came, wearing Valerie's best jewellery', author interview with Honey Bell.

33 A concept of belonging

'I was eighteen storeys up', Interview with Michael Sharkey, *Southerly Magazine*, July 1989; 'I loved him. He was a special person', *Delinquent Angel*, p. 236; 'The concept of "belonging"', *Delinquent Angel*, p. 244; 'I'm penniless but have arranged a fare back', *Delinquent Angel*, p. 252; 'Shelton just persists in having babies', Diana Georgeff interview with Brett Lea [1995]; 'Diana disagrees', author interview with Diana Georgeff.

35 The drifter and the career woman

'I wasn't surprised', author interview with Moana Wilson; 'They were staying in the room where they used to punish me', Diana Georgeff interview with Brett Lea; 'His behaviour wasn't what I expected of a husband', author interview with Moana Wilson.

36 He could make a weekend feel like a year

'According to Barrett Reid', *Delinquent Angel*, p. 279; 'Shelly would not complain about Valerie', *Delinquent Angel*, p. 280; 'lurching toward maturity', *Delinquent Angel*, p. 279; 'an affirmation of life', *Delinquent Angel*, p. 304; 'I had heard about him as a troublesome poet', author interview with Leith Woodgate; 'he wasn't there for long periods', author interview with Leith Woodgate; 'Diana Georgeff expressed surprise and admiration', author interview with Diana Georgeff; 'We were looking for a big family', Diana Georgeff interview with Valerie Lea [1995].

38 Brothers and sons

'People know we exist, they just don't know why we exist', *The Age*, 29 August 1992, p. 34; 'They can't do what we can do', *The Age*, 29 August 1992, p. 34; 'I wasn't great scholastically', author interview with Lael Lea; 'There is a photograph that Jason Lea Jnr treasures', author interview with Jason Lea Jnr.

39 Reunion

'Chuck Bell was long gone', author interview with Honey Bell.

40 Mothers

'Diana Georgeff first heard about Shelton Lea when she was fourteen', author interview with Diana Georgeff; 'He was nearly fifty', *Delinquent Angel*, p. 3; 'I'm going to tell her', Diana Georgeff interview with Brett Lea; 'She came in after we founded the charity', author interview with Jo Darvall [2017].

41 He wanted to clear the air

'Moana woke suddenly', author interview with Moana Wilson; 'Jason put $500 on the bar', author interview with Lael Lea.

42 Bad blood

'It was a question of how much', author interview with Jason Lea Jnr.

43 Circles of our death and life

'Shelton and Leith had been holidaying', author interview with Leith Woodgate; 'And they did come', *Delinquent Angel*, p. 354; 'I asked him if he wanted me to read some of the biography', author interview with

Diana Georgeff; 'No one loved poetry as much as Shelton', *Melbourne Times*, 25 May 2005; 'We did not hear everything we could have from Shelton Lea', *Blue Dog: Australian poetry*, volume 4, number 8, November 2005; 'Shelton's poetry was more about a search for love and beauty than rage', author interview with Diana Georgeff.

45 Charryce and Gaela

'If you have one dog', author interview with Lael Lea.

Author Note

Permission to reproduce excerpts of Shelton Lea's poetry within these pages was sought, but unfortunately terms could not be agreed upon.

Thanks to Black Pepper Publishing for permission to reproduce Shelton Lea's poem 'Nebuchadnezzar' on p. 383.